DATE DUE

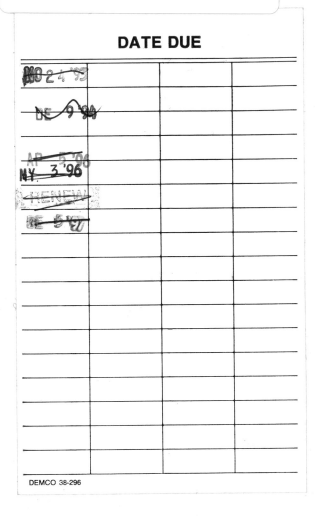

NO 24 '93			
DE 9 '94			
AP 3 '00 NY 3 '96			
RENEW			
DE 5 '07			

DEMCO 38-296

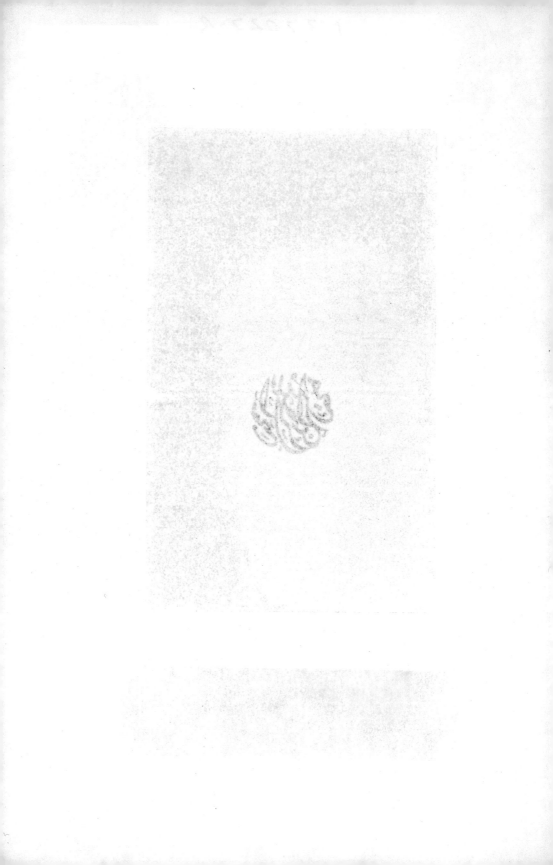

POLITICS, ADMINISTRATION & DEVELOPMENT IN SAUDI ARABIA

Edited by
Ahmed Hassan Dahlan

POLITICS, ADMINISTRATION & DEVELOPMENT IN SAUDI ARABIA

Edited by
Ahmed Hassan Dahlan

Copyright© 1990 by Ahmed Hassan Dahlan
Library of Congress Catalog Card Number 90-085306
ISBN No. 0-915 957-07-8

Amana Corporation
Brentwood, MD, U.S.A.

Dar Al-Shorouq
Jeddah, Saudi Arabia

Printed in the United States of America

Dedication

To the Warm Waters

of the Red Sea

and the Arabian Gulf

"IT IS THE DUTY OF THE STATE TO BE RESPONSIVE TO THE NEEDS AND DEMANDS OF ITS CITIZENS."

Fahd bin Abd al-Aziz

"SAUDI ARABIA, ITS PEOPLE AND GOVERNMENT, BELIEVES DEEPLY THAT THE FREEDOM OF OPINION AND EXPRESSION IS GRANTED TO ALL, FOR ISLAM GUARANTEES SUCH FREEDOM."

Abd Allah bin Abd al-Aziz

PREFACE

The future of Saudi Arabia, which occupies the greatest part of the Arabian Peninsula, is rooted in its history and culture since the emergence of Islam in the seventh century. Following its reunification in 1926 (1345 AH), Saudi Arabia turned into a virtual "workshop", and the government has made sound strides toward development, particularly after the rapid increase in oil revenue in the early 1970s. Saudi Arabia has experienced "phenomenal economic development", and similarly the 1990s are going to witness comparable political development. In addition to its spiritual and financial wealth, life in Saudi Arabia is characterized by stability, security, progress and participation (SSPP).

This book draws from a wide range of disciplines including humanities, the law, and social and political sciences. Articles discuss the ancient history and culture of Saudi Arabia, the Islamic environment and value system, political and administrative development, industry and business— government relations, the women's movement and other issues.

The purpose of the book is twofold. First, is to illustrate and examine, in one handy reference, different aspects of development in Saudi Arabia. While current issues are the main focus, several articles provide the reader with adequate historical and cultural backgrounds. Still, paradoxically, whereas some articles draw from Western schools, close examination reveals the interaction between, and the impact of the Arab and Islamic civilization on, the world's cultures and enlightment.

Second, the articles suggest for researchers, planners, and decision-makers in Saudi Arabia areas for continued improvement and future development. The reunification of the Arabian Peninsula under the Saudi government has brought hope that the Peninsula will regain its historical and powerful position among the world's nations, and resume a leading and pivotal role in the international community. This depends, first of all, on how responsive and creative the Saudi society will be in meeting its current needs and prospective ambitions in light of its precious heritage. It is the hope of the editor, and all contributors to this volume, that their studies will be taken into account by planners and researcher community toward a brighter future.

ACKNOWLEDGEMENTS

In the 1970s and 1980s, the scientific research movement in Saudi Arabia, along with the development plans and processes, has taken a new direction and pattern. In terms of volume, scope and quality, research has increased, covering a wider range of fields and disciplines, and generally in more depth and detail.

Gratitude and thanks go first to the authors and other contributors who brought this work to light as an attempt to fill part of the vacuum in the literature pertinent to Saudi Arabia. While a great deal of research on Saudi Arabia has been done by non-Saudis, it is undisputable that much of it lacked adequate knowledge concerning real-life conditions in the country. It has been a major interest of the editor and contributors to have such work written by Saudis published, so as to be available to the Saudi reader as well as to those who are interested in other cultures. Thanks again to the contributors, without whose efforts, cooperation and trust this work could not have been accomplished.

Individually, I would like to thank the following people:

Dr. Ali M. El-Saflan, Chairman of the Department of Public Administration, College of Economics & Administration, King Abd al-Aziz University (KAU), Jeddah, Saudi Arabia. His valuable suggestions and endless support were of great help in carrying on and finishing this work.

Drs. Mohammed Badran, Hesham Milyani, and Mohammed Haddad, all Assistant Professors of Public Administration; Dr. Wahid H. Hashim, Assistant Professor of Political Science; Dr. Omar Al-Khouli, Assistant Professor of Law; and Dr. Walid A. Hashim, Assistant Professor of Economics, all of KAU. These intellectuals deserve my deepest gratitude for their criticisms and suggestions, and for the time they spent in evaluating the articles I provided them.

I would like to extend my gratitude and respect to the following scholars and professionals for their encouragement and support:

Prince Bandar Bin Sultan, the Saudi Ambassador to the U.S.; Dr. Reda Obaid, KAU President; Dr. Hassan Aburokbah, Professor and Secretary General, KAU; Dr. Ghazi Madani, Professor of Management, KAU; Dr. Hashim B. Hariri, Dean of the College of Education, Umm al-Qura University, Makkah; Dr. Muneer S. Khashogje, Dean of the College of Education, Madinah Campus, KAU; Dr. Saleh Bin Nasser, Vice President of the Presidency of Youth; Drs. Alawi Abu al-Saud, Kamal Filemban, and Abdullah Al-Ghamdi, all Assistant Professors of Public Administration, and in fact all my colleagues in the Department of Public Administration, KAU; Mr. Anas H. Dahlan, Director of Administrative Development, the National Guard, Jeddah; Drs. Hassan Balkhi, Faruq Al-Khatib, Wadi Kabli, all Assistant Professors of Economics; Dr. Fatina Shaker, Assistant Professor of Sociology, and Hayyat Rajekhan, Lecturer of Public Administration, all of KAU.

Special thanks go to those who assisted me in the copy editing of the articles: Constance Joy; Kristin Guss of the American University, Washington, D.C.; Dr. Melva Peterson, Director of Adult Education, SAIS; Donald Lehnhoff of Professional Writing, Minneapolis, MN. My sincere appreciation goes to Seham Fatani, Sabah Oun and Asma Al-Abdullah, all Lecturers at the English Department, KAU, who edited, proofread, reviewed, and translated material for this book.

Finally, I am indebted to the prompt response of several members at the departments of Political Science and Urban Studies, Temple University: Carolyn Adams, Professor and Chairperson of Urban Studies; Conrad Weiler, Professor and Director of M.P.A.; Charles Joiner, Professor of Public Administration; and Harry Bailey, Jr., Chairman and Professor of Public Administration.

Thanks to all.

Editor

CONTENTS

xiii

مقدمة عن كتاب

السياسة ، الادارة ، والتنمية في المملكة العربية السعودية

إعداد : أحمد بن حسن دحلان

يقدم لنا الكتاب الذي بين ايدينا محاولة جيدة لاستعراض تاريخي وسياسي وإداري لدولة نامية هي المملكة العربية السعودية. وعلى الرغم انه من الصعب لكاتب مهما كان أن يضم كل مثل هذه الموضوعات في كتاب واحد الا أن معد الكتاب قد بذل جهداً في انتقاء الموضوعات التي تغطي في مجملها كافة الجوانب المختلفة التي توضح للقارىء وخاصة القارىء الغربي المعالم المختلفة لدولة نامية في مفهومها حديثة في طموحاتها.

ولعل أهم ما يُعنى به الكتاب هو فكرته الأساسية والتي تتبلور في إلقاء الضوء على عناصر مختلفة تمثل ركائز التطور الحديث في المملكة العربية السعودية. فالكتاب بعد ان يقدم لنا منظوراً تراثياً لتاريخ المملكة العربية السعودية يتدرج بعد ذلك في فصول متعددة لنمائج مختلفة من ركائز النهضة الحديثة في المملكة.

ويمكن القول ان معالم هذا الكتاب تتحدد في ثلاثة جوانب رئيسية اولاها الباحثون جلّ اهتمامهم وهي:

● الدولة السعودية تاريخاً وسياسة وإدارة.

● معالم التطور الحديثة في المملكة في مجالات بناء المواطن السعودي، وبناء الهياكل الادارية والتنظيمية اللازمة للتنمية.

● صور ونماذج من التطور في مجالات التعليم والقوى البشرية، الصناعة وإنماء المدن.

وربط هذه الجوانب في الغالب الذي يظهر به هذا الكتاب هو مساهمة رائعة في إثراء المكتبة الغربية قام بها معد الكتاب الأستاذ احمد بن حسن دحلان الذي أبّت قدرة فائقة في الاتصالات والاقناع لمجموعة الباحثين المشاركين في المادة العلمية للكتاب.

نرجو ان يحقق الكتاب اهدافه ـ وان يطور فيما بعد لتتبعه سلسلة من الكتاب المختلفة التي تعطي صوراً مشرقة للمملكة العربية السعودية حاضرها ومستقبلها.

أ.د. مدني عبد القادر علاقي
عميد كلية الاقتصاد والادارة
جامعة الملك عبد العزيز بجدة

FOREWARD

Few definitive books exist in English on the processes of government in Saudi Arabia. Many of those that do exist are either outdated or written by those with only superficial knowledge of their subject. Nonetheless, this collection of essays by native authorities is certainly unique and should be of great assistance to researchers in the future. The history of the Arabian Peninsula; the impact of Islam on every aspect of our life; and our unique process of participation are all of immense importance in any analysis of Saudi Arabia. Most of these concepts and forces can be traced back to the principles of Islamic government and the traditions of our ancestors. This collection of essays by Saudi scholars will be valuable to Western attempts to understand the basis of our political system and culture since these are interconnected with each other.

The over-whelming importance of the majlis (council), as a mechanism to promote participation and, indeed, partial distribution, is one of the most important examples of the major differences in our political model as compared to the political machine in Western countries. Access, as afforded by the majlis, is a primary pillar of the Saudi governmental system. The majlis offers access to either the King, the Crown Prince, a Minister, or the Emir of a Province to all citizens. On a regular weekly schedule, these officials meet in their city of residence with citizens who wish to greet them or present a particular need or problem. Any complaints against government departments, special family needs for either monetary assistance or health assistance or other, or ideas about any aspect of government are among the functions of any majlis. Issues are discussed, both domestic and international. Perhaps the concept of true democracy comes closer to being realized in this system of personal contact with the rulers than in the so-called Western democracies where access to the head-of-state is almost impossible and where individual opinions or problems are not so easily aired.

Of course, our population is not in the hundreds of millions. However, even for its size, the Saudi system must be unique in its attention to the individual. We believe the Saudi governmental system is a very effective and useful model. It is based on our needs and traditional patterns of authority. This book should be an important part of any research involving an understanding of that system.

Bakor O. Al-Amri
Professor of Political Science
Dean's College of Economics & Administration
King Abd al-Aziz University
Jeddah, Saudi Arabia

PART I: HISTORY, LAW, and CULTURE

INTRODUCTION:

Part I furnishes a general background on Saudi Arabia. The articles included here trace human settlement in the Arabian Peninsula since early history, present the validity of Islamic law regard the environment, and highlight the growth and importance of Arabic both as a native and as a second language. In *"THE HISTORY & DEVELOPMENT OF HUMAN SETTLEMENT IN SAUDI ARABIA,"* Dr. Masry sketches cultural history and human settlement in different regions of the Arabian Peninsula since the *Stone Age*. Recent discoveries in the mid 1980s indicate that Arabia might have witnessed the earliest Stone Age settlements yet found. Dr. Masry examines the role each region of Arabia played in the cultural circuit of the time (e.g. Egypt, the Levant, Mesopotamia).

Then Dr. Masry outlines the cultural legacy of the Neolithic settlements in Arabia, and its definite link with other civilizations beginning in the *third millennium B.C.* During this period, the first truly urban settlements in Arabia appeared, and the commercial activities that followed could be regarded as the highest "international" trade of the time.

Dr. Masry proceeds to the *second millennium B.C.* and points out the decline of the major cultural centers in Mesopotamia and its impact on the eastern region of Arabia. Meanwhile, the other regions experienced the development of large walled town-complexes supported by oases cultivation and animal husbandry.

Focusing on early Arabian history, Dr. Masry depicts the *first millennium B.C.* as characterized by complexity due to rapid internal developments and cultural influences. Growth of the walled town-centers continued, and commercial and cultural interactions began to evolve, leading to the emergence of the early Arabian States in the various regions of the Peninsula. Different centers in Arabia had connections with other civilizations of Assyrians, Babylonians, and Greeks among others. The most significant developments of the first millennium B.C., however, took place in northwestern Arabia (Midian) which was part of the Nabataen Kingdom. This kingdom superseded the earlier successive states, and its language and writings are the most direct predecessor of modern Arabic. Ultimately, the Nabataen Kingdom was invaded and liquidated by the Romans.

The era from early Christianity to the emergence of Islam, as Dr. Masry briefly mentions, was influenced by the struggle between the eastern and

3

western empires of the time. As in the previous stages, many settlements vanished only to appear again.

Finally, Dr. Masry delineates how the emergence of *Islam* in the seventh century rescued the fragmented segments of the Arabian Peninsula, leading, within a decade, to its consolidation in Medina. Though the capital of the Islamic State, and, consequently, the political power, moved to Syria and later to Iraq, many town-centers reemerged and expanded in the different regions of the Peninsula. In addition, new urban settlements were established. Dr. Masry considers the caravan link between Kufa in Iraq and the Holy Places of Makkah and Medina as the most spectacular development during the early Islamic State. That road, later named after Zubayda (the wife of a Muslim leader at the time), was about 1,000 miles long with more than 70 rest stations. It reflected high standards of engineering.

Dr. Masry concludes with the decline of the Islamic Empire. This event deeply divided the Peninsula, which was not reunited until the rise of the present *Saudi State* in the early 20th century.

Dr. Bakhashab, in his article *"ISLAMIC LAW & THE ENVIRONMENT: SOME BASIC PRINCIPLES,"* attempts to explain the rationale for the existence of Man on the Earth, and to provide a framework and set of guidelines for his duties and actions. God, the Supreme Being, as He created the Heavens and the Earth, created Man, equipped him with certain capabilities, and charged him with authority to utilize (rationally) the resources therein.

Dr. Bakhashab presents the concept of the stewardship of Man on Earth, emphasizing that no individual, family, or nation has privilege over another except by rightous deeds. The author highlights the significance of work, and the freedom of action and knowledge, with freedom exercised in accordance with Islamic Law and the public interest.

As Dr. Bakhashab discusses an individual's dugies, he underscores Man's responsibility and accountability for the preservation and conservation of the natural environment. The universe is created in order. Man is encouraged to explore it and speculate about its abundant resources, magnificent phenomena, and delicate interactions, so he would eventually consider their systematic relationships and great benefits.

Dr. Bakhashab addresses the main elements of nature—soil, water, flora and fauna—and their interrelationships.While soil is a dynamic support system for both plants and animals, water, in its different forms, is essential for all life. Plants and trees, another component of the natural environment, provide food and wood, and affect climates and soil, among other

4

things. Lastly, animals, like plants, provide food, medicines and many other benefits.

Dr. Bakhashab, citing several verses of the glorious Quran, warns that misuse of resources is harmful to oneself and others, and might disturb the balance of different sub-systems of life. The extravagant waste of resources, or the pollution of water caused by modern industry, for example, are violations of the welfare of others. The message of Islam, the author concludes, is universal: Man should live in harmony with others as well as with nature, and environmental conservation is a sacred duty of both individuals and government.

Concluding Part I of this book, Dr. Oraif, in his article *"THE DEVELOP-MENT OF ARABIC AS A FOREIGN LANGUAGE INSTRUCTION IN SAUDI ARABIA,"* highlights several dimensions of the significance of the Arabic language. Arabic is one of the seven major world languages. Today, it is the religious language of more than 900 million Muslims.

As Dr. Oraif analyzes, Arabic has influenced Eastern and Western cultures and knowledge since the seventh century, when the Arabic language held ancient Greek culture and learning in a virtual custodianship. Eventual English and Spanish translations were derived from the Arabic version. At present, several languages in Asia and Africa make use of Arabic script. Furthermore, both Spanish and English use many words of Arabic origin.

Dr. Oraif, joining other Western scholars, encourages students all over the world to learn Arabic for its etymological richness, powerful rhetoricism, and musical rhythm.

Dr. Oraif presents the different institutions and programs in Saudi Arabia which teach Arabic as a foreign language. In addition to the privileges they offer, some of these institutions have branches beyond the borders, e.g. in Indonesia, Pakistan and Japan.

THE HISTORY AND DEVELOPMENT OF HUMAN SETTLEMENT IN SAUDI ARABIA
by Abdullah H. Masry, Ph.D.

The land of Saudi Arabia has been settled by man since the remotest period from our present era. Perhaps only the Horn of East Africa can be claimed to possess equal depth of antiquity. This fact is attested to by the spectacular discoveries of sites containing evidences of settlements dating back more than one million years. Despite these recent discoveries, however, we know very little about the details of the oldest development of man and culture in Saudi Arabia. This is so because scientific research was very late in coming to focus on the area. Until quite recently there did not exist even the barest outline of chronology of its pre-Islamic periods.

There exists, of course, extensive literature on pre-Islamic history from Arabic sources. Al-Hamdhani, al-Istakhri and al-Tabari were among the early Muslim geographer-historians who were deeply interested in recording and analyzing evidences of ancient settlements in Arabia. Among contemporary historians one may single out al-Ansari and al-Jassir as particularly original and thorough in their approaches to the early history and epigraphy of Arabia. Their findings are disseminated in their respective scholarly publications, "al-Manhal" and "al' -Arab."

The recent advent of systematic and controlled investigation in Arabian antiquities, particularly in Saudi Arabia (Masry 1974; Department of Antiquities Surveys 1976-1986) and the Gulf States (Frifelt 1968, 1970a, 1970b, 1985; Kuml series 1956-70 on Bahrain, Kuwait, Qatar and Abu Dhabu; De Cardi 1974, 1979; Kapel 1967; al Turki 1985), has brought to light new and important information on the Peninsula's history which must be integrated with previously known information in order to construct a historical chronology that includes the Age of Islam in Greater Arabia. One must hasten to add that the effort is quite far from satisfactory even in its preliminary stages, but the knowledge thus far gained justifies the attempt.

It is with these limitations clearly in mind that the following brief outline of cultural history in Greater Arabia is prepared. The outline will represent summaries of extant and recent evidence bearing on the various chronological periods, from the early Stone Age through the Age of Islam.

Special significance is attached to the respective role each part of Arabia played in the cultural orbit of its most contiguous cultural-civilizational area outside the confines of the Peninsula. This provides the most useful, and ultimately the most relevant context in which to consider the long evolutionary cultural history of the region.

It was inevitable that a great land mass such as the Peninsula, on whose western, northern and eastern peripheries existed formidable nuclei of ancient civilizations (Egypt, the Levant, Mesopotamia, Persia and the Indus Valley) would have been variously influenced by, and in turn have affected the inception and growth of, these major centers. Admittedly such considerations would appear to compromise the indigenous role of the pristine culture of Arabia, presumably centered in the inner impregnable plateau or heartland of Arabia; yet it is argued here that this sub-region of Arabia, characterized by its insularity and remoteness from the mainstream of historic events transpiring on its boundaries, was indeed the pivotal part and catalyst of long-drawn processes of external contacts. Hence, one is tempted to articulate a perspective of Arabian history that emphasizes a central component of a homogeneous pristine culture based on the settlements of the inner plateau.

This component was always in constant dialogue with the far-flung parts of its peripheries. The dialogue could have encompassed population movements and migrations prompted by changing ecological and climatic variables. In turn, whole systems of different relationships were formed by Arabian populations with regions beyond the Peninsula. The different orientations resulted in complex cultural adaptations, but essentially the dialogue with the "heartland" remained constant. This may explain, as we shall see, the periodic emergence, disappearance and resurgence of many settlement centers along the margins of Arabia throughout the last six thousand years. In fact, the immediate pre-Islamic period is a recorded historic case in point.

THE STONE AGE IN ARABIA: 1,000,000-10,000 B.P.

There is no doubt that the Arabian Peninsula was very extensively settled by early man, probably to a greater extent than the already impressively large corpus of evidence would suggest. It may also be the case that the highlands of southwest Arabia provided a significant link between the early hominid forms in South Asia and East Africa during successive geological periods up to the Pleistocene (Overstreet 1971).

8

Aside from this, the extent record on Stone Age settlements in Arabia abounds in evidence ranging from Lower Paleolithic- pre-Acheulian, Acheulean and predominantly levallois Mousterian industries — to more recent Neolithic (ca 5,000 to 2,000 B.C.) As stated above, a number of preliminary investigations and collections have been undertaken in this regard since the 1930s (Field 1956; Smith and Maranjian 1962; Sordinas 1973; Overstreet 1971; Kapel 1967, 1973; Whalen 1984, 1986).

Curiously, the largest concentration of Stone Age settlements was found along the margins of the great deserts; e.g. the Nafud in the north and the Empty Quarter in the south, southwest and southeast. The earliest of these settlements was found along the northern boundaries of the Nafud Desert (in the vicinity of the modern pipeline crossing northern Saudi Arabia into Jordan and Syria). Recent investigations in 1985 and 1986 have located in Dawadmi (Central Province) and Shuwaythia in Wadi Sirhan (Northern Region) extensive series of what might conceivably be the earliest Stone Age settlements yet found (ca 1,000,000 — 300,000 B.P.). Another area of concentration of early sites is on the northeastern peripheries of the Empty Quarter around the natural oasis of Yabrin.

Fig. 1 Acheulean Stave Tools from Dawadmi, Central Arabia.

9

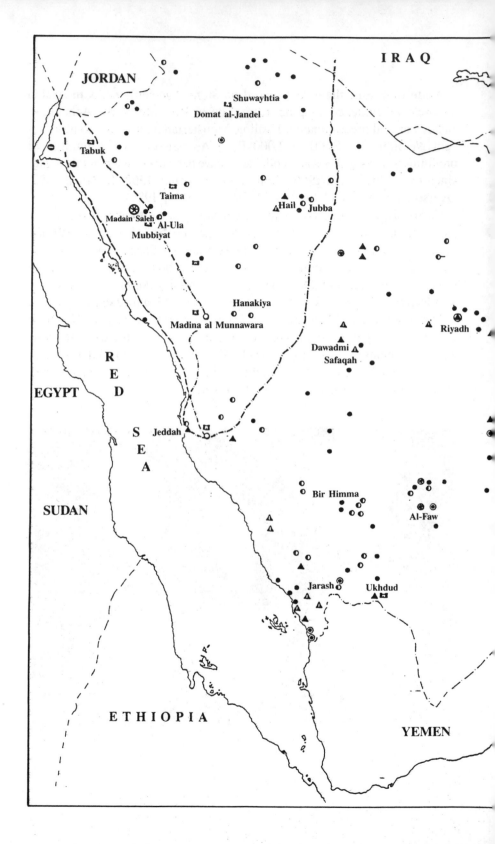

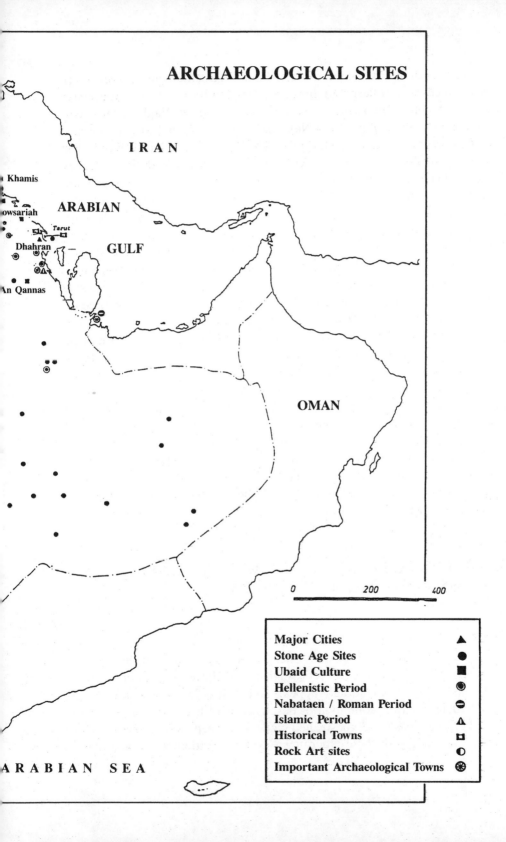

ARCHAEOLOGICAL SITES

IRAN

ARABIAN

GULF

OMAN

Khamis

owsariah

Tarut

Dhahran

An Qannas

ARABIAN SEA

Major Cities	▲
Stone Age Sites	●
Ubaid Culture	■
Hellenistic Period	◉
Nabataen / Roman Period	⊖
Islamic Period	⚠
Historical Towns	▥
Rock Art sites	◐
Important Archaeological Towns	✳

0   200   400

The pattern of distribution for later Stone Age settlements, however, appears to be more widespread throughout the Peninsula. Thus, Mousterian and a few upper Paleolithic sites are found in southern Najd, eastern 'Asir, the central plateau of northern Najd and Hail, the Wadi 'l-Sirhan drainage and elsewhere, dating to ca 30,000 B.P. The Lower Paleolithic of Wadi Sirhan shows parallels with Olduvi of Africa dating to ca 1,000,000 B.P. The key factors to the distribution of these sites are fossil ecological settings of ancient lacustrine lake beds, extinct Wadi drainages and raised terraces (McClure 1976). Hence the real understanding of Stone Age settlements in the entire region is dependent upon our knowledge of the environmental and geomorphological processes of change occuring within Arabia since the middle pleistocene. Regrettably, the gap in our knowledge in this regard is very great. Except for brief and largely hypothetical outlines of early environmental and human settlements, there exists no reliable source on the subject (McClure 1971, 1976; Chapman 1971).

Thus, our present conclusion on the early Stone Age in Arabia may be described as only reasonably adequate. It suffices to observe that the region was indeed extensively exploited by human population as early as one million years B.P. (Whalen 1986), and that this pattern was to increase throughout the Paleolithic period, with changing environmental conditions governing their distribution within the Peninsula. As such conditions accelerated toward the end of the Paleolithic, coinciding with the termination of the Ice Age, there may have appeared new processes that induced Arabian populations to migrate to adjacent regions in the north and west. This could have provided the setting for wider contacts with the external cultures in the early Neolithic period (Diester-Hass 1973).

THE PRE-POTTERY NEOLITHIC IN ARABIA: CROSS REGIONAL CONTRACTS

The chronological dimensions of the Neolithic with its accepted implications regarding settled life, domestication and agriculture cannot be accurately defined in Arabia as yet (Singh 1974). However, certain evidence that has recently come to light appears to confirm the belief that by 9,000 B.P. partially settled communities based on small-to-medium sized mammal herding (possibly domesticated cattle and sheep) were already underway. Attendant with these emerging Neolothic settlements was a pattern of seasonal, probably long-range movements neccessitated by climatic factors. The chief centers for these settlements were the eastern, central, and to a lesser extent the northwestern wadi systems in Arabia. It is possible that at this time population movements from these areas accounted for gradual diffusion and perhaps settlements into the adjoining, ecologically more optimal setting to the north of Arabia, e.g. the southern Levant and lower Mesopotamia. The site of Bayda in Jordan (Kirkbride 1966) with its characteristic similarities to some of the Neolithic settlements in northern Arabia, could be a case in point for such a process. Likewise, the extensive contacts that developed between eastern Arabia and lower Mesopotamia during the later 'Ubayd period could have been foreshadowed by a similar pattern of movement/settlement in the preceding pre-pottery Neolithic period.

The cultural legacy of the Neolithic settlements in Arabia, aside from the chipped-stone industries, is represented today by the unusually massive and widely spread rock art (petroglyphs in low relief) particularly in the northcentral, northwestern highlands and northeastern sandstone outcrops of Saudi Arabia (Anati 1968; Rhotert 1983; Courtney-Thompson 1975; Ingraham et al 1982; Kabawi et al 1985-86). The finest example of these settlements is at a complex site, "Jubbah", 100 km. north of the town of Hail in the Great Nafud. Here a wide variety of finely carved relief figures depicting humans in naturalistic and schematized styles, long horned bovids, equids and other complex motifs crowd the cliff faces of low-lying sandstone outcrops. Nearby a composite of small pre-pottery surface sites lines the edges of a fossil lake bed. It is quite likely that the rock art is related to these settlements which may be reasonably in the range of between 11,000 −8,000 B.P.

Fig. 2 Neolithic Rock Art from Jubbah, Saudi Arabia. Human figure holding a boomerang and a cow behind him.

13

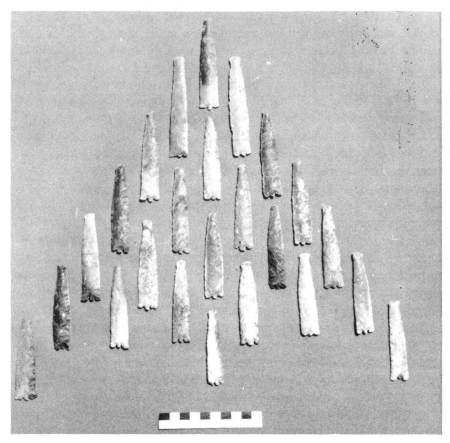

Fig. 3 Late Neolithic Stave artifacts from Tummama.

It is during the 7,000 − 5,000 B.P. time range in Eastern Arabia that we begin to find settlements with pottery, namely 'Ubayd period sites alluded to above (Masry 1974). Thus, and for the first time, a region of the Peninsula starts to be definitely linked to an external zone − i.e. the 'Ubayd culture of southern Mesopotamia - for which we possess a well established chronological framework. It is this relationship that would later account for Arabia's partial entry into the historical record by the middle of the third millennium B.C. during the height of the Sumerian civilization in Mesopotamia. This contact with Mesopotamia was continued with few interruptions and gaps from the 'Ubayd period all the way to the Islamic period.

The inception of Arabian external relations during the 'Ubayd period (7,000 − 5,500 B.P.) is also significant in another way. It identifies the

14

beginning of a process in which the Peninsula throughout its various regions came to be linked with divergent civilizational centers beyond its peripheries. The ensuing dialogues were very crucial, not only in defining the character of each specific region in Arabia, but also in the development and growth of the concerned external entity. Thus, while the east became intertwined in the Mesopotamian based cultural orbit, the north and northwest were to develop crucial ties and interdependencies with the lands of Palestine and the Levant. Likewise, the western coast and its littorals established early links with the Nile Valley, probably across the Red Sea, as well as through the Sinai Desert (Rothenberg 1970). In the southwest an altogether different cultural complex developed and came to be fully recognized by the middle of the second millennium B.C. as the independent indigeneous civilization of southwestern Arabia (Cleveland 1965; Jamme 1962; Van Beek 1969).

The extant archeological record and the continuing primary explorations of Arabian archeology afford ample data to illustrate these wide and divergent networks of cultural relations which the Peninsula had witnessed since prehistoric and early historic times. In the following sections, brief descriptions of that evidence are offered in the context of successive chronological periods.

EARLY HISTORY: CHALCOLITHIC TO MIDDLE BRONZE AGE

The first truly urban settlements in Arabia appeared during the third millennium B.C. The principal ones were concentrated along the Arabian Gulf and its littorals. These had come about as a direct result of the earlier links with the Mesopotamia on the one hand, and the widening horizon of "international" relations (centered on the Gulf trading lanes during the third millennium B.C.) on the other. The important city-state of Dilmun, now partially equated with the island of Bahrain, was one such thriving center (Bibby 1970). Indeed, it was the Sumerian connections with this cultural entity, as evidenced in the former's written records, that historically established the identity of Arabian-Mesopotamian relationships. On the Arabian coast there also existed a series of well defined and highly developed cultural centers spanning its length from souther Oman, all the way to the latitude of modern Kuwait. Notwithstanding their respective cultural differences, these various settlements centers shared one common characteristic that defines their development and growth. They were essentially a constellation of coastal and semi-coastal urban settlements that assimilated the natural and human resources of the vast, thinly populated Arabian hinterlands in response to the extensive and growing networks of trade in rare materials and finished products between the nuclear areas of Mesopotamia, the Indus Valley and southwestern Iran. Perhaps it is not an exaggeration to describe the commercial activities that took place along the Gulf coasts during this period as the highest "international" trading process to occur in the history of ancient civilizations.

The Arabian coast settlement-centers played major roles in this process on two different levels of interaction. For one, they provided basic raw materials, e.g. copper from Oman and other natural resources (fishing, marine products and probably agricultural crops from the productive regimes like al-Hasa and Qatif in Saudi Arabia), which may have been channeled into short-range trade between the settlements themselves, as well as long-rang trade to Mesopotamia and other destinations. Secondly, the Gulf harbours of these settlements served as ports of call, or "enterports", for long distance trade and commerce between the nuclear areas (Crawford 1973). Thus, the settlement of Tarut island off Saudi Arabia's Qatif coast could boast of the availability of such luxury items as steatite, alabaster and lapis lazuli; as well as copper, both as a raw material and in finished forms, within the context of a highly developed prosperous urban setting (Burckholder 1971).

In the meantime, far in the northern and northwestern regions of Arabia, other semi-urban settlements were appearing; once again based on the exploitation of productive oases regimes and mineral resources, and producing yet another trading network with the Levant and Egypt. Although no specific records have been established thus far, preliminary evidence indicates that the settlements of Qurayya, Wadi al-Sirhan, and northern Midian in Saudi Arabia could very well be cases in point. Copper mining sites of possibly early Bronze Age date were found in northwest Saudi Arabia, which seem to indicate a relationship with similar findings in the Wadi Araba and Sinai (Rothenberg 1970, 1972).

The "stone circle" and stone kite" structures so widely spread in central, northern and northwestern Arabia had perhaps first emerged as well during the third millennium B.C. Intial systematic and comprehensive study has been undertaken of these phenomenon (Adams, Parr et al 1976; Zarins et al 1979; Ingraham et al 1981). It seems very likely, on the basis of the

16

present evidence, that these were permanent structures associated with semi-settled populations who were culturally inter-related. The majority of archeological remains found on these structures is composed of stone tools with scanty, and as yet undetermined pottery types. The earliest material dates from the Chalcolithic period and final, intensive occupation ceased after the Middle Bronze Age period (ca. 1850 B.C.). In a side commentary, it is possible to imagine those populations with their stone structures and domesticated sheep, goat, cattle and donkey to have been the forerunners of the more mobile Arabian Bedouins — the nomads of the camelhair tents — who arguably appeared much later in history (Ronen 1970). To be sure, the "stone circle" structures were sporadically reoccupied during later prehistoric periods, and possibly could be associated with the widely distributed Thamudic people.

SECOND MILLENNIUM

The heightened growth of settlements in the various parts of Arabia during the third millennium as described above came to a slow and gradual demise by the middle of the second millennium, particularly in the eastern Gulf region. This was partly due to the overall disruptions and/or collapse that afflicted the major cultural centers in Mesopotamia, the Indus Valley and southwestern Iran. The earlier wide network of trade slackened and came to a virtual halt by the end of the millennium. For good reasons, this era was dubbed the "Dark Age" in Mesopotamia. It is quite likely that, partially as a result of this decline, a great migration of population from eastern Arabia took place at this time. However, some settlement continued to thrive and to maintain contact with Mesopotamia, though on a much curtailed basis.

In the central, north and northwestern regions of the Peninsula this process of diminishing settlement growth does not seem to have been as severe as it was in the east, for in those regions we begin to see the development of large walled town-complexes by the mid-to-late second millennium. In this category we can include Tayma, Dedan (modern al-Ula), Khayber, al-Jawf (the Biblical Duma), and the earlier settlement of Qurayya, where possibly the oldest irrigation network system in Arabia was first known (Parr et al 1972). It is not yet clear by what process of local population aggradations, or terms of external relations with the established urban centers

17

in the Levant to the north and possibly in the Nile Valley across the Red Sea to the west, these town settlements achieved their emergence. What is evident, however, is that they were firmly established entities based on oases cultivation and animal husbandry along what later became the lengendary Arabian trade routes of Classical Times. Furthermore, it was from these combinations of fortified towns that a succession of truly Arabian states (as established by the epigraphic records) was to emerge by the middle of the first millennium B.C.

Fig. 4 A view of excavated early Islamic site of al-Magiyal

Fig. 5 Decorated/painted pottery from Tayma.

18

In the middle of the second millennium B.C., at the time of the disruption and curtailment of settled life in eastern Arabia, the indigenous civilization of South Arabia, as witnessed again by the epigraphic record, began to be consolidated. This cultural complex, with its multiple successive states, was later to expand and spread its influences and hegemony over much of western Arabia up to the land of Midian in the north.

FIRST MILLENNIUM: EARLY ARABIAN STATES

The first millennium B.C. was a very complex period in early Arabian history, both in terms of the intensity of external cultural influence and the rapid internal development of "state" entities. When the millennium came to a close, one end of Arabia was already partially Hellenized and the other apprehensively awaiting the onslaught of Roman expansion.

First in the east, where settled life remained a very truncated version of what was a millennium earlier, significant cultural influences, through a local dialogue with nuclear Mesopotamia and later Persia, continued unabated. Literary evidence from Mesopotamia leads us to suspect that sizeable movements of largely nomadic populations (i.e., Arameans, Chaldeans and others), from this part were coming into frequent and sometimes disruptive contacts with the frontiers of settled life along the alluvium (Brinkman 1968). Indeed, it was in one of the Assyrians annals, dated to the middle of the ninth century B.C., that we first encounter a mention of the Arab nomads who engaged the imperial army of Assur in one of the many clashes that punctuated the history of the period. The pattern usually ended with Assyrian regulars pushing the nomads back to the oblivion of the vast north Arabian deserts, but the latter would, within a short interval, resume their swift attack upon the frontiers of the imperial domain.

Fig. 6 Painted wares from the site of Obeid, Eastern Province

The evidence of external cultural influences upon the few settlements that continued to thrive along the Gulf ranges from Assyrians, Babylonian, Achemenid and later Parthian periods, i.e. from the ninth to the second century B.C. It was in the period of the Selucids, successive to Alexander the Great who reportedly had a dream of conquering Arabia, that the east once again witnessed a sizeable increase in settlements. The famed emporium of Gerrha (al-Jarha), still to be accurately located along the Saudi Arabian coast, belongs to this era of expansion. Other Selucid-influenced cities and many smaller settlements dot the length of the Gulf coast. Some are even located far in the interior, the most prominent of which is the large, massively walled city of Thaj, some 100 km. inland from the coast (Bibby 1968, Dickson 1948). The interior location is significant in terms of the trade that criss-crossed the Peninsula in a southwest-northeast direction ending in southern Mesopotamia. Along the southwesterly expansion from Thaj there thrived many trading towns (e.g. al-Faw and Najran) during the same period. The selucid influence in the east lasted well into the third century A.D. and was succeeded by the Sassanians. Settlement growth continued during this period virtually to the beginning of Islam.

In central and northern Arabia the first millennium B.C. witnessed an accelerated growth of the walled town-centers which saw their beginning in the previous millennium. The towns were now engaged in multiple networks of trade and cultural interactions with South Arabia on the one hand, and the combined Mesopotamian and Levant regimes on the other which were under the successive rule of the Assyrians, Chaldean and Achemenid empires. New town centers also appeared. The settlement of Hail (or "Are Kome" in later Greek sources) located in the central Jabal Shammar area is a good example of this later development. The other towns along the Wadi al-Sirhan (dubbed later the Gateway of Arabia), such as al-Jawf, were also expanding at a great pace and by the middle of the millennium came to control the whole area of central and northern Arabia, thus marking the earliest recorded appearance of an independent Arabian state.

At the same time similar developments of unified entities were also occurring in the Najd plateau along the Tuwayq escarpment-Wadi al-Dawasir system leading into the highland of the southwest. The famed Kingdom of Kinda, centered perhaps at the trading town of al-Faw, was the earliest identifiable politico-cultural component of the Arabian heartland. The site of al-Faw is being excavated by Dr. Abdul Rehman Ansari of the University of Riyadh. The results confirmed a succession of settlements starting in the mid-millennium and lasting until pre-Islamic times. The recovered

20

artifacts indicated strong links with Parthian, Hellenistic, and Sassanian, in addition to the nearby South Arabian cultures.

The hegemony of the Kingdom of Kinda could have also included the well known trading towns of Najran and Jarash which appeared at about this time and provided the direct link between South Arabia and the rest of the Peninsula. Located along the lower eastern slopes of the fertile 'Asir highlands, at the pivotal juncture of the major trade routes to the north and northeast, Najran and Jarash figured prominently in the historic contacts between south Arabia and Palestine. It is quite possible that their surrounding highland region represents the land of Ophir, famous for its timber, silver, spices and gold during the time of Solomon (ca. 1,000 B.C.). The Romans, under Aelius Gallius, invaded Najran in the second century A.D. seeking to control the trading system. However, the attempt ended in total failure.

Fig. 7 Incense burner from Dhahran

It was in northwestern Arabia, or the land of Midian, that the most significant developments of the first millennium B.C. took place (Parr et al 1972, Zarins et al 1979). As we observed above, the previous millennium saw the rise of several important town settlements located along the eastern slopes of the Hejaz mountains. By the middle of the first millennium, they had become sizeable and had acquired access to the Red Sea through numerous coastal settlements scattered along its shores, from the latitude of modern Jeddah northward to the Gulf of Aqaba. Those centers began to be assimilated and unified under a succession of trading states early in the

21

first half of the millennium. Thus, the Dedanite Kingdom centered in modern al-Ula was followed by the Lihynate. Parralleling these localized state developments was the expansion of the South Arabian states. Hence, we have Minaean and Sabean influence widely spread throughout Midian. The states of this region also extended their domain into the interior of central north Arabia and sometimes controlled the Wadi 'L-Sirhan settlements.

Perhaps the most illustrous example of all the northwestern settlements was that of Tayma'; the chief reason being its association with Nabonidus, the last king of the Neo-Babylonia Empire, which collapsed by the middle of the sixth century B.C. as a result of the Achemenid invasion. The story of Nabonidus' flight is well recorded in history thanks to the inscriptions found in Harran, Turkey. The details of Nabonidus' retreat from Babylon, including his ten year sojourn in northwestern Arabia, principally at Tayma', are clearly set forth in that important document. We learn much about the then thriving towns of the region e.g., Adumatu (modern Jawf), Yathribu (modern Medina), and a host of others as yet unidentified in the archeological record. Future investigations at Tayma', itself a site of considerable dimensions, should throw significant light on the history of this region during the first millennium.

By the closing centuries of the millennium there appeared in northwestern Arabia a dominant unifying force, represented by the Nabataen Kingdom which supplanted the earlier successive states. The magnificence of its culture and achievements is echoed in the monuments left behind at Petra in Jordan, and Mada 'in Salih in Saudi Arabia. Their language and writing styles are the most direct predecessor of modern Arabic. The domain of the Nabataen, a state based on the control of trade, has been traditionally recognized as extending from the Syrian Desert and Jordan Valley to northwestern Arabia. Recent discoveries have established their dominion also in the interior Wadi 'L-Sirhan and Jawf settlements.

The Nabataen Kingdom fell victim to Roman expansion and was subsequently liquidated by the second century A.D., with its historic trade diverted to North Africa. The eclipse of the Nabataen signalled the end of the independent early Arabian state-system, and the beginning of rivalries between the great empires of Byzantium and Persia over control of the Peninsula.

IMPERIAL CONFLICTS OVER ARABIA: 200-632 A.D.

Much of the history of northern Arabia, and to a lesser extent elsewhere, during the early Christian centuries up to the emergence of Islam, was reflected in the fierce struggle between the eastern and western empires over the control of trade in Arabia. There were successive Arabian vassal states which attached and frequently switched their allegiance to either of the two dominant powers. The case of the Ghassanids in the northwest and that of the Lakhmids in the northeast are prime examples. As a result, the history of this period is very confusing and is ironically much less understood than the previous era of independent states.

Eastern and south Arabia fell under Sassanid suzerainty during this period until the Islamic conquest. The east, particularly as observed above, achieved a remarkable revival of settlement growth. Many substantial sites of this period were found along the Gulf coast and in the interior.

The known archeological sites of this period found in central and southwestern Saudi Arabia are very few. The settlement of Faw existed only until the fourth century A.D. The center of Najran collapsed well before the rise of Islam. A few seaport sites along the Red Sea are known from this period, e.g. al-Jar (Modern Rais) and al-I's (modern Yanbu). However, these too appear to have terminated before Islam.

During this period in Arabia's history the pattern of growth in town centers and other settlements shows a decisive decline. Undoubtedly, this was part due to the confusion and chaos that befell trade as a result of the enduring conflict between the declining great empires. Furthermore, traditional explanation frequently associates this decline with the recession of the incense trade in the Christian markets of the western empires. However, this may have been only a secondary factor. A more plausible primary cause could well have been a slight climatic change which could have produced devastating effects upon town growth in the context of an ever precarious ecological balance attending Arabian settlements, and which might have led to sizable dispersion. Unfortunately, the state of our knowledge of climatic history for this period is not much better than for the earlier or later ones. In fact, it is most impoverished.

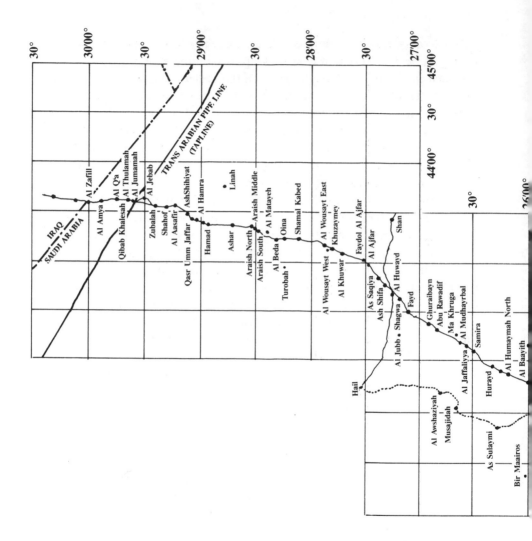

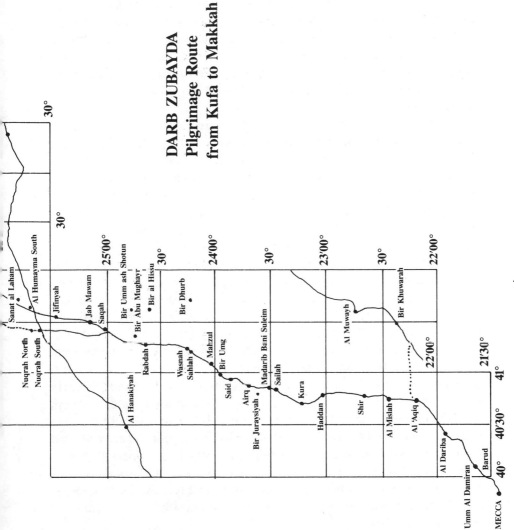

DARB ZUBAYDA
Pilgrimage Route
from Kufa to Makkah

THE AGE OF ISLAM

From a purely geopolitical point of view, the rise of Islam represents the most significant juncture in the history of the Arabian Peninsula. Within barely a decade of its consolidation in Medina, the recent Islamic state was able to accomplish the unique feat of assimilating the various segments of the Peninsula that had been for millennia entangled in the orbits of divergent external cultures. Without a deep appreciation of the segmentary pattern of ancient Arabian history, as has been attempted in the skeletal outline above, one would not readily perceive the impact of Islam from this angle of consideration.

Islamic archeology in Arabia has long suffered a distinct disadvantage, resulting from the analytical deductions propogated by historians of the Empire. The prevalent view is that beyond the initial stage of the formation of the Islamic state, Arabia came to play an increasingly minor role in the epoch making processes of expansion and achievement of the subsequent Golden Age. Once the center of gravity had shifted from the Peninsula to the Levant, and later to Iraq, the former became merely a backwater region throughout the various stages of global Islamic history.

This assessment, while it might be partially true from a grossly generalized political view, does not even narrowly reflect the now growing record of material evidence of extensive growth and achievement in Arabia during the early and middle Islamic period. In general, the evidence indicates the re-emergence and expanded growth of many formerly renowned town centers throughout the Peninsula. Furthermore, new urban settlements were created especially during Ummayad and Abbassid times (e.g., Samira, Sadriya in the Najd). Particularly in eastern Arabia, hundreds of early Islamic sites were found during the comprehensive archelogical surveys (1976-79) of the region and the majority are of substantial size. In fact, the traditional oases settlements of al-Hasa and Qatif appear to have achieved their greater settlement density during this early Islamic period.

In the southwest, many new settlements were founded around the ancient gold mining areas in the highlands. Presumably, substantial amounts of gold were mined and shipped to the minting towns of Wasit in Iraq and Rayy in Iran.

Along the western coastline many new towns were established near the earlier pre-Islamic sites. Moreover, along the western pilgrimage route from Egypt and the Levant there appeared a great number of settlements, some

26

supplanted the earlier towns of the ancient trade while others were newly founded.

The most spectacular development during the early Islamic Age in Arabia, however, took place in connection with the caravan link between the Holy Places and Iraq (Darb Zubayda Surveys 1977-82, Department of Antiquities and Museums). Along a stretch of road nearly a thousand miles long, later known as the Darb Zubayda, the late Umayyads and early Abbassids undertook a gigantic work project for the benefit of the pilgrimage caravans. Over seventy stations were built at intervals of no more than twenty five miles apart between Kufa in Iraq and Makkah. The water reservoirs and pools erected at each of the stations reflected the highest engineering achievements of the age. In addition, palaces and large public buildings or "caravansarai" appeared as smaller service units were established at each station. Since the road at its northwestern end traversed the barren, treacherous Nafud Desert, large sections were paved with flag stones, presumably for the benefit of donkeys which provided the main transport of provisions but do not travel easily over sandy tracts. Accurate milestones were posted at each station indicating the distance to and from Kufa and Makkah. Near the Makkah end, the road went through heavily settled communities where complex and grandiose architectural monuments were erected. In one such settlement, an Ummayyad palace with stucco decorations was discovered (Darb Zybayda Survey 1977, Department of Antiquities and Museums).

The decline and fragmentation that the Islamic Empire experienced at the end of the middle, and throughout the later periods, was also felt in the Peninsula. Various independent hegemonies were created within the Peninsula with partial Ottoman control. The peninsula was not united until the coming of the present Saudi State (Philby 1955). And once more, this was achieved only through the same spiritual idea system — "the purity of the faith" — which orginally gave impetus to unity during the initial rise of Islam.

CONCLUSION

The foregoing account is, admittedly, a sketchy chronological outline of ancient and recent Arabian history; it is also greatly generalized. Its purpose is less to offer a meaningful synthesis of content than to propose a framework of spatial chronological systematics.

The dominant theme recurring in this account is the emphasis on one major process which shaped the evolving form of cultural history in this very important, though still little known area of the world, "The Arabian Peninsula". The process in question is defined as the multiple cultural dialectics with the external world that underlined and differentiated the cultural histories of the Peninsula.

Hopefully, future investigations will help us to articulate this theme more fully, and thereby afford us a more detailed chronological outline than the one at hand.

ISLAMIC LAW AND THE ENVIRONMENT: SOME BASIC PRINCIPLES

by Omar Abubakar Bakhashab, Ph.D.

Say: "He is God, the One and Only;
God, the Eternal, Absolute;
He begetteth not, nor is He begotten;
And there is none like unto Him"...(112: 1-4)

THE DIVINE RATIONALE FOR THE EXISTENCE OF MANKIND ON THE EARTH

The Almighty, praise be unto Him and glory, created Man and placed him on this Earth, providing him with the capability to make use of its resources. This is refered to in the Holy Quran:

". . . It is He Who hath produced you from the earth and settled you therein. . ." (11:61).

"It is He Who has made the earth manageable for you, so traverse ye through its tracts and enjoy of the sustenance which He furnishes: but unto Him is the resurrection. . ." (67:15).

Man was created and placed on Earth to settle thereon and to make use of its resources but for a certain period only, until the time comes for the Lord to redeem the Earth and that which is on it. Indeed, all things including the Earth and all its resources are owned by the Lord:

"To Him belongs what is in the heavens and on earth and all between them, and all beneath the soil." (20:6).

29

The Lord created the Heavens and the Earth and all that is between them and entrusted their creation to Man, making him their steward:[1]

"Behold, thy Lord is to the angels: "I will create a viceroy on earth". They said: "Will Thou place therein one who will make mischief therein and shed blood? — Whilst we do celebrate Thy praises and glorify Thy holy (name)?" He said: "I know what ye know not."
(2:30).

In so doing, the Almighty gave Man authority over all things created by Him, for his welfare and benefit.[2]

"It is We Who have placed you with authority on the earth, and provided you therein with means for the fulfillment of your life. . ."
(7:10).

The Holy Quran indicates that the Almight ordered Man to settle the face of the Earth and to build dwelling places in which to find shelter, and to procreate and benefit from that which is to be found on the Earth, caring for it generation upon generation, until the Lord redeems the Earth and that which is upon it. This is the divine rationale for the existence of mankind on the face of this planet.

"And remember how He made you viceroys after A'ad and gave you station in the earth. Ye choose castles in the plains and hew the mountains into dwellings. So remember (all) that bounties of Allah and do not evil, making mischief in the earth." (7:74).

THE SOURCE OF MAN'S DUTIES TOWARDS THE NATURAL ENVIRONMENT

By bestowing upon Man such benefits and authority, the Lord honoured Man above all other creatures:

"We have honoured the sons of Adam; provided them with transport on land and sea, given them for sustenance things good and pure; and conferred on them special favours, above a great part of our Creation. . ." (17:70).

This in turn generates an obligation upon, and a commitment of Man to shoulder his responsibilities with regard to the Lord's creation, to perserve and conserve the natural environment, and to make it a source of welfare

30

for all of the Lord's creatures. And hence whereas Man has been given the privilege to benefit from the resources to be found on the Earth and those which are stored within it, he is also bound by the Lord to preserve all these resources which the Lord has provided for his use.[3] Reference is made to this in the Holy Book:

"He it is who hath placed you as viceroys of the earth. . ." (6:165).

All that which can be seen in this universe is an expression of the greatness of the Creator; indeed the universe has been made according to God's divine plan. The planets, including the Earth, move in a precise and definite pattern, and on the Earth night follows day regularly. The heat of the sun evaporates waters from the oceans and rivers; through the atmosphere they are carried by the winds in the form of rain which succours God's creatures from the torments of thirst, and waters the earth to produce food.[4] The Holy Quran refers in elaborate detail to many of these phenomena and to their importance.[5]

"He merges night into day, and He merges day into night; and He has full knowledge of the secrets of (all) hearts." (57:6).

"And we send the fecundating winds, then caused the rain to descend from the sky, therewith providing you with water (in abundance) through ye are not the guardians of its store." (15:22).

The interaction of all these factors, in accordance with rules established by the Almighty, guarantees the continuity of life on Earth. If Man looks about him and considers everything which surrounds him on this Earth, he will observe that he lives in constant interaction with other forms of life and the physical elements of the environment, each of these components contributing to the functioning and balance of nature. This is referred to in the Holy Book:

"And the Earth we have spread out (like a carpet); set thereon mountains firm and immovable; and produced therein all kinds of things in due balance." (15:19).

The Almighty also created the universe for Man to explore, in order that by doing so he should discover the majesty and greatness of the Creator in His guidance of this universe, and in the laws and rules governing its proper functioning. The subjection of the Heavens and the Earth and all that lies between them to Man is also intended to urge him to contemplate these creations and to become acquainted with the Laws and rules to which

31

they are subject. Thus the Lord enabled Man to learn the secrets of the Heavens and the Earth, in order to make more profound his faith in the oneness of the Lord.[6] This is also referred to in the following verses:

"We created not the heavens, the earth, and all between them, but for just ends . . ." (15:85).

"Not without purpose did We create heavens and earth and all between . . ." (38:27).

"Behold! In the creation of the heavens and the earth; in the alternation of the night and the day; in the sailing of the ships through the ocean for the profit of mankind; in the rain which God sends down from the skies, and the life which He gives therewith to an earth that is dead; in the beasts of all kinds that He scatters through the earth; in the change of the winds, and the clouds which they trail like their slaves between the sky and the earth; — (Here) indeed are signs for a people that are wise . . ." (2:164).

". . . Moreover His design comprehended the heavens, for He gave order and perfection to the seven firmanents; and of all things He hath perfect knowledge . . ." (2:29).

The Almighty ordered man to benefit from the Lord's blessing and to use them, warning him, however, that he would be liable to reckoning and punishment if he were to misuse them: Man is bound to behave in a manner acceptable to the Lord, for which he shall be richly rewarded.[7] "Good is (the reward) for those who do good in this world. Spacious is God's earth . . ." (39:10)

In addition, misuse might result in unjustly depriving future generations of the ability to benefit from them, and thus would also contradict the teaching of the True Faith and the stewardship of Man on the Earth.[8] God has not created everything and placed it at the service of some individuals, but in the service of all mankind. Thus, benefitting from God's blessings but depriving others of them is disregarding one's responsibility towards other humans, and future generations as well. In the Islamic perspective, people in a community can be compared to passengers on a ship, having a common responsibility. Each passenger has to ensure the ship's safeguard not only for his own safety but that of others as well.

Hence, when individual interests at times come into conflict with public interests, the individual interests should be brought into line with those of the community. Failing this, the interests of the individual would become unlawful. Islamic law gives precedence to communal interests over those of the individuals, without detriment to his rights; and it is established in Islamic jurisprudence that the rights of the individual are closely inter-related with, and restricted by, those of others.[9] Past events provide examples of the consequences deriving from not respecting the limits prescribed by God. The Holy Quran relates many accounts of past nations which spoiled and damaged the blessings of the Lord, instead of being thankful for them. Their end came amidst destruction and ruin. Man should learn from the past and avoid such errors.

Conservation of the environment is essential for Man to exercise his duty of care towards the blessings of the Lord which the Earth and its resources constitute, and ultimately is essential to his own survival.[10] Any damage caused by Man is considered an ingratitude and a disavowal of the blessings of the Lord, for which the abuser shall be punished in this world and in the hereafter. Disruption of the environment and of the delicate balance of natural systems not only endangers all forms of life,—and as such as contrary tc the will of God and is a form of ingratitude for his blessings—, but in addition contradicts the principles that one should not cause environmental harm (embodied in Islamic Law 'Shari'a').[11] While it is true that the Lord ordered man to go foth on the face of the Earth, to work and to endeavour and to observe the majesty of cration, this is conditional upon his observing the balances of nature and not harming them.[12]

The Islamic law is tolerant and grants Man freedom of action and knowledge, but the concept of freedom in Islam is embodied in the honour bestowed on Man in the True Faith. This freedom is also subject to the principle of not causing harm. Man was entrusted with fulfilling the responsibilities placed upon him by the Lord, and as such he should discharge his duties in this respect in a responsible manner, and in a spirit of true faith in his Creator, dealing peacefully with the other creatures of God.[13]

> "O mankind! We created you from a single (pair) of a male and a female, and made you into nations and tribes, that ye may know each other (not that ye may despise each other). Verify the most honoured of you in the Sight of God is (he who is) the most righteous of you. And God has full knowledge and is well acquainted (with all things). . ." (49:13).

Islamic law also devotes great attention to the question of neighbours, and calls upon the faithful to be charitable to their neighbours and to avoid causing them harm or discomfort.[14] As the Holy Book encourages us to:

33

"Serve God, and join not any partner with Him; and do good —
to parents, kinsfolk, orphans, those in need, neighbours who are
near, neighbours who are strangers. . ." (4:36).

The same principle is mentioned in the Traditions of the Prophet: "He
who believes in God and the Day of Judgement shall honour his
neighbour. . ."[15] It is, therefore, the duty of all Muslims to honour their
neighbours, to be charitable towards them and to avoid harming them and
their property. Harm here is intended to include mataerial harm such as
causing harm to the neighbours' health, or disturbing their peace and comfort
in various ways. This fully conforms with the general principle outlined
above and stated so clearly in Islamic law that prohibits causing harm of
any sort: "Ye are all shepherds and each of you is responsible for his
flock. . ."[16] Any violation of the Law is punishable in this world and the
hereafter.

The precepts outlined above constitute the fundamental tenets of Islamic
Law as applicable to the conservation of the natural environment as a whole.
The natural world and its component ecosystems, however, are comprised
of a multitude of interlinked elements. Significant impact upon any of these
elements of the processes through which they interact have repercussions
on the functioning of the ecosystems considered, and ultimately on the
natural world itself. Hence, the precepts above are and must be applicable
as well to human behaviour in regard to all component parts of the natural
environment. Guidance is thus also provided for safeguarding all natural
resources — renewable such as air, and non-renewable such as minerals
— in a manner guaranteeing against wastage and in cognizance of the rights
of others, within the divine scheme of the Almighty.

MAN'S DUTIES TOWARDS SPECIFIC RESOURCES

In addition to being covered by the general precepts outlined in the
previous section of this paper, specific elements of the natural world —
soil, water, flora and fauna — are also particularly addressed by Islamic
Law. These resources have a common characteristic: they may be continually
used for the benefit of mankind if wisely conserved, while they are subject to irrecoverable depletion if not. The following section traces the specific
treatment given by Islamic Law to these resources, while at the same time
recalling the application of the general precepts outlined above in each case.

Soil

The Holy Quran contains numerous references to the importance of soils and land and their relationships with water and living resources. It indicates that God created Man to populate and settle the Earth, generation upon generation. To this end, He caused the Earth to produce food and drink for his sustenance by cultivation of its soil. To do so He brought life to the hitherto lifeless soil in which no plants grew, with the water which He caused to descend from the sky. He then brought fourth the seeds which constitute Man's main food.[17] The Holy Book summarizes it this way:

> "And God sends down rain from the skies, and gives therewith life to the earth after its death: verily in this is a Sign for those who listen." (16:65).

> "Seest thou not that God sends down rain from the sky, and forthwith the earth becomes clothed with green? For God is He Who understands the finest mysteries, and is well-acquainted (with them). . ." (22:63).

In addition to being the material from which Man was created (He created Man from Clay), soil is a crucial life support system; a living and dynamic medium. It supports plant and animal life and is the origin of the main food resources for both Man and animals. Formed very slowly by physical, physico-chemical and biological processes, soil is easily destroyed or degraded, and centuries may be needed for its reconstitution. As the soil is one of the components of the environment entrusted to Man, he must take care to preserve, protect, and conserve it:

> "He it is Who hath placed you as vicroys of the earth. . ." (6:165).

Thanks and gratitude to the Almighty can only be expressed fully if this is accomplished, so that it can be passed on to future generations.[18]

> "A sign for them is the earth that is dead: We do give it life, and produce grain therefrom, of which ye do eat. And We produce therein orchards, with date-palms and vines, and we cause springs to gush forth therein: that they may enjoy the fruits of this (artistry): it was not their hands that made this: will they not then give thanks?" (36: 33-35).

The Lord enjoined Man to make the soil thrive, by planting and cultivating it. Failure to do so in a proper manner, however, would damage the soil and cause it to deteriorate, which is prohibited by the Almighty and by his Prophet:

". . . So eat and drink of the sustenance provided by God and do not evil nor mischief on the (face of the) earth. . ." (2:60).

And Man shall be rewarded for this care, as the traditions of the Prophet also state: "He who shall bring life to a lifeless soil shall have a reward therefrom", and "Who shall bring life to a lifeless soil shall have it for himself".[19]

It is important to note that this duty does not only address lack of proper agricultural care, but also pollution and other degradation that would cause soils to lose their fertility and ability to produce. Degradation of land and soil brings about harm to the life they support: Man, animals and other forms of life alike. This, in fact, is causing harm to others, which is prohibited by God and his Prophet who said "Cause not damage or harm" and "No Muslim shall intimidate another Muslim".[20] The Holy Book explains it this way:

"It is He Who produceth gardens, with trellises and without, and dates, and tilth with produce of all kinds, and olives and pomegranates, similar (in kind) and different (in variety): eat of their fruit in their season, but render the dues that are proper on the day that the harvest is gathered. But waste not by excess: for God loveth not the wasters." (6:141).

Water

There is no life without water, which is essential for Man as well as animals and plants alike. In addition, freshwater systems support important inland fisheries and other aquatic resources, as well as provide nutrients for floodplain agriculture. Many verses of the Holy Book mention in great detail the waters which God brought down from the heavens, then established in the Earth, in the form of springs, streams and rivers to quench Man's thirst, to provide sustenance for animals and plants and to irrigate the soil.

All the civilizations of Man have had their origins in the basins of rivers[21]; it is one of the blessings of the Almighty that he allows water to run on

36

the face of the Earth. Water descends as ordained by the Almighty, as mentioned in following Holy verses:

"It is He Who sends down rain from the sky: from it ye drink, and out of it (grows) the vegetation on which ye feed your cattle. With it He produces every kind of fruit.". . . (16:10-11).

"And we send down from the sky water in measure and we give it lodging in the earth, and Lo! We are able to withdraw it". . . (23:18).

Freshwater resources are, however, unevenly distributed, scarce at times and places, and not inexhaustible. In addition, increasing demands are made on such resources to meet the needs of expanding industrial and agricultural activities. Significant reduction of quantity or impairment of quality of waters — surface or underground, running or still — jeopardizes freshwater systems and benefits they provide.

Man, therefore, must do his part by using water economically and by protecting it from pollution.[22] This duty is all the more important as Man also needs water to clean and to purify himself, and to perform the ritual ablutions before praying to his Lord, to Whom prayers are not acceptable from one who has not thus cleansed himself. The Almighty clearly showed His desire in this repect in several verses in the Holy Book.[23]

God created water for all people; it is therefore the right of all to benefit from it in the lawful manner ordained by the Creator.[24] Reference is also made to this in the Traditions of the Prophet: "People (share) have three things in common: water, pasture and fire."[25] Water is therefore considered communal property, with all people sharing the right to use it in all the lawfully prescribed manners. This also is in the Traditions of the Prophet, according to Al-Bukhari: "(There are) three who will be disregarded on the Day of Judgement, for whom there will be no attestation and who shall be sorely punished: he who has water by the roadside and refuses it to a wayfarer. . ."[26]

Pollution of water such as that caused by the disposal of vast quantities of wastes created by industries and other developments of modern life may also infringe upon this right, and is thus also a transgression of the rights of all. This is a clear contradiction of the will of the Almighty and, while it is sinful to refuse water to a wayfarer, for which one deserves to be sorely punished on the Day of Judgement, spoiling water by polluting it is punishable by the wrath of God.[27] In addition, pollution by Man of the water resources and systems and their wastage are, in fact, an expression of ingratitude for the blessings bestowed by the Lord. God created water to enable Man and fellow creatures to live, and he should therefore turn towards his Maker and express his thanks and his gratitude for this blessing. He should do this by using water properly, in accordance with the Divine will, and by preserving it from pollution in order that it may serve the purpose for which it was created.[28] This is expressed in the following verses:

"Do not mischief on the earth, after it hath been set in order, but call on Him with fear and longing (in your hearts): for the mercy of God is (always) near to those who do good.". . . (7:56).

". . . But waste not by excess: for God loveth not the wasters." (6:141).

It is also the duty of Man to take good care of this water that was created by God, so as to avoid causing harm to others who depend on it for their various needs. Pollution of water not only makes it often unfit to fulfill the objectives for which it was created, it also destroys its purity which is essential for the performance of ritual ablutions.[29] Man should refrain from such action, since the earth has been set in order.

The same precepts apply to marine environment, including coastal wetlands and shallows, which provide food and shelter for waterfowl, fishes, crustaceans, molluscs and other marine resources to which many verses of the Holy Quran refer, stating that the oceans and the seas were created to enhance Man's life and to provide him with food and means of communication.[30]

"It is He Who has made the Sea subject, that ye may eat thereof flesh that is fresh and tender." (16:14).

"Your Lord is He that maketh the Ship go smoothly for you through the sea, in order that ye may seek of His Bounty. . ." (17:66)

Today, pollution of the oceans by vessels, dumping, land based sources and seabed exploitation represents a serious threat to marine living resources and the marine environment as a whole. Numerous verses of the Holy Quran speak most clearly about spoilage and degradation, and on how they are, in fact, a form of ingratitude for the blessings of the Almighty.[31]

Flora

The Almighty created vast numbers of trees and plants, each playing a role in the natural systems of which they are part, to confirm man's faith in the majesty of God who created this universe, and for man's admiration and pleasure.[32] Trees provide not only food, but also wood which Man uses for innumerable purposes. Vegetation and forests have, in addition, an essential role in natural processes: they comprise elements of the habitats of animal species, they play a part in determining local and regional climates, they assist in keeping water resources, they protect soil cover. Watershed forests, by their regulating effects on water, also protect downstream areas and assist in preventing siltation of reservoirs and irrigation systems.

Many wild plant varieties are of medicinal value and are components of pharmaceutical products, and the usefulness for these purposes of many others has not yet been investigated. In addition, the genetic material contained in cultivated varieties and their wild relatives is essential to the future and the improvement of Man's cultures. Man and all living creatures also need oxygen, which is produced through plant species. All these benefits are essential to the continuation of Man's life on the Earth, that he may settle it generation upon generation until the day on which the Almighty redeems it and all that is upon it.[33]

The Almighty hence caused water to descend from the heavens, thus giving life to the soil and causing gardens, forests, palm trees, olive trees and various other plants to grow which are essential to Man's existence, as well as that of other creatures.[34]

> "And We send down from the sky Rain charged with blessing, and We produce therewith Gardens and Grain for harvests; and tall (and stately) palmtrees, with shoots of fruit — stalks, piled one over another; — as sustenance for (God's) servants; — and We give (new) life therewith to land that is dead: thus will be the Resurrection.". . . (50:9-11).

The blessings provided by plants and trees and their genetic materials are innumerable and any impoverishment of these committed either directly or indirectly, is an expression of ingratitude to the Almighty. God created such plant species in conformity with precise laws. In the same manner that Man needs pure air, appropriate food and a healthy habitat to lead a peaceful life, plants and trees need a specific and favourable habitat to enable them to continue to play their role as regards the life of Man, that of other species and the natural system of which they form a part.[35] In turn, each species has a role to play in the effective functioning of these systems and the processes which take place within them. For nothing was created in vain, and the Lord produced all things in due balance.

Any person who causes damage shall pay the price for it; he shall be punished in this world and in the hereafter. Even if he escapes punishment in this world, in no way can he escape the latter, as this would violate the laws established by the Almighty. The prohibition against spoiling and damaging stated in many verses in the Holy Book embodies an obligation of Man to preserve the blessings bestowed on him by the Creator. For example, cutting down a fruit-bearing tree is harmful to others, as doing so deprives them of fruit which would have otherwise been available to them. Causing such harm is contrary to the Divine laws which not only prohibit felling fruit-bearing trees, but also the destruction, directly or indirectly, of all plants that are, now or potentially, beneficial to Man.[36]

Fauna

Animals constitute an important element of nature, and all have a part to play in the continuation of life until the day that the Lord redeems the Earth and that which is on it.

"Verily, all things have We created in proportion and measure."
(54:49).

The natural environment is an entity whose components complement one another. It must be preserved in such a way as to maintain its balance as required by the teachings of the True Faith, which require that the animal species created by the Lord be properly conserved, as they were not created whimsically, nor did they appear by chance on the face of the Earth.[38] "And God has created every animal from water. . ." (24:45).

The blessings provided by animal species are innumerable. As in the case of plants they provide food, medicines and countless useful objects made from their products. In addition they form an essential element of the natural system in which they are integrated, playing an important role in the processes which make them function.

40

"There is not an animal (that lives) on the earth, nor a being that flies on its wings, but (forms part of) communities, like you. . ."

(6:38)

These communities — of animals, plants and micro-organisms — that interact in a particular ecosystem cannot be readily substituted by others. This is particularly so because of the processes associated with such interaction, such as pollination and naturally occurring pest control. The role of insects in nature is noted by Islamic jurisprudence,[39] and the Holy Quran contains numerous references to the Bee, created by the Lord to act and make honey for the benefit of mankind:

"And the Lord taught the Bee to build its cell on hills." (16:68).

The Lord also prohibited the killing of bees.[40]

Misuse of pest control substances may have inadvertent harmful effects on the ecosystems and processes referred to above, causing unintended environmental harm, and is thus a contravention of the will of the Creator.[41] Aggression against the blessings provided by animals species, directed or indirected, are indeed an expression of ingratitude of Man towards the Lord. As in the case of plant species, aggression against animal species may take several forms: indirectly by degradation or destruction of their habitat, introduction of alien species, or directly by their over-exploitation.

Habitat destruction is today the most serious threat to species. Major tools in fighting this threat are the provision of sufficient and sufficiently large protected areas, together with careful land use planning and allocation outside these areas. The stewardship which Man exercises over species which he holds from the Almighty mandates action towards such threats.

With regard to exploitation, the True Faith permits hunting of birds and animals to use their flesh for food, and also to make use of their hides and skins, wool, hair and bones in all lawful manners prescribed by the Almighty.[42]. However, the Almighty created animals and made it lawful for Man to use them subject to certain restrictions, including those put upon him by the stewardship which he holds from the Lord. These restrictions require that the benefits derived from such use be continual and hence sustainable exploitation.

In addition to these restrictions, hunting for mere pleasure or as a hobby is reprehensible in both the Malki and Hanbali jurisprudence, as it is an offense to the Almighty. The Traditions of the Prophet are also clear on this point, in accordance with the principle of not causing any harm: "I cannot conceive of hunting wild animals except by those who are in need,

41

and for whom therein lies their sustenance."[43] It is therefore very clear that hunting for mere pleasure is an expression of ingratitude for the blessings bestowed by God, and an offense punishable in this world and in the hereafter.[44]

It is stated in the Traditions of the Prophet that he urged Man to be good and kind to animals, for which he would be rewarded. This, in effect, confirms the reprehensibility of hunting whimsically or for pleasure. A hadith states it this way: "Should a man be walking on his way and be over-taken by severe thirst, and should he descend to a well slake his thirst, and should he upon ascending from it find a dog panting with thirst and digging the earth in despair, and should this man say to himself: 'Observe this dog, he is indeed as thirsty as I was', then should he again descend to the well and fill his shoe with water and give it to the dog to drink, meanwhile thanking the Lord, Who thereupon forgave him his sins". So shall he be rewarded for slaking the thirst of any living creature."[45]

CONCLUSION

Man has been entrusted by God with the Earth and its resources as its steward and is bound to preserve and conserve the natural environment. By so doing he expresses his gratitude for that which was entrusted to him by the Almighty, and for which he is enjoined to give thanks:

"But the bounty of thy Lord rehearse and proclaim! (93:11).

Perhaps the best manner in which Man can express his gratitude to the Lord for blessings He has bestowed upon him is by being an active member of society, working constructively and following the teachings of the True Faith. In this, divine inspiration relates all activities to belief in the oneness of God.[46] Reference is made to this in the Holy Book: "And say: Work (righteousness) soon will God observe your work, and His Apostle, and the Believers." (9:105), and in the Traditions of the Prophet: "God urges you to seek perfection in your work."[47] This and the concept of conservation of the natural environment as ordained by the True Faith is evidenced by the wisdom of the successor of the Prophet of God, Abu Bakr al-Siddiq. In his speech of farewell to the Muslim army headed by Zaid Ibn-Haritha, he ordered the army not to destroy any trees by cutting or burning, or by taking their fruit unnecessarily and unlawfully, except for food. This is proof of a genuine desire to preserve the integrity of nature with which the Almighty blessed Man, and is a revelation of the morality of the True Faith as regards safeguarding the natural environment.[48]

To sum up, Islamic law urges Man to have faith in the Almighty, to be thankful for his blessings and to live in harmony with others and nature, and to act righteously for the happiness and well-being of all. This message of Islam is universal and is not restricted to any particular nation.

It follows that Man, as a believer, should care for the Earth and God's creatures and the elements on which they depend; and conserve them until the day that the Lord redeems the Earth and that which is upon it. Conservation of the environment is thus a sacred duty and harm to the soil, the air, the water and the plants or animals is a violation of this duty, and a contradiction of the injunction to worship the Lord and thank Him for His blessings. Informing people, and making them aware of the fact that safeguarding their environment is also an act of worship, is essential. Indeed, environmental conservation cannot be obtained through the efforts exerted by the state alone. Individual efforts and support are also required, and this will be facilitated by the awareness of people to the fact that environmental conservation is an act of worship and a way of adhesion to God's teachings. It also follows that the enactment of legislation directed towards the conservation of the natural environment through the regulation of resource use, or the control of pollution and other forms of degradation, is a worthy pursuit deriving from the spirit of Islam, and that the observance of such legislation and its effective enforcement equally derives therefrom.

Different events take place over the ages and new developments take place every day. The Holy Quran and the Traditions of the Prophet are clear in their message; scholars of Islamic jurisprudence should undertake research into Islamic law to show and develop its application to modern environmental conditions and its compatibility with all aspects of modern contemporary life.

FOOTNOTES

1. Al-Tabari, *Jami' Al-Bayan*, Cairo, 1373 A.H./1953.
2. Al-Jauzi, *Zad al-Masir fi Ilm al-Tafsir*, Damascus and Beirut, 1384 A.H./1964.
3. Ibid.
4. Ibn Kathir, *Tafsir al-Quran*.
5. See al-kassany, *Badai' al-Sanai' fi Tartib al'Sharai'* Cairo 1327 A.H./1907.
6. See Al-Qurtubi, *Fi al-Jami' li-Ahkam al-Quran* Cairo, 1372, A.H./1952.
7. Ibn Kathir, *Tafsir Al-Quran Al'Azim*, Cairo (ND).
8. Sayyed Kotb, *Zhilal Al-Quran*, Beirut, 1386 A.H./1966.
9. Al-Shatbi, *al-Murafagat*, and, *Majallat Usbu' al-Figh al-Islami* (Weekly Review of Islamic Jurisprudence), article by Dr. Fothi al-Durunini, Cairo, 26 Muharram 1387 A.H./1967.
10. Ibn Kathir, *Fi Tafsir al-Quran*.
11. Al-Shatbi, *al-Murafagat.*.
12. Abdel Razik Nofal, *al-Quran wal Ilm al-Hadith*, Cairo
13. See al-Shirazi, *Al-Mazhab*, Cairo.
14. al-Tabari, Jami' al-Bayan, Cairo, 1373 A.H.
14. al-Tabari, Jami' al-Bayan, Cairo, 1373 A.H.
15. *Sahih* al-Bukhari, Cairo, 1348 A.H./1928 and *Sahih* Muslim, 1332 A.H./1912.
16. Ibid.
17. al-Tabari, *Tafsir al-Quran al-Karim*, and Ibn Kathir, *al-Jami'.*
18. al-Shirazi, *al-Mazhab*, Cairo, N.D.
19. Ibn Hanbal, *al-Masnad*, Cairo, 1386 A.H.; *Sahih* Muslim, 1332 A.H.; Sahih al-Bukhari, 1348, A.H.
20. al-Tabari, *Jami' al-Bayan*.
21. Ibn Kathir, *Tafsir al-Quran*.
22. al-Tabari, *Fi Jami' al-Bayan*.
23. See, the Holy Quran (5:6), (8:11). For more details see, Ibn Qidama, *al-Mufti*, Cairo, 1367 A.H.
24. Al-Kassany, *Kitab al-Shurb*.
25. *Sahih* al-Bukhari, Cairo, 1348 A.H.
26. Ibid.
27. The *Sunan* of Ibn Dawud, Cairo, 1369 A.H.
28. Al-Tabari, *Jami' al-Bayan*.
29. Al-Kassany, *Badai' al Sani' Fi tartib al-Sanai'*, Cairo, 1327 A.H.
30. Al-Tabari, *Jami' al-Bayan*, and al-Qurtubi, *al-Jami' li-Ahkam al-Quran*, Cairo, 1372 A.H.
31. Al-Qurtubi, *al-Jami' li-Ahkam al-Quran*, Cairo, 1372.
32. Ibid.
33. Al-Razi, *Ahkam al-Quran*, Cairo, 1347 A.H.
34. Ibn Kathir, *Tafsir al-Quran.* . . .
35. Al-Qurtubi, *al-Jami' li-ahkam al-Quran.* . . .
36. Al-Ghazaly, *Ihya' Ulum al-Din*, Cairo, 1352 A.H.
37. Al-Baji al-Manfi, *Sharh Muta Malik*, Cairo, 1331 A.H.

44

38. Al-Mardawy, *al-Insaf,* Cairo, 1374 A.H.
39. Al-Jauhari, Fi Tafsir al-Quran al-Karim, Cairo, 1350 A.H.
40. Al-Tabari, Jami' al-Bayan, Cairo, 1373 A.H., and Al-Jauhari, Op. Cit.
41. *Bidayat al-Mujitahad wa Nihayat al-Muktasad,* Cairo, N.D.
42. AlSarkhay, al Mabsut, Cairo, 1324 A.H.
43. *Sahih* al-Bukhari, Cairo, 1348 A.H. and *Sahih* Muslim, Cairo, 1334 A.H.
44. Al-Baji, *Fi al-Muntaga li-Sharh Muta Malek,* Cairo, 1391 A.H.
45. The sunan of Ibn Majid, Cairo, 1372 A.H. and Abi Dawood and al-Tirmizi, Cairo, 1372 A.H., 1369 A.H.
46. Abdul Razik Nofal, *al-Quran wal 'Ilm al-Hadith* (The Quran and Modern Science) Cairo, and Sayed Qutb, *Fi Zilal Al-Quran.*
47. *Sahih* al-Bukhari, Cairo, 1348 A.H.
48. Al-Tabari, *Jami' al-Bayan,* and Ibn Kathir, *Tafsir Al-Quran..*

THE DEVELOPMENT OF ARABIC AS A FOREIGN LANGUAGE INSTRUCTION IN SAUDI ARABIA

by Mohammed K. Oraif, Ph.D.

. . .No language I know comes even near to Arabic in its power of rhetoricism, in its ability to penetrate beneath and beyond intellectual comprehension directly to the emotions and make its impact upon them. In this respect, Arabic can only be compared to music.

Raphael Patai, 1976

THE IMPORTANCE OF ARABIC IN PRESENT TIMES

Present day Arabic is one of the major world languages and some consider it the most important Semitic language. Its importance comes from the large population that speaks it, from its influence in many places in the world and from its historical development. Badawi and Younis argue that the importance of Arabic at the present time comes from its ability to survive for more than sixteen centuries with no *major* changes in its structure, due in large part to the standard provided by the Koran.

> We read Arabic poetry today that was written in the pre-Islamic period, as well as the poetry of the early Islamic periods. We can understand this ancient poetry as well as we do our modern poetry. The credit for this is given to the holy book, Koran, through which Arabic poetry was preserved for these long centuries.[1]

In part, it is the tie between the language and Islam that provides the basis for the significance and spread of Arabic. Historically, Arabic was successful in representing the entire Islamic and Arab culture for more than sixteen centuries.

> In order to understand the power of the Arabic language. . ., one must cast a brief glance back into history. Until the appearance of the Prophet Muhammed, Arabic was spoken only in Arabia, and not even in all parts of that vast, arid, half-inhabited peninsula.

47

After Islam became the dominant religion in the peninsula, the newly-converted Arabs embarked on a conquest of a major part of the world.[2]

Moslems consider Arabic the language of their religion. Since it is the language of the Koran, the holy book of Islam, a very powerful relationship was established between this language and Islam early on. Arabic became the language of worship for the entire Moslem nation. The language has been reinforced powerfully by Islam wherever it exists, and has followed wherever the religion has spread, since it is a religious obligation for all Moslems to use this language in many acts of worship. Although there are several translations of the Koran into other languages, it is believed that complete understanding of and contact with this holy book can only happen by reading or hearing it in the original Arabic. Translations of the Koran into other languages vary to a great extent in their accuracy, particularly as regards the Koranic verses.

The historical importance of Islam has also been compared to the cultural importance of Greek:

> Arabic, with its literary heritage, is one of the major languages of the world. Since the Middle Ages it has enjoyed a universality that makes it one of the world's great languages, along with Greek and Latin, English, French, Spanish and Russian. This status reflects not only the number of Arabic speakers, but also the place the language has occupied in history and the important role it has played — and is still playing — in the development of Arab-Moslem society.[3]

Throughout history, Arabic has had a great impact on Western human knowledge and culture. Greek science and philosophy were translated into Arabic early during the first century A.D. Lost in Europe during feudal times, they were re-introduced through Arabic documents and various translations which had been made from Arabic into Latin during the Middle Ages. Arabic can truly be said to have been the guardian of Greek philosophy and logic which eventually catalyzed the "enlightenment."

The Arab world covers a huge geographical area that includes the entire northern part of Africa and the western part of Asia. Among the languages spoken in the world, Arabic is considered the sixth largest in its number of speakers. It is the most widely spoken language in Africa and western Asia. It is the national or official language of at least nineteen nations. It is estimated that "Arabic is the mother tongue for about 139 million people, out of 150 million living in the Arab world today; and among those, only 11 million people speak another language."[4] In addition, Arabic is the *religious* language for about one billion Moslems in today's world.

Arabic has also had a significant influence on many other languages. According to Toiemah,

> Arabic is considered the mother of the existing Semitic languages. Its impact on many other languages has been extensive. Many languages, such as Persian (in Iran), Urdo (in Pakistan and North India), Punjabi (in Punjab), Pushtoo (in Afghanistan), Malay (in Malay Peninsula), Kanuri (of the Nile-Chad group in Africa), Hausaa (of the Negro-Chad group), make use of Arabic script. In Hebrew, thousands of words are pronounced with slightly different accents as in Arabic. Arabic has also left its impact on many western languages. In Spanish there are an estimated 6,500 words of Arabic origin. In Spanish, most words beginning with "al" are from Arabic. It is well known that Arabic gave technical words for subjects unknown in Europe, and for which there was no Latin or Spanish equivalent.[5].

As far as English is concerned, for example, it is well known that it contains literally hundreds of words which have derived from Arabic, many of which entered the language through everyday use among merchants and travellers as well as through science and learning. Below are listed illustrative examples of several words in English of Arabic origin, along with their etymological definitions. All these words have been taken from *Webster's Third International Dictionary:*

admiral	(amir al bahr) prince of the sea
alcazar	(alquasr) the palace
alcohol	(algaoul) getting drunk
algebra	(al jabr) same meaning in Arabic
algorism	(al Khawarizmi) name of a famous Arab mathematician
almanac	(almanakh) weather
apricot	(burkouk) same meaning in Aabic
cable	(habl) rope
camel	(jamal) same meaning in Arabic
candy	(quandi) sugar
carat	(quirat) a weighing unit
coffee	(qahwa) meaning originally wine
cotton	(qutn) same meaning in Arabic

49

gazelle	(ghazal) same meaning in Arabic
giraffe	(zarafa) same meaning in Arabic
jar	(jarra) a container
jasmine	(yasmeen) same meaning in Arabic
lemon	(laymoon) same meaning in Arabic
lime	(laym) same meaning in Arabic
magazine	(makhazin) storage
massage	(massa) to touch
matress	(mafrash) same meaning in Arabic
safari	(safariy) travel
sesame	(simsim) same meaning in Arabic
spinach	(ispinakh) same meaning in Arabic
sugar	(succar) same meaning in Arabic
syrup	(sharab) a drink
tariff	(taarif) to inform
zenith	(samt) same meaning in Arabic
zero	(sifr) same meaning in Arabic

Many scholars describe the tremendous ability of Arabic to derive words from their roots:

> The power of word-building takes one to the..incredible wealth of words we face when we learn Arabic. These many roots, plus the innumerable changes that can be made with them, make Arabic one of the great languages of the world, and for this alone, it is worth learning. . . it is one of the great classical languages, and ranks along with Greek and Sanskrit.[6].

Internationally, Arabic has become both an offical and a working language of the General Assembly and its main committees in the United Nations.[7]

For all of the above-mentioned reasons, Arabic has become one of the most important languages in the world. It is, therefore, not uncommon to find that institutions have been established in many different areas of the world to teach this language. Many of these institutions teach it as a foreign language. A great number of students come to these institutions from different nations and this is the case in Saudi Arabia, where many students come especially to learn Arabic.

SAUDI ARABIA AS THE MOTHERLAND OF ARABIC AND ISLAM

The Kingdom of Saudi Arabia lies like a wedge between the continents of Africa and Asia. The Kingdom occupies four-fifths of the Arabian Peninsula and comprises 865,000 square miles. This is about the size of the United States east of the Mississippi River. Some of the country's area is covered by scrub desert, not unlike that of the southwest in the U.S. Saudi Arabia's geography is surprisingly varied. Rugged mountain ranges, grasslands, and vast seas of sand all characterize the landscape.

Despite its fame in the classical world as a gateway to the East and as a land of fabulous wealth, it was from the spread of the Holy Koran and the message of Islam that old Arabia first became widely known internationally. The Prophet Mohammed was born in Makkah in the sixth century, A.D. By the time of his death in 632 A.D., the new religion had been carried to the West across North Africa and to the East towards Iran and the Indian subcontinent, thereafter spreading as far east as Indonesia and the Philippines. "From that time on, the faith of Islam has radiated its light throughout the world and, as if in response, pilgrims by the hundreds of thousands have converged on Makkah and Medinah from all points of the compass."[8]

Since its foundation in 1926 by King Abd al-Aziz, modern Saudi Arabia has been following the Sharia, or religious law in running the country's affairs. The country is ruled at present by one of the founder's sons, King Fahid bin Abdulaziz. It has actively participated in international organizations and committees. "Saudi Arabia is a founder member of the Congress of the Islamic World, the Arab League, the United Nations, the international Monetary Fund, and a wide range of other international organizations."[9]

Because of its religious and linguistic roots and importance in the Arab and Islamic world, Saudi Arabia has offered several educational programs for the purpose of teaching Islam to Moslems from all over the world. All Saudi universities are open to students who come from everywhere in the Islamic world to learn more about Islam and Arabic. One of these universities, The Islamic University in Medinah, specializes in Islam and Arabic. More than 90% of this university's students are non-Saudi citizens. They are of 78 different nationalities.[10] This makes the Islamic University a very distinguished example of an international university, although it is 100%

financially sponsored by the government of Saudi Arabia. Other universities offer significant financial aid and scholarships for students from all over the world, not only to study Islam and Arabic, but to enroll in any specialization that these universities offer.

THE CURRENT PRACTICE OF TEACHING ARABIC AS FOREIGN LANGUAGE IN SAUDI ARABIA

As of 1986, there are five programs that offer Arabic as a foreign language (AFL) in Saudi Arabia. The programs are found in the following universities: King Saud University and the Islamic University of Imam Mohammed Bin Saud, both in Riyadh; Umm Al-Qura University in Makkah; the Islamic University in Medinah, and King Abdulaziz University in Jeddah. Presented below are some statistics on programs and enrollment current as of 1986.

1. King Saud University at Riyadh

The AFL Institution at King Saud University is the largest in the nation. The total enrollment in this institution is 750 students from more than 50 different countries. The institution was established in 1974, and includes four units (departments): **a) The Unit of Arabic and Arab Culture:** Teaches Arabic as a foreign language to non-native speakers of Arabic. There are two programs in this unit: a morning program for full-time university students and an evening program for part-time students. **b)** Students graduating from **the Teacher Training Unit:** become teachers of Arabic as a foreign language. **c) The In-Service Training Unit:** provides in-service training for Arabic teachers in teaching Arabic as a foreign language. **d) The Research Unit:** publishes research in teaching Arabic as a foreign language and other areas related to this field. The total number of staff members in this institution is about fifty.[11]

2. Umm Al-Qura University, Makkah

The second largest AFL program in the nation is the one offered by Umm Al-Qura University. This program was established in 1975. At present, the total number of students in this institution is about 400, of 65 different nationalities. It has the following departments: **a) The Department of Arabic as a Foreign Language:** teaches Arabic to non-native speakers at three

52

levels: beginning, intermediate and advanced. Each level is covered in one year, so the program can be completed in three years. **b) The Department of Instruction:** trains teachers to teach Arabic as a foreign language. **c) The Unit of Curriculum and Research:** publishes reseach in the field of AFL. It aslo helps in planning for the institution and developing its curricula. The total number of staff members in this institution is sixty-four.[12]

3. The Islamic University of Imam Mohammed Bin Saud, Riyadh

This institution teaches only Arabic as a foreign language to non-native speakers of Arabic. It does not offer other programs. This institute has three branches: one in Riyadh, one in Indonesia and a third in Japan. The Riyadh branch has about 300 students. The total number of students in all three branches is about 900, meaning this university has the largest program enrollment of any in the nation. As regards programs with students inside the Kingdom, however, King Saud University has a larger enrollment.

There are three levels of instruction offered at this institution: beginning, intermediate, and advanced, and the program can be completed in three years. The staff has about thirty-five members.[13]

4. The Islamic University, Medinah:

The AFL Institute in the Islamic University in Medinah was established in 1966, which makes it the oldest in the nation. Ninety-eight students from twenty-nine countries are enrolled in this program. There are four levels of instruction and the entire program can be completed in two years. There are about thirty staff members.[14]

5. King Abdulaziz University, Jeddah

This university does not have an independent AFL institute. AFL is taught in the Department of Arabic at the Faculty of Arts and Humanities. The AFL program started in 1976, and it was very active at that time; there were more than 200 students enrolled. At the present time, the total number of students is about twenty-six of six different nationalities and there are five staff members. There are three levels of course instruction in this program: beginner, intermediate and advanced, and the entire program can be completed in three years.[15]

CONCLUSION

Arabic is one of the most important languages in the world today due to a variety of religious, historical, linguistic and political factors. Because of its extreme importance, it is the view of the author that Arabic ought to be spread as much as possible to speakers of other languages and among world Moslems in particular.

The Kingdom of Saudi Arabia is the motherland of Arabic and Islam and as such has a greater responsibility than any other nation to aid in the spread of Islam. Educational planners in Saudi Arabia are aware of this great responsibility and have established five institutions in the nation to teach Arabic to non-native speakers. These institutions are considered the best in the entire Islamic and Arab world. Most of them contain research departments that conduct and publish research in the field of AFL and some of them have branches in different countries such as Japan, Indonesia and Pakistan.

The AFL program in Saudi Arabia not only offers free language instruction to non-native speakers, but also provides monthly salaries and free housing and meals to students. This is entirely different from any program that teaches English as a second language anywhere in the world. EFL students usually pay a fortune in order to complete their studies no matter where they study. It is the hope of the Saudi Government and of teachers and researchers in these programs that the reputation of the AFL centers in Saudi Arabia will gradually spread. Saudi Arabia is attempting to play a major role in spreading the classical Arabic language and in helping scholars, linguists and Moslems to learn it and teach it to others.

Footnotes

1. A. Badawi and F. Younis. *The Major Textbook in Teaching Arabic as a Foreign Language,* (in Arabic), Tunis, The Arab Organization of Education, Culture and Science, 1983 p. 1.
2. R. Patai. *The Arab Mind,* New York, Charles Scribner and Sons, 1976, p. 46.
3. A. Chejne. *The Arabic Language: Its Role in History,* Minneapolis: University of Minnesota Press, 1969, p. 1.
4. M. Hijazi. "The Role of Arabic in Today's World Languages," (in Arabic), an unpublished paper presented at the Arab-German Conference in Cairo, 1977, p. 1.

5. R. Toiemah. *Lexical and Cultural Principles of the Teaching of Arabic Language.* (in Arabic), Makkah, Umm Al-Qura University, 1978, p. 5.
6. T. Irving. "How Hard is Arabic?" *Modern Language Journal,* no. 6, 1957, p. 289.
7. United Nations Resolution −3190 (XXVIII) of December 18, 1973.
8. *Saudi Arabia,* The Ministry of Information in Saudi Arabia, Riyadh, 1978, p. 2.
9. Ibid., p. 3.
10. *The Islamic University Bulletin,* (in Arabic), Medinah, The Islamic University Press, 1980, p. 179.
11. *The Bulletin of the AFL Institute at King Saud University,* Riyadh, King Saud University Press, 1985, pp. 1-2.
12. *The Bulletin of the AFL Institute at Umm Al-Qura University,* Makkah, Umm Al-Qura University Press, 1986, pp. 7-42.
13. Directors, in an interview, January 10, 1986.
14. *The 1985-86 Report of the Islamic University,* Medinah, Islamic University Press, 1986., p. 34.
15. Directors, in an interview of January 15, 1986.

References

Abu-Absi, S. "Language-in-Education in the Arab Middle East." In Kaplan, R. ed., *Annual Review of Applied Linguistics,* Rowley, Newbury House Pub., 1982.

The AFL Institute at King Saud University, *The Bulletin of the AFL Institute at King Saud University,* Riyadh, King Saud University Press, 1985.

The AFL Institute at Umm Al-Qura University, *The Bulletin of the AFL Institute at Umm Al-Qura University,* Makkah, Umm Al-Qura University Press, 1986.

The AFL Institute at Umm Al-Qura University, *The Common Linguistic Writing Errors Among Advance Students at the AFL Institute at Umm Al-Qura University,* (in Arabic), Makkah, Umm Al-Qura University, 1983.

Altoma, S. "Language Education in Arab Countries and the Role of the Academies." In Sebek, T., *Current Trends in Linguistics,* The Hague, Mouton, 1970.

A. Badawi and F. Younis. *The Major Text book in teaching Arabic as a Foreign Language,* (in Arabic), Tunis, The Arab Organization of Education, Culture and Science, 1983.

55

A. Chejne. *The Arabic Language: Its Role in History,* Minneapolis: University of Minnesota Press, 1969.

Encyclopedia Britannica. "The Arabic Language," vol. 1, 1981.

M. Hijazi. "The Role of Arabic in Today's World Languages," (in Arabic), an unpublished paper presented at the Arab-German Conference in Cairo, 1977.

T. Irving. "How Hard is Arabic ?" *Modern Language Journal,* no. 6, 1957.

The Islamic University in Medinah. *The Islamic University Bulletin,* (in Arabic), Medinah, The Islamic University Press, 1980.

The 1985-86 Report of the Islamic University, Medinah, Islamic University Press, 1986.

The Ministry of Higher Education in Saudi Arabia. *Higher Education in the Kingdom of Saudi Arabia,* (in Arabic), Riyadh, The Ministry of Higher Education.

The Ministry of Information in Saudi Arabia. *Saudi Arabia,* The Ministry of Information in Saudi Arabia, Riyadh, 1978.

Oraif, M. *The Structure of Arabic Discourse,* unpublished master's thesis, San Diego State University, 1982.

Patai, R. *The Arab Mind*, New York, Charles Scribner and Sons, 1976.

The Royal Embassy of Saudi Arabia, Washington, D.C. "For the Record," *Saudi Arabia,* no. 4, 1986.

Seeni, M. *Arabic for Life: A complete Curriculum in Teaching Arabic for Non-Native Speakers,* (in Arabic), Riyadh, Deanship of Library Affairs at King Saud University, 1984.

Seeni, M. *Simplified Arabic Grammar: A Series in Teaching Arabic Grammar for Non-Arabs,* (in Arabic), Riyadh, Deanship of Library Affairs at King Saud University, 1983.

Seeni, M. *Teacher Guide in Teaching Arabic for Non-Native Speakers: Practical Application.* (in Arabic), Riyadh, Arab Bureau of Education for the Gulf States, 1985.

Seeni, M. *The Use of Visual Aids in Teaching Arabic as a Foreign Language.* (in Arabic), Riyadh, Deanship of Library Affairs at King Saud University, 1984.

Toiemah, R. *Lexical and Cultural Principles of the Teaching of Arabic Language,* (in Arabic), Makkah, Umm Al-Qura University, 1978.

Toiemah, R. *The Use of CLOZE to Measure the Proficiency of Students as a Second Language in Some Universities in the United States,* unpublished doctoral dissertation, University of Minnesota, 1978.

Toiemah, R. and Annaqua, M. *Teaching Arabic as a Foreign Language.* (in Arabic), Makkah, Umm Al-Qura University, 1982.

PART II:

GOVERNMENT, BUREAUCRACY & PARTICIPATION

INTRODUCTION

The major theme of this book is to present cultural, political and administrative forces operating in Saudi Arabia. Articles in this section move from the central and regional levels to municipal and individual roles. First, Ahmed Dahlan presents his article about the development of the Consultative Council and the Council of Ministers. Dahlan outlines some dimensions of the Islamic value system and several players in the political network. Then, Seham Fatani submits her book review about the Saudi political system and assesses its responsiveness. Third, Nizar Samman discusses the regional emirates of the country and highlights the role of governors and omara in social and economic development. Next, Aidaros Al-Sabban outlines the organizational structure and functions of municipalities. As municipalities are given greater responsibilities, resulting in the expansion of the entire municipal system, they need the promotion of the municipal council system. Membership in these local institutions could be obtained via election and appointment.

As Robert Saunders summarizes the current trends:

> "Local government management is facing a new age demanding creativity. Not only are new functions and services being added to its responsibilities, but a more educated, sophisticated, and aware citizenry is being served . . . and, certainly, the citizen who seeks to participate in the affairs of government which affect him most must find a response which will encourage and develop his commitment to local government."

In a succeeding article, Dahlan asserts the significance of citizen participation in local affairs. He includes a variety of reasons and dimensions, i.e., human, political and economic, among others. He supports and praises the "Open-Majlis" technique, and introduces also other mechanisms, i.e., neighborhood councils, municipal councils, the mosque, and the media. Finally, on similar lines, El-Saflan highlights the significance of tribal leaders' participation in policy formulation and program design.

THE SAUDI ARABIAN COUNCIL OF MINISTERS: ITS ENVIRONMENT, ITS ROLE AND ITS FUTURE

by Ahmed Hassan Dahlan, M.P.A.

The Islamic consultative system has to be revived again, so the *ahl al-hall wa al'agd* (committee to loose and bind) can participate in building the new state and oversee the work of other branches of authority in a way that fits the level of development to be attained by the people.

Faisal ibn Abd al-Aziz

INTRODUCTION

The Council of Ministers was established in Saudi Arabia in 1954. At present it is the most powerful political institution in the Kingdom, having both the power to legislate and to implement laws, as well as to formulate government policy on internal and foreign affairs. The Council of Ministers represents a type of governing body which is perhaps unique in the world. Its powers and functions are in part the result of the conservative religious environment in which it operates and partly due to the historical and political situation in which it was established and subsequently developed. In this article an overview and discussion of this important institution is organized in the following way:

First, a brief account is given of the founding of the present kingdom. Secondly, a discussion of Muslim values is presented emphasizing in particular their affect on government in Saudi Arabia. Thirdly, a description is given of the historical and structural environment in which the Council emerged with special attention to the function and roles of the Consultative Council and the Ulama. Fourth, special mention is made of the ways in which the bureaucracy, the royal family and the citizenry have influenced the Council. Next, a review is given of the establishment of the Council of Ministers and a history of its early years. Finally, the present roles, functions and powers of the Council are described.

HISTORICAL BACKGROUND

The Saudi Arabian Council of Ministers can be better understood given a brief background of the recent political history of the country. After the decline of the Islamic State in the thirteenth century, the Arabian Peninsula, with the exception of the Hijaz, had no form of central government. This condition lasted for centuries and negatively affected educational, economic and political institutions. This was seen in the low levels of citizen involvement in and experience with establishing, developing and running a modern sophisticated form of government.

It was not until the beginning of the twentieth century that Saudi Arabia became the political entity that it is known as today. This occurred in 1926 when Abd al-Aziz Ibn Saud took control of the Hijaz or Western area of the Arabian Peninsula ending a long course of battles to consolidate a vast but torn and fragmented territory.[1] He started rebuilding the nation when he seized Riyadh in 1902 in the central area known as the Najed. In 1916 he conquered Al Hasa on the East coast, and in 1921 he annexed Hail in the Northwest. The southwest area of the Asir was taken in 1922.[2]

"As he conquered Al-Hijaz, (Abd al-Aziz) found a more advanced political organization than that of Najed. In order to maintain the advanced institutions of Al-Hijaz, he issued the Organic Instructions of Al-Hijaz or the 1926 Constitution. According to this Constitution, the existing institutions and practices were to be guaranteed and safeguarded."[3]

One of these institutions and probably the most significant one was the National Assembly. However, this assembly was dissolved and the Constitution issued in 1926 stated that a Consultative Council in the Holy City of Makkah should be formed in its place. As will be seen later, this council was subsequently to have a profound effect and influence on the establishment and functioning of the Council of Ministers.

THE VALUE SYSTEM

In all aspects of life in Saudi Arabia, Islamic values dominate ways of thinking and behavior. As regards the Council of Ministers, or indeed any government organization, the inseparability of politics and religion profoundly affect goals and actions. The inseparabaility of religion and politics is so crucial to the mechanics and dynamics of the political life in Saudi

Arabia that religion is, in fact, the "Supreme Constitution" for the people and government. No single official decision can be issued by any institution or any of its members, if it contradicts the principles of Islam. If such a thing happens, *ipso facto* that decision is illegal. Government is regarded as a requirement of Islam and necessary to keep order, achieve justice and enact the public interest. Islam provides clear guidelines for leadership and responsibility; it explains to Muslims the relationship between rulers, offficials and the public; and it provides government with a framework for formulating duties, policies, plans and activities. Islamic government involves administering the law of God according to Islamic justice as cited in the Qur'an and the Hadith. All actions of government officials are judged according to criteria from these sources.

"A major aspect of the efficacy of the Shari'ah law is the fact that it is considered divine by the general population. This creates an automatic equilibrium between the state and the people because the functions of the state are based upon the precepts of the Shari'ah. As a result of this balance, stability of the political system prevails and the legitimacy of the sovereign will be respected, just as the sovereign will respect the rights of the people according to the teachings of the Shari'ah."[4]

The Vicegerency Theory

Islam affirms that under the sovreignty of God, man is the representative or Caliph of God. According to the Qur'an, God said:

"We made you vicegerents in the land. . . (10:14).

To illustrate what this entails, Al Mawdudi explains: "Let us take the case of an estate of yours which someone else has been appointed to administer on your behalf. Four conditions invariably obtain: First, the real ownership of the estate remains vested in you and not in the administrator; secondly, he administers your property directly in accordance with your instructions; thirdly, the administrator exercises his authority within the limits prescribed by you; and fourthly, in the administration of the trust he executes your will and fulfill your intentions and not his own. Any representative who does not fulfill these four conditions will be abusing his authority and breaking the covenant which was implied in the concept of representation."[5]

According to Islamic principles, all individuals are vicegerents. Each person has to bear and play his role in his or her community. Citizens have

63

no choice but to participate. This does not, however, negate the concept of leadership. The Qur'an and the traditiion of the Messenger make it clear that communities should have representatives who are charged with authority. Several Muslim scholars, among them Omar Ibn Al-Khetab, the second Right-Guided Caliph, have explained, however, that being a Muslim leader means being a servant for the people.[6] Other learned Muslim scholars have considered a ruler or leader in Islam to be a) a representative, b) a vicegerent, and c) an employee of the people. In Saudi Arabia, government officials operating at any level, (including ministers and governors), should keep these concepts in mind when working.

Furthermore, in practice, all kings of Saudi Arabia absorbed these Islamic concepts. King Abd al-Aziz asserted his claim to being a public servant to the people. Citizens, including beduin, addressed him as "the Sheikhs." King Faisal, subsequently, while speaking to citizens in his open *majlis,* begged them to consider him as just a brother and servant for the public. He asserted that the title "Majesty" belongs to God alone.[7] King Fahd, in 1986, made a practical and historical step when he rejected the title of "His Majesty" and changed it to "the Servant of the Two Holy Mosques." Such a step contributes towards both restoration of Islamic concepts and propulsion of political development in Saudi Arabia.

Al-Shura or Mutual Consultation

According to Muslims, to be regarded as legitimate a government must be based on Islamic principles. Therefore it must be consultative and should enforce the rule of consultation at every level of government operation. As Muhammed Asad stated: "[Mutual consultation] is so comprehensive that it reaches out into almost every department of political life, and it is so self-expressive and unequivocal that no attempt at arbitrary interpretation can change its purport."[8] The predominant opinion among Muslim jurists is that the rulers and officials, including those in the central government such as the king, the ministers, etc., are obligated to consult their citizens on public matters and abide by agreements made in consultation. Citizens, moreover, must express their views on matters of concern to them, even if not asked to do so. In short, the Islamic concept of *shura* deals precisely with the questions of representation and citizen participation.

Responsibility and Accountability

Islamic principles also charge every citizen with different responsibilities and make them accountable for their actions. The Apostle of God said: "Behold, every one of you is a shepherd, and every one is responsible for his flock. Thus the imam that has been placed over the people is a shepherd and is responsible for his flock." It follows logically that the government is responsible for enforcing the law in all its transactions and that it has to be held accountable for its practices. It also follows that each member of the Council of Ministers is responsible for carrying out the duties he is charged with and is accountable for his actions.

The Principle of Freedom

Islam, the "Supreme Constitution" of Saudi Arabia, requires the establishment of government to achieve public interest and keep order. It provides, in addition, several principles to be realized in the relationship between government and the public, such as consultation, equality and justice. Furthermore, the fundamental right of freedom is granted by Islam. This right includes freedom of thinking, expression and scientific research; freedom of ownership, freedom to work and in general economic freedom with the exception of monopoly. Also, freedom of transportation and traveling are Islamic rights. These types of freedom are granted to males as well as females as long as they are in compliance with other principles and teachings of Islam. Islamic history is full of ideal examples to be followed today. King Fahd, who strongly believes in Islamic freedoms has asserted, since his arrival to office, his beliefs. On June 14, 1987 King Fahd explained to citizens in a meeting in his Peace Palace in Jeddah all of these principles.

HISTORICAL AND STRUCTURAL PRECEDENTS TO THE COUNCIL OF MINISTERS

Ahl al-hall wa al-agd:

It should be noted here that a group of people who have been commonly recognized from the earliest days up to the present time to constitute "the powers that be" in the Kingdom are the *ahl al-hall wa al-agd* or the "people who bind and loose". Together these people can be said to be the chief decision makers. They are composed of the Al-Saud family (the royal fami-

65

ly), the 'Ulama, the chiefs and judges of courts, the Council of Ministers members and the Consultative Council members.

1. The Consultative Council

"Saudi Arabia's experiment with a modern administration started only after the annexation of the Hijaz in 1924. The Hijaz was the first province to confront Abd al-Aziz with the problem of having to run a far more complex region with little preparation."[9] Abd al-Aziz felt that it was in the best interest of the people to leave responsibility for government in the hands of the citizenry. The idea of a consultative council of elected religious scholars, notables and merchants emerged and in January 1925 representatives of the three groups in Makkah elected 15 members to form the Council. The regulations of the Council specified that the King maintained control over foreign and military affairs but that power over other affairs was granted to the Council.

This Council lasted only six months before it was dissolved and new rules for election, to form a new council, were adopted. The second Consultative Council was composed of 18 members: 15 elected by the people and 3 appointed by the king. The elected members were two from the 'Ulama group, one from the merchants and twelve members each representing one neighborhood of Makkah.

The functions of the new Council included study of the following: the courts system, the internal security, education, health, trade, communication, and municipal affairs. The King, again kept for himself the administration of military and foreign affairs.[10] Soliman A. Solaim, the Minister of Commerce, explains the significance of this Council: "The importance of the Makkah Consultative Council is that it was the nucleus of the General Consultative Council which played an important legislative part prior to the creation of the Council of Ministers. The Makkah Consultative Council became the model for other major cities of the Hijaz after the completion of its annexation. Thus, Abd al-Aziz officially announced the establishment of consultative councils in Medina, Jidda, Tayif and Yanbu, in addition to the one in Makkah. . . Electoral rights were limited to the 'Ulama, merchants, notables and the "chiefs of professions." A General Consultative Council was then to be chosen by these consultative councils."[11]

These plans were not carried out, however, since another proposal was being considered. The Constituent Assembly proclaimed the "Organic Instructions" or constitution of the Hijazi Kingdom. The Constituent Assembly consisted of thirteen members, eight of whom were chosen via secret ballot

66

by representatives of the various cities of the Hijaz, and the other five, including the chairman, appointed by the king.[12]

In September 1926, seven months after its formation, the Constituent Assembly completed its task, and the Organic Instructions were issued. They consisted of nine sections, the fourth of which established certain councils at different levels, in particular: the Consultative Council, administrative councils, district councils and village and tribal councils.[13]

In July 1927, the "Commission on Inspection and Reform" submitted its recommendations for reforming the administrative system to the king. Following this, a new statute of regulations for the Consultative Council was issued leading to the dissolution of the old council and the formation of a new one consisting of eight members.[14] Yet another method for election of its members was adopted. As Soliman A. Solaim explains it:

"It stipulated that four members of the Council were to be chosen by the government after consultation with 'the people of integrity and experience', while the other four were to be chosen by the government at its discretion. . . It is not clear to what extent the government (planned to) go into the matter of consulting "the people of integrity and experience" before appointing the first group of four. But from a speech by the King on the same day the statute of the Council was issued, one might conclude that the intention was to expand this kind of consultation to include an electoral process."[15]

The work which the government proposed for the Council was to include the following: (1) budgets of public agencies, including amendments to the annual budget, (2) licenses and concessions for economic and construction projects, (3) expropriation of property for public interest, (4) decisions regarding employment of foreign nationals, and (5) legislation of laws and statutes. In addition, the Council was authorized to "draw the attention of the government" to any mistakes in the application of laws and statutes.[16] Soliman A. Solaim summarizes the development of the Consultative Council at this stage: "The new statute of the Consultative Council was an improvement on the original section IV of the instruction in the sense that it was given more specific duties and explicit rights to differ from the government."[17]

The preceeding discussion indicates the importance of the following points: (1) Abd al-Aziz maintained it was in the best interest of the people to leave for themselves the control over their local affairs. (2) Abd al-Aziz supported, in many ways, the establishment and development of a consultative council, chosen through elections, to help run the country. Elec-

67

tions were therefore recognized in the early days of Saudi government. (3) Electoral rights were confined to the 'Ulama, merchants, notables and chiefs of professions. (4) Prior to the foundation of the Council of Ministers, the Consultative Council played an important legislative role. One of its functions was to legislate laws and statutes. (5) Once formed, the Consultative Council had the right to "draw the attention of the government", the executive branch, to any mistakes in the application of laws and statutes. As a matter of fact, the Consultative Council had the right to reject or amend any proposed bills submitted by the government.

The division of power created through the establishment of the Consultative Council prevailed for a period. By now, however, the powers of the Council have substantially faded. According to Soliman A. Solaim:

"It was only after the decision was taken to create a Council of Ministers in 1953 that the Consultative Council began to decline. But before this took place, the Council left its permanent imprint on the country. . . Some of the laws and regulations now in force may be traced back to the Council. The Council still exists today. It meets three times a week and has three committees: legislative, financial and administrative. But, in practice, it is subservient to the Council of Ministers."[18]

2. The Royal Family

The power of the Al-Saud emanates from several factors. Historically, their ancestors, since 1745, asserted profound leadership over different tribes in fragmented Arabia, basically in the Najd. In modern Arabia, when Abdul Aziz succeeded in unifying most parts of the Arabian Peninsula in 1926, he acquired both international and local respect and attention. His successors and descendents, in addition, proved to have the insight to overcome conflict and stand united.

For Saudi people, as well as many Arabs and non-Arabs, several members of the Al-Saud inherited Abd al-Aziz's charisma. King Faisal is one example. He is considered outstanding cosmopolitan personality, at least in the Arab and Islamic Worlds. Recently, many members of the family have acquired high levels of education, in addition to experience gained through running government offices. Administratively speaking, they can be considered a pressure group which participates in designing state public policy through their involvement in the Council of Ministers. The average frequency of their membership in this Council since the year 1955 has been six. (see table one)

TABLE 1

Frequency of Royal Family Members in the Council of Ministers	Total Number of Council of Ministers Members	Year
6	11	1955
5	13	1960
6	16	1965
6	22	1970
8	27	1975
7	26	1980
6	26	1981
6	26	1982
6	26	1983
6	26	1984
6	26	1985
6	31	1986
6	31	1987
6	31	1988
6	31	1989

In 1989, six highly qualified seniors of the Royal family were members in the Council of Ministers, including the King. The ministries of Interior and of Defense, in addition to the National Guard, have always been headed by members of the royal family. The power of the royal family is very evident as compared to that of other political and religious groups in the *ahl al-hal wa al-agd* when it is time to choose the King, the Crown Prince (who is the first deputy of the President of the Council of Ministers), and the second deputy. It is expected that the family will maintain their traditional average total membership in the Council of Ministers.

3. The 'Ulama and Chiefs and Judges of Courts

The 'Ulama are those men who are, presumably, very knowledgeable in religious affairs. Since courts' chiefs and judges share this knowledge to a certain extent, they are also discussed in this section, under the title of 'Ulama. The 'Ulama in Saudi Arabia are closely tied in with the political organizations in the country. The Minister of Justice, a member of the Council of Ministers, for example, has always come from this group. The 'Ulama continue to have their influence on the country's day-to-day political and

69

judicial practices and "theoretically they are responsible for making sure that the government adheres to Islamic doctrine."[19] Nizar Samman explains their influence as follows: "The wishes of the 'Ulama naturally carry a great deal of weight in the government decision-making process. They represent the conservative force with which the government must always reckon".[20]

Historically the 'Ulama have been actively involved in the following: (1) The judicial system. They play a vital role in the administration and implementation of Islamic law. In fact, their control in this area is exclusive. (2) Islamic law. In particular they oversee the adherence of government to the law as it pertains to its social and economic activities, such as in the banking system. (3) The Religious Guidance Group, which has affiliated offices all over the Kingdom. (4) Religious education. In particular, they regulate legal and theological education at all levels. (5) Islamic scientific research. (6) Girls' education. All texts and curriculum are supervised by them. (7) Mosques. They supervise the running of mosques throughout the Kingdom. (8) Religious jurisprudence. (9) Islamic proselytizing. They regulate the preaching for Islam abroad. (10) Notary public activities. (11) Supervision of the mass media.[21]

Two episodes from the modern history of Saudi Arabia help to clarify the role played by the 'Ulama. First, in 1950, when an attempt was made to introduce an income tax, the influence of the 'Ulama forced the tax to be assessed to foreigners only since Islam requires Zakat from Muslims. Zakat is defined as alms giving of 2.5 percent per year on cash or capital which is beyond one's immediate needs. To the present day there is no tax required of Saudi citizens and the giving of Zakat is left to the individual conscience.[22] Secondly, "the 'Ulama were substantially responsible for the transfer of executive powers from King Saud to Crown Prince Faisal in 1962 and for the deposition of King Saud in 1964. This power to legitimize authority continues to be important today."[23]

The "Supreme Judicial Council" was established in 1971 consisting of twenty members chosen from distinguished jurists and 'Ulama. The legal decisions of all courts, notary publics and judges now come under the jurisdiction of this Supreme Judicial Council, and the Courts of Appeal are supervised by them as well. It is through this council, mainly, that Saudi Arabia has been able to expand its traditional legal system to include modern institutions and regulations that are in conformity with provisions and the spirit of Islamic law. The Saudi 'Ulama role, in this regard, is parallel to that of the medieval scholars who carried out their responsibilities through

70

ijtihad, or independent legal interpretation, as one source of Islamic law.[24] In short the 'Ulama have had an influential role in shaping, directing and running the government, and they are consulted on a variety of issues which might be political, economic or social.

THE ROLE OF THE BUREAUCRACY

Bureaucracies, in developing countries in particular, have had a great impact on the formulation, execution and evolution of public policy. Bureaucrats have gained their influence for at least two reasons. First, due to the lack, or in some cases the absence, of competent legislative institutions. Second, through their involvement in day-to-day government operations, they have acquired expertise which makes them more qualified than anybody else to participate in determining public policy. Many scholars have discussed these issues and according to one specialist:

"In every country a great expansion of governmental agencies and a proliferation of functions has taken place, especially in the new nations, (however), a phenomenon of the utmost significance. . . is the lack of balance between political policy-making institutions and bureaucratic policy-implementing structures. . . (Thus, in their turn), bureaucrats have (gained) more influence in politics — although the extent of such influence varies from precious little to a great deal. In the developing countries the extent of bureaucratic involvement in politics is exceptionally high."[25]

Another writer, Ahmed Tawati, has discussed the influence of bureaucrats on policy making process. He advocates that public administrators be responsible for interpreting and applying general policies and rules formulated by legislatures to meet the demands of the people. Administrators are in constant contact with the public which makes them well aware of their demands and what should be done to satisfy them.[26] Tawati summarizes his point of view by stating:

"In both developed and developing countries public administrators exercise influence on the formulation of public policy. In some developing countries where. . . political institutions such as parliament. . . do not exist, bureaucracy's role in policy making is high. In Saudi Arabia, for instance, the power of government lies in the public administration. Administrators are involved directly in the policy making process. They recommend programs to the Council of Ministers. They offer expert advice to both the King and the Council of Ministers. In fact, all members of the Council are administrators; each is in charge of a certain ministry. This Council, at present, is the only legislative body in Saudi Arabia. Thus, administrators decisively affect the policy making process."[27]

THE COUNCIL OF MINISTERS

The "Organic Instructions" (or Constitution), as mentioned earlier, were issued in September 1926. In the following year, in July 1927, the "Commission of Inspection and Administrative Reform" submitted its recommendations to the King, to reform the administrative system. One of its recommendations concerned the development of the Consultative Council as a legislative body.

Another recommendation was to establish an organ to assist in the administration and development of executive affairs and consequently, the Council of Deputies, *majlis al-Wukala,* was formed in 1932. "This Council could be considered the precursor of the Council of Ministers of 1954."[28] Soliman A. Solaim describes the political institutional development at that stage as follows: "The emergence of a central administration for the first time in Saudi Arabia was the result of the gradual change in the character of internal administration . . . the Organic Instructions. . . the Consultative Council and the Council of Deputies, might be regarded, from a historical perspective, as necessary transitional institutions leading to the final centralized administration."[29]

One of the major developments that led toward centralization was the increasing complexity of government affairs. Another reason for centralization was that more control and coordination on a central level were needed in order to build the nation and provide it with stabilization and modernization.

Thus, a number of centralized departments were founded which eventually paved the way for the establishment of the Council of Ministers. The Ministries of Foreign Affairs and Finance had already been in existence since 1930 and 1932, respectively. World War II necessitated the transformation of the Agency of Defense into the Ministry of Defense in 1946. During the period from 1951 to 1954, the Ministries of Interior, Education, Agriculture, Communication, Commerce and Industry, and Health were founded.

Other subordinate organizations were also established, such as the Department of Labor, the Directorates General of Petroleum and Mineral Affairs, and of Broadcasting, Press and Publications. All of these were to be developed years later into the Ministries of Labor and Social Affairs,

72

Petroleum and Minerals, and Information, respectively. "When the decision to establish the Council of Ministers was made, the component elements were already in existence. All that was needed was to pull these different departments together into a coordinated and centralized body."[30]

The Establishment of the Council of Ministers

In 1953, King Abd al-Aziz announced that the public interest of the country required the establishment of a council of ministers. He stated that "It would be composed of all those ministers of state charged. . . with the conduct of the affairs of ministries entrusted to them so that they may look into all the affairs of the nation whether foreign or domestic."[31] According to the Royal Decree issued, the Presidency of the Council of Ministers was to be under the Crown Prince. Furthermore, the Council was given a comprehensive mandate to look into both the foreign and domestic affairs of the nation, but its decisions were to be valid only after the President approved them and the King sanctioned them. Thus, the President and the King were to have veto power over the Council.[32]

As the final steps to inaugurate the Council were being taken, King Abd al-Aziz died and a delay ensued in initiating the Council. The new King, Saud, however, continued his father's efforts and the first session of this first Council of Ministers was held on March 7, 1954. It was attended by high officials as well as the 'Ulama. In his speech the King sketched out public policy for his government and asserted the principle of *shura* or consultation prescribed in Islam.

The functions of the Council of Ministers, according to the Statutory Regulations of 1954, included: (1) the state policy within the country and abroad, (2) the approval of the annual budget, and the making of new appropriations, (3) the approval of international treaties and agreements, (4) the appointment and dismissal of high officials, (5) the acceptance of donations, and (7) the examination of draft regulations prepared by the Consultative Council or the concerned ministries and departments for their approval, amendment or rejection.[33]

Several important comments should be made regarding the first (1954) Statute of the Council of Ministers: (1) though the Statute is a brief document marked by the lack of detailed rules of procedure, it might be considered an acceptable framework for the working council which had started without any previous experience behind it;[34] (2) the powers of the Council of Ministers mentioned above extended over all legislative, executive

73

and financial affairs; (3) according to the Statute, the position of the King is clearly dominant—he is the President of the Council and he appoints ministers and dismisses them; (4)the authority of the Consultative Council, according to this Statute is further reduced to the process of merely preparing regulations which may or may not be approved by the Council of Ministers;[35] (5) the Statute, in its final part, deals with the establishment of a bureau, or *diwan,* for the Council of Ministers. It is composed of four divisions. These are as follows: the Secretariat General, the Office of the Comptroller of State Accounts, the Technical Experts, and the Grievance Board.[36]

The New Statute of the Council of Ministers, 1958

The newly established Council of Ministers continued to operate under the Statute of 1954 for some four years and a half. However, in 1958, the financial and monetary crisis compelled King Sa'ud to call for evaluating and developing the organization. This process led to complete replacement of the old statute.[37]

"The Council of Ministers as originally founded was not a formal policy making structure, but rather an advisory body in which the appointed Ministers were only to recommend to the King their opinions considering the affairs of the country. . . In 1958, the Council of Ministers, following a major reorganization, was developed into a formal decision-making body, with legislative, executive and administrative functions."[38]

The Council of Ministers in the Eighties

At the end of the 1980s, the Council of Ministers continues to be the only dominant political institution in the Kingdom with powers both to legislate laws and to implement them. The Council is responsible for formulating state policy pertinent to internal and foreign affairs, national economy, education, social welfare and all public affairs and oversees their execution. It possesses regulatory, executive, and administrative authority. It is the final authority for financial affairs and for all matters connected with the various ministries of state and other government departments.[39]

An organizational chart of the current structure of the Saudi government is provided below. The chart illustrates the following: (1) The Saudi political structure at present has only two branches, one of which is legislative-executive combined, and the other is the judiciary. Prior to 1954, however,

74

the power was shared by three branches, the Consultative Council being legislative, the Council of Deputies being executive and the judicial system running independently; and (2) On the cabinet level, the principles of specialization and division of labor prevail. Besides the twenty Ministries, there are some twelve independent bureaus, and the heads of six of these bureaus are members of the Council of Ministers.

In addition to what can be viewed on the chart, there are more than thirty public corporations which are linked to various ministries in the government structure. These government corporations enjoy somewhat greater latitude in day-to-day operations than is the case with other agencies. Some of these public corporations are: The Saudi Arabian Monetary Agency (SAMA), the Institute of Public Administration (IPA), and the Saudi Arabian Agricultural Bank (SAAB), all under the supervision of the Ministry of Finance and National Economy. In addition, for the welfare of Saudi citizens, three financial public corporations were established in 1973 and 1974 which are the Saudi Credit Bank, The Real Estate Development Fund, and the Saudi Industrial Development Fund, all of which offer interest free loans. Other examples of public corporations include: The Public Corporation for Petroleum and Mineral Resources (Petromin) under the authority of the Ministry of Petroleum and Mineral Resources, the General Organization for Social Insurance under the Ministry of Labor and Social Affairs, Saline Water Conversion Corporation under the Ministry of Agriculture and Water, Saudi Arabian Airlines under the Ministry of Defense and Aviation, the Saudi Arabian Railroad Agency under the Ministry of Transportation and all universities in the Kingdom under the supervision of the Minister of Higher Education.

Regarding this great expansion of governmental agencies in the Kingdom, which is considered to be the governmental response to meet the needs and demands of the Saudi nation, Nyrop wrote: "The gradual development of the ministerial system is often cited as the major political accomplishment achieved by past kings of Saudi Arabia and by King Khalid, who expanded the Council of Ministers from fourteen into twenty ministries in October 1975. The existence of these ministries, however, should not be taken to imply that each is fully developed and efficiently organized. What had emerged by the mid-1970s was a diverse system of central government that attempted to respond to the needs of the country and its people, and this system had become more effective over time."[40]

The Saudi Arabian Government Structure, 1990

The Holy Qur'an
The Tradition of the Messenger

The Judicial Branch

The Legislative-Executive Branch

The Council of Ministers

The King (Prime Minister)
Crown Prince & First Deputy Prime Minister
Second Deputy Prime Minister
Ministers of various Ministries
Ministers of State
Ministers without Portfolio
Royal Advisors
Heads of Important Independent Bureaus

The Consultative Council

MINISTRIES

Planning
Health
Education
Housing & Public Works
Information
Transportation
Posts, Telephone & Telegraph
Labor & Social Welfare
Pilgrimage & Endowments
Justice

Finance & National Economy
Higher Education
Municipal & Rural Affairs
Interior
Foreign Affairs
Defense & Aviation
Petroleum & Mineral Resources
Commerce
Agriculture & Water
Industry & Electricity

BUREAUS

Comptroller General
The General Bureau of the Civil Service
Grievance Board
Disciplinary & Investigation Board
Public Authority for Ports
National Guard
Presidency For Youth Welfare
Presidency For Girls Education
Public Morality Committee
Religious Supervision at the Two Holy Mosques
Ifta & Religious Guidance Dept.
Intelligence Department

76

Centralization and Decentralization

Up to the middle of the 1970s, the Council of Ministers preserved for itself jurisdiction over many minor issues such as promotion of all higher level public employees from grades 11 to 15. The administrative process between ministries and other central organizations on the one hand, and local and field agencies on the other, was gradually characterized by an excessive centralization of authority. This led to delay of activities in the field and to unjustifiable routine work at the central level.[41]

In the beginning of the eighties, however, especially since King Fahd came to office, the government has taken brave steps towards decentralization. The Council of Ministers has delegated much of its personnel to the General Bureau of the Civil Service. Also, in the financial arena, the flexibility of the procurement system has substantially improved; government agencies, on all levels, are given greater authority to secure their needs. District and local agencies, in general, have assumed more responsibility and have been more effective and responsive in meeting people's needs as a result of the greater authority being delegated to them. Thus, the Council of Ministers has been relieved of being overburdened by minor details and now has more time to devote to important public policy issues.

Administrators of the present and future face many challenges stemming from development. "Growth, technology and population mobility are forcing geographic interdependence; and interdependence forces centralization in public policy."[42] It will be a complicated challenge to move toward both centralization and decentralization at the same time. As F. Mosher summarizes the situation: "Continuing centralization seems inevitable; yet decentralization is a plain necessity. Only a small share, in number if not in importance, of public decisions should or can be made in [the capital]. . . A challenge for administrators of the present and future is to devise, test, effect, and operate mechanisms whereby we can move in both directions at the same time. That is: devices for communities to initiate and make community decisions within [district and local] guidelines, standards, and policies and within nationwide objectives and standards."[43]

CHECKS AND BALANCES

Since the establishment of the Council of Ministers in 1954 through the end of the 1980s, the only political division of power existing in the Kingdom has been between the legislative-executive branch on the one hand and the

77

judicial system on the other. "The Council of Ministers may be regarded as the core of the political system, as the central body that correlates work of all departments and enacts statutes in conformity with Islamic law and supervises their implementation."[44]

Since the beginning of the 1960s, however, the government intent has been to revive the general consultative system and the Consultative Council in particular. All former kings of Saudi Arabia pledged to reactivate the Consultative Council which their own father established; the high illiteracy rate was one of the constraints.

Today, a committee which was established during King Khalid's reign exists, whose responsibility is to prepare a new Basic Law or constitution. Such a constitution would contain regulations governing the Consultative Council. The members of this Council should be elected in a manner similar to that set in the early days of King Abd al-Aziz in 1926 when its members were chosen through free election, while a small portion was appointed by the king. To be effective and productive, other prerequisites for the establishment of the Consultative Council should include: (1) specification of its power and functions; (2) clarification of its interrelationships with the Council of Ministers, the bureaucracy and the judiciary system as well as of the channels of communication with these institutions; (3) establishment of several committees and sub-committees to study and evaluate all state activities, i.e. religious, educational, economic, industrial, agricultural, commercial, housing, civil service, etc.

The Saudi government has made the commitment to revive the Consultative Council, and the 1990s are going to witness steady political development, since establishing the new Council would allow the division of power to prevail again. Such a step and reform is not conclusive yet momentous. Surely it would sustain the political system.

Footnotes

1. The present official name, the Kingdom of Saudi Arabia, was given in 1932 when a group of notables, after Friday prayer in the Holy Mosque of Mecca, drew up a petition to King Abd al-Aziz. They suggested a change from the name the "Kingdom of the Hijaz and of Najed and its independencies" to something that better represented a new unified country.

2. See Willard Belling, ed. *King Faisal and the Modernization of Saudi Arabia,* Westview Press, Inc., Boulder, 1980, pp. 25-29 and 75-79. See also George Lipsky, *Saudi Arabia − Its People, its Society, its Culture,* HRAF Press, New Haven, 1959, pp. 8-18.

3. Fatina Amin Shaker, "Modernization of the Developing Nations: The Case of Saudi Arabia", Ph.D. dissertation, Purdue University, 1972, p. 124.

4. Hamad Sadun Al-Hamad, "The Legislative Process and the Development of Saudi Arabia", Ph.D. dissertation, University of Southern California, 1973, pp. 187-188.

5. Abul Al'a Mawdudui, *Human Rights in Islam,* Islamic Foundation, London, 1980, 2nd ed., p. 10.

6. Thus, this Muslim leader, Ibn Al Khetab, 633-643, preceded Max Weber and other western scholars to present the concept of public servant.

7. Ahmed H. Dahlan, *Dirasa fi al-Siyasa al-Dakhiliya Li'l Mamlaka al-Arabiya al-Saudiya* (A Study of the Internal Political System of the Kingdom of Saudi Arabia), first ed., in Arabic, Dar Al-Shoruq, Jeddah, 1981, pp. 35-39.

8. Mohammad Assad, *The Principles of State and Government in Islam.* Dar Al-Andalus, Gibraltar, 1980, 2nd ed. p. 44.

9. Soliman A. Solaim, "Constitutional and Judicial Organization in Saudi Arabia", Ph.D. dissertation, John Hopkins University, Washington, D.C., 1970, pp. 7-8.

10. Ibid., pp. 12-13.

11. Ibid., p. 13.

12. Mohammad Tawfiq Sadiq, *Tatawur al-Hakum wa al-Idarah fi al-Mamlakah al-Arabiyyah al-Saudiyyah,* (Development of Government and Administration in Saudi Arabia), Institute of Public Administration Press, Riyadh, 1965, p. 29.

13. Ahmed Dahlan, op.cit., pp. 120-123.

14. Soliman A. Solaim, op.cit., p. 27.

15. Ibid., p. 28.

16. Ahmed Dahlan, op.cit., p. 154-155.

17. Soliman A. Solaim, op.cit., p. 30.

18. Ibid., p. 34-35.

19. Ibrahim Al-Awaji, "Bureaucracy and Society in Saudi Arabia", Ph.D. dissertation, University of Virginia, 1971, p. 120.

20. Nizar Samman, "Saudi Arabia and the Role of the Imarates in Regional Development", Ph.D. dissertation, Claremont Graduate School, 1982, p. 70.

21. Fouad Al-Farsy, *Saudi Arabia: A Case Study in Development,* Stacey International, London, 1978, pp. 66-67.

22. George Lipsky, op.cit., p. 129.

23. Richard Nyrop, *Area Handbook for Saudi Arabia,* U.S. Government Printing Office, Washington, D.C., 3rd ed., 1982, p. 171.
24. Hamad Al-Hamad, op.cit., pp. 185-187.
25. Fred Riggs, "Bureaucrats and Political Development: A Paradoxical View", in Joseph La Polombara, ed., *Bureaucracy and Political Development,* Princeton University Press, Princeton, 1967, pp. 120-121.
26. Ahmed Tawati, "The Civil Service of Saudi Arabia: Problems and Prospects", Ph.D. dissertation, West Virginia University, 1976, p. 47.
27. Ibid., pp. 52-53.
28. Soliman Solaim, op.cit., p. 36.
29. Ibid., p. 40.
30. Ibid., p. 42
31. Royal Decree, October 9, 1953, *Umm al-Qura,* Makkah, October 16, 1953.
32. Soliman A. Solaim, op.cit., pp. 43-44.
33. Charles Harrington, "The Saudi Arabian Council of Ministers", *The Middle East Journal,* vol. 12, no. 1, Winter 1958, Washington, D.C., pp. 8-9.
34. Soliman A. Solaim, op.cit., p. 48.
35. Ibid., pp. 53-54.
36. Charles Harrington, op.cit., p. 10
37. Soliman A. Solaim, op.cit., pp. 65-66.
38. Othman Y. Rawaf, "The Structure of Saudi Government", *Middle East Insight,* vol. 3, no. 1, Washington, D.C., 1983.
39. Article 18 of the Statute of the Council of Ministers, 1958, Royal Decree 380, May 11, 1958, published in *Umm al Qura,* May 16, 1958, translated in Samman, op.cit., p. 606.
40. Richard Nyrop, op.cit., p. 178.
41. Al Awaji, op.cit., pp. 206-207.
42. Frederick Mosher, "The Public Service in the Temporary Society", *Classics of Public Administration,* Jay Shafritz and A. Hyde; eds., Moore Publishing Co., Inc., Oak Park, Ill., 1978, p. 378.
43. Ibid., p. 378.
44. Majid Khadduri, *Arab Personalities in Politics,* The Middle East Institute, Washington, D.C., 1981, p. 52.

A STUDY OF THE INTERNAL POLITICAL SYSTEM OF THE KINGDOM OF SAUDI ARABIA

by Ahmed Hassan Dahlan, Jeddah, Dar al Shuruk, 1984, 288 pp.

Book Review by Seham M.S. Fatani

Ahmed Hassan Dahlan's *A Study of the Internal Political System of the Kingdom of Saudi Arabia,* is a book that closely examines the internal policy of the Saudi government. Dahlan, a young Saudi specialist in Public Administration, looks at how the Saudi monarchs were able to build a strong Islamic government and at the background from which the Saudi constitution evolved. He stresses the fact that the Islamic political system is based on equality, social justice and service to the people. Dahlan first compares the Saudi government with the ideal form of government in Islam. He then analyzes in depth its Islamic constitution to convince his readers that the Saudi monarchy is a "constitutional monarchy" and not an absolute one. Saudi Arabia, Dahlan explains, has an Islamic form of government with power divided between the leader, the council of ministers, the *majlis al shurah* (or Conslultative Council), and the judicial legal system. The *Shariah,* derived from the Quran and the Sunnah, forms the basis of the Saudi constitution. The Saudi constitution which is under the strict inspection of the body of Islamic scholars and *Ulama* limits and divides the king's power, the power of his council of ministers and the power of his governors and the chiefs of public institutions. All laws conform with the constitution. Royal decrees are announced when new political procedures are initiated.

Dahlan's book makes the issues alive and important. It provides an analytical survey of the development of Islamic institutions and lays the historical and conceptual framework for more systematic research in contemporary Saudi Arabian Islamic life. The author deals with a wide array of topics on religion, state and politics. His book is divided into five major sections.

Chapter one summarizes the history of the Arabian Peninsula, its importance and its development. The author points to Makkah as the cradle of Islam and discusses the Arabian Peninsula before its unification up to the creation of the Saudi state. He divides the history of the Saudi state into three different periods. The first, from 1157 to 1233 A.H. (1745-1818 A.D.), centers on the birth of the first Saudi State, and the desire of the leaders of that time to unify the Arab tribes and to restore the Islamic doctrine to the land. The second, from 1240 to 1309 A.H. (1824-1891), is the time when a new surge of national and religious sentiments which were fully realized. The third stage, from 1319 A.H. (1902) to the present, is the period when the unification process of the Arabian Peninsula and the creation of the Kingdom of Saudi Arabia under the leadership of King Abdul Aziz al Saud came about.

Chapter Two discusses the duties and the responsibilities of the government of the Islamic State, past and present, from the time of the Prophet until the present. The author concentrates on substantive issues related to leadership and important characteristics of a muslim leader in the government of the Islamic State. Both leader and citizen in his firm opinion, are equal under Islamic jurisdiction and the leader is viewed as a servant to the people he governs. Dahlan affirms a continuation of traditional Islamic practices and gives as examples the political behavior of modern Saudi Monarchs. He repeatedly states that there is a direct linkage between past Islamic tradition and the present day system of Saudi constitutional monarchy and also between public and traditional opinions, or *shurah,* and policy making. He asserts that open channels of communication exist in the Kingdom and the Islamic egalitarian spirit is alive. The Saudi government and its people abide by and consult their constitution. Strict judicial penalties are imposed on those who deviate.

In this chapter Dahlan also defines the duties and internal responsibilities of the government and illustrates how they are all based on principles of Islamic rule and doctrine. Saudi Arabia is an excellent example of a theocratic state and Islamic principles continue to be the generating and unifying force in the Saudi government. Islamic doctrine remains the supreme law of the land. Accordingly, all political issues are shaped by the teachings of Islam. Through many examples, Dahlan demonstrates how Saudi leaders and government have implemented Islamic values and principles found in the Quran and the Sunnah in the administration of the Saudi State. He also explains how Saudi jurists, using these religious sources, possess and impose a body of law which regulates all aspects of Muslim life.

Dahlan provides a detailed study of the method employed by the king to express his will in the affairs of the nation. He examines the shape and structure of the Saudi government and reveals the controls under which Saudi leaders and bureaucrats operate.

He also describes one aspect of the legislative system, namely how statutory laws are promulgated through the Council of Ministers. The Saudi Council of Ministers is a central administrative body of the kingdom. The head of each ministry, three ministers without portfolio and selected administrators and advisors constitute the membership of this council. The Council's decisions are subject to royal sanction. Dahlan examines the procedures followed by the Council of Ministers and enumerates five major stages in promulgating new regulatory or statutory rules.

1. The Ministers of the Council must constitute a quorum prior to submitting any regulatory proposals. Each Minister has the right to propose new regulations deemed important to his ministry (Article 22 of the Statute of the Council of Ministers, 1958.) This regulatory proposal is then transmitted to the Council of Ministers to be reviewed more thoroughly before a decision can be reached.

2. After reviewing and evaluating the regulatory proposals and hearing the resolutions, all decisions and resolutions must be voted for by the majority of the attending members in order to become effective. (Article 21).

3. The king's approval is sought. The decisions of the Council of Ministers are not effective until they have been sanctioned by the king. The king, however, has the right to veto the Council's resolution within thirty days of its issue date. If the Council does not receive the king's approval within thirty days, the Council's resolution is deemed to be in effect and the Head of the Council may take all appropriate measures to enact it. (Article 23).

4. At this point, the President of the Council of Minsiters gives orders to issue the new regulation, rendering the Council's decision final.

5. The new regulation must then be published in the official government gazette and becomes effective upon the date of publication. (Article 24).

Chapters three through five analyze in depth the system of government in the Kingdom and its constitution in the light of the true meaning of government in Islam. Dahlan explains how Islamic ideology shapes the Saudi constitution and how in turn it influences both ruler and people. He notes that the constitution speaks of "Islamic principles" and that Saudi rulers prefer to be viewed as servants of the people rather than as kings and monarchs. King Fahd's 1986 decree, changing his title from "his Majesty the King" to the "Servant of the Two Holy Mosques" supports Dahlan's claim that the king's will is the people's will and that Saudi political leaders listen to the "voice of the people".

It is the author's contention that Saudi Arabia is unique among major world states. Saudi Arabia is a theocratic constitutional monarchy: As a theocracy, religion and politics are inseparable and Islam is the State's governing principle. As a monarchy it allows its king to acquire and retain power. As a constitutional government, it invites the king and his cabinet, the Council of Ministers, the Consultative Council and jurists to set policy and to govern the nation. It also assures a role for public opinion and that of religious factions to divide, separate, diffuse and limit the power of the king and his bureaucratic government. In other words, the constitution keeps the government close to the people by allowing for their participation and providing numerous areas for decision-making. After formal consultation with the Council of Ministers and the conservative religious leaders and Ulama, the Saudi king enacts laws according to the Shariah.

Dahlan also looks at how opinion is formed and affects the Saudi political system. He believes that Saudis' principles and values come directly from their great Islamic heritage and is expressed in the local political and religious culture in which they have all grown up. Islam has exerted a tremendous power over the individual will as well as on the collective institutional will in Saudi Arabia and the power of Islam is indisputable. It governs every sphere of life.

Finally, the author provides new appendices of great value. These appendices outline the regulations of the Consultative Council, of the Council of Ministers and those governing the provinces. The last two appendices deal with the general regulations of the municipalities and the special list of privileges given lately to the governors of the provinces.

Dahlan's book is a useful introduction to the reader on the Saudi political system. It covers the development of the Saudi State and constitution as well as other aspects of, and linkages between, the political system, the nature of Islamic values, and public opinion, *shura*. The book reveals important information about institutions and leaders and how they affect decision-making and the internal policies of Saudi Arabia.

SAUDI ARABIA AND THE ROLE OF THE EMIRATES IN REGIONAL DEVELOPMENT*

by Nizar Hasan Samman, Ph.D.

"Local government management is facing a new age demanding creativity. Not only are new functions and services being added to its responsibilities, but a more educated, sophisticated, and aware citizenry is being served. . . And, certainly, the citizen who seeks to participate in the affairs of government which affect him most must find a response which will encourage and develop his commitment to local government."

Robert J. Saunders

Throughout several centuries of history, cities and villages on the Arabian Peninsula have traditionally been ruled by "omara", known generally in English as princes (amirs), or governors. Their rights, duties and responsibilities have been locally defined within their emirates and usually not written down. After the unification of the Arabian Peninsula by Abd al-Aziz, there began to be more central government, and the roles of regional and local omara began to change. The Consultative Council was established in 1926 and later the Council of Ministers was created.

Around 1932, the Central government began to set up lines of authority and connection between the Ministry of Interior and the emirates. By 1975, the government recognized fourteen major "regional" (mantikat) emirates reporting to the Ministry of Interior and these were divided into a total of 592 emirates and marakez. (Makkah and Medina in the Western Province; Asir, Al Baha, Jizan, and Najran in the Southern Province; Al Jawf, Tabuk, Al Qurayyat and the Norhtern Frontiers in the northern Province; Riyadh and Hail in the Central Province; Qassim in the Qassim Province; and the Eastern Province: see chart one). The country was administratively divided into six provinces (mokataah). These provinces were further divided into districts (mantikah) and sub-districts (marakez), and by agreement an Amir was appointed to be the "juristic person" who headed each. Province governors (hakim) were to be appointed and provincial councils established. In 1963, the Provincial Statute was written to establish guidelines

---

*Based on the author's Ph.D. dissertation, Claremont Graduate School, 1982.

as to the lines of authority between these various provincial heads and other branches of government and to specify clearly roles and duties for each. To date, the Statute has not been fully implemented because, almost immediately, it was under criticism and recommended for review. It did not stipulate chains of command, provide specific plans for implementation of the regulations, and was generally inadequate.

As part of this dissertation work, fifty or more persons who worked directly with the emirates in 1981 were interviewed and their opinions of the present role of the omara and emirate functions in the Kingdom were solicited. Thirty-three of these people, who are closely quoted in the disser-

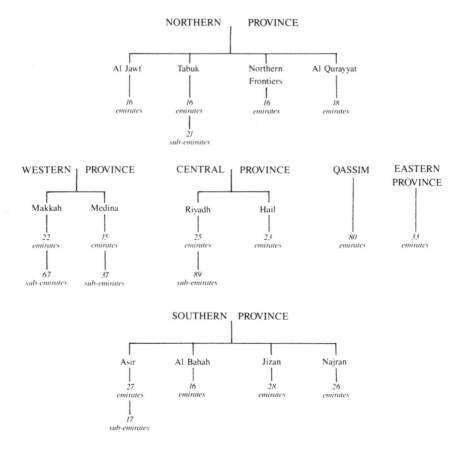

Administrative Divisions of Saudi Arabia

86

tation, are listed on the chart at the end of this paper. In particlular, an attempt was made to see whether or not there were differences in the role as seen from the point of view of the Ministry of Interior representatives, ministers of other Ministries, the omara (amirs) themselves, and the representatiaves of local or regional branch offices or municipalities.

In the section that follows, an integrative summary is made of the major points presented in all interviews and at the end of this paper a summary table is given. This summary identifies chief differences between the groups interviewed and calls attention to some of the main areas of conflict and agreement regarding the role of the emirates. The primary issues regarding the role of the omara and of the emirates are listed by number, usually in the order by which they were most often mentioned by those interviewed. The numbers correspond to those listed on the chart at the end of the paper.

1. At present there is nothing in writing which defines or specifies the relationships between the branches of government and the omara or emirates, or the job specifications of the omara. More than two-thirds of the people interviewed stated this point. Most regretted it considerably and were looking forward to the issuance of clear regulations from the central government, hopefully with input from all elements concerned. The issue was discussed by all types of persons interviewed and not by one group more than the others. All agreed that at present the role of the amir is so undefined that basically what he does in his own province is up to him. In some provinces, this has resulted in an active and interested prince supervising the day to day activities of ministry projects, getting involved with planning and budget and participating in law enforcement. In others, the Amir has been less active. The functions and quality of work performed by the emirates vary radically from one end of the Kingdom to the other, depending most often on the nature and personal qualities and skills of the omara involved.

2. The preservation of peace and security for local citizens. This was the role most often cited by all ministers and the omara themselves, though not the branch representatives. Most interpreted this to mean the amir should be involved in the settlement of disputes and the assurance of police protection. Disputes might be between government branches, between citizens themselves or between citizens and government agencies.

3. The enforcement of laws and court decisions. All Ministry of Interior officials, half of the omara and a few of the branch officials brought

87

up this point and saw it as one of the main functions as long as it was in agreement with shariah. Both the Mayor of Jeddah and the Mayor of Makkah made the point that this was basically not an emirate function and that omara and their administrations should refer all minor problems of this type to the municipal government rather than trying to solve them. In both these cities there are mayors, municipal councils and well-established city governments which function separately from the amir's office. These mayors saw the amir's duties as lying in other directions.

4. The amir is the representative of both the King and the Minister of Interior and executes orders passed down by these two persons. This function was strongly stressed by all the representatives of the Ministry of Interior, however it was not mentioned by any of the omara and only rarely mentioned by the branch representatives or other ministers. Apparently it was not thought of as a "chief" function or at least not as one of the most important functions. Furthermore, a couple of those interviewed mentioned that there is a general discussion in the Kingdom as to who exactly is in charge locally. Prince Majid Ibn Abdul Aziz, the Amir of Mantikat Makkah, for instance, stated that a big question in people's minds is whether the Amir is a representative of the King and thus in charge of all ministries in the regional fucntions or whether he is the representative of the Ministry of the Interior only and is supposed to pass information via him to other departments.

5. The amir and the emirate coordinate activities locally between the emirate and the local branches of the ministries and also between ministries so that overlap, confusion and waste are avoided. The amir can and often does act as chief of the committee of planning for the region (this is the case in both Abha and the Eastern Province) to ensure better coordination. He also sets up meetings locally between the branches. All but three persons mentioned this as a major function of the emirate. In general, the Ministry of Interior representatives stressed that the amir did such work while working through the Ministry of Interior while others seem to imply this was done through all ministries.

6. The amir acts as a chief reference source to the Ministry of the Interior (or other Ministries) and provides support and back-up to the branches, while at the same time supervising their services. Again, nearly everyone interviewed mentioned this as a prime duty of the amir and his office. At the same time, most stressed that the role was one of support and administrative execution, not of policy-making. Policies for the branches were seen as having their final authority stem from the central govern-

88

ment and ministries in Riyadh, although they needed (and often took) input from the regions. The amir of Al Jawf stated that the role was one of supervision and guidance, however both the mayors of Jeddah and Makkah said the omara had no role in planning as this was done by the municipal council.

7. Evaluate the activities of the branches. This fucntion was mentioned from a number of points of view. Some felt the amir had a direct role of assessment while others felt his role was to report to the ministry involved on issues of need for services and problems encountered in providing services. Still others stressed that the amir had a duty to assure that his citizens were provided with what they most needed and that branch activities were assessed in this light.

8. Explore possible areas for development and assess regional needs for development. This aspect of the omara's role was cited by all but three persons interviewed. It was particularly stressed by the representatives of the branches and the officials of the Ministry of the Interior. A few omara, such as Prince Khalid al Faisal, Amir Mantikat Asir, emphasized it as his key role and the chief means by which he could help his people. On the other hand, both mayors interviewed (of Jeddah and Makkah), felt that for their cities and regions, this was a role better left to the mayor and the municipal government. It should be noted that in some regions the amir is chairman of the planning council (Abha) while in others he is not (Makkah). Some mentioned that an amir's plans for development may be forwarded to the Ministry of Planning for input into the five-year development plan.

9. Supervise development projects. Again, most persons interviewed saw this as a most important function of the emirate in general, however, people were careful to stress that the role was one of guidance with a view to regional needs, not of technical input or of general policy, both of which were made by the ministries responsible.

10. The amir represents the Ministry of Interior. This point was mentioned by each of the representatives of the Ministry of Interior, but was not mentioned by any of the branches and only by one amir and two ministers outside the Ministry of Interior. Apparently, this is a regulation issued in the 1963 promulgation but it is not taken literally by most concerned in emirate activities. Most felt that an amir's authority stemmed from multiple sources, not simply the Ministry.

11. Screen citizen requests based on need. Aside from security, responding to citizen requests was seen as the primary duty from the point of

view of the omara themselves. Everyone of them mentioned this function. Others seem to agree. About two-thirds of the other groups also cited this as a role. The method by which omara should screen needs was seen to vary quite a bit. In some cases, the amir solved the problem himself. In others, he sent requests to the local branches of government, and in still others, he sent requests straight to the Ministry concerned in Riyadh. Most interviewed thought that this is one area of confusion which should be addressed in the new regulations governing emirates, which they hoped would be issued before too long.

12. Look after citizens' welfare and daily livelihood. Again, all of the omara mentioned this as one of their chief duties and indeed they often saw it as being intertwined with providing peace and security to their region. Prince Saud Ibn Abdul Mohsen Ibn Abdul Aziz, the vice governor of Makkah District saw this as his most important job. It is interesting that this function is rarely mentioned by most other groups. Perhaps the function simply seems "obvious" or it was assumed under other aspects in the interviewees minds. It is true that nearly everyone agreed that the amir was the chief authority of his region and held the ultimate responsibility for what occurred within it.

13. The amir has a direct relationship with the Minister of the Interior who then routes requests on to other ministries. The topic of which Ministers the amirs have direct contact with was the subject of much discussion during the interviews. Some said direct contact was with the Minister of Interior only (point 13); some said with each of the Ministers (point 14); still others said contact could be made both ways (point 15). A couple of those interviewed (both with the Ministry of Education), emphasized that direct contact only with the Ministry of Interior accorded with the regulations but rarely did anyone think that this was what was practiced in real life. As a result, several of those interviewed felt there was much confusion and lack of coordination.

14. The amir has a direct relationship with each of the ministers. Many of those interviewed implied that direct contact with each of the ministries separately helped to increase efficiency. However, two people from the Ministry of Education stated that there was no direct relationship with the various ministries and they emphasized the need for the emirates to be subordinate to the central government and to follow lines of authority in carrying out their functions. It became clear in the interviews that there were several opinions regarding whom the amir should contact at different levels in the ministries and when or how he should contact them.

15. The amir contacts all ministers directly or he may choose to make contacts through the Ministry of Interior. When reviewing the overall situation in the Kingdom, it was, in fact, agreed that this is what most omara did. This was perhaps confusing for some, but it was generally seen as the amir's right to contact whomsoever he wished. Eight out of nineteen persons expressing an opinion on this subject stated that this was how things were done.

16. Report local problems to the Ministry of Interior. Again, most of those interviewed thought the omara should contact whomever they thought necessary to get the job done or the problem solved. In most cases this was the Minister or branch office in any particular ministry where a problem originated. Also, the kinds of problems may pertain to citizens, to planning and implementation of projects, or to laxity or mismanagement in the discharging of duties by employees of the government or involved with projects. All are thought to be within the rights of the amir.

17. The amir is the head of the district (al-mantikah) and the central authority in his region. This fact was mentioned by nearly every minister, but rarely by anyone else. Perhaps it is so obvious a fact that it is merely taken for granted. What it means to be "head" also was clearly viewed differently, as is demonstrated by the opinions in the other points mentioned in this paper.

18. The amir does not have direct executive authority from the central government. This fact was mentioned by about half of each group interviewed. Many were careful to state that the central government was the chief authority in the Kingdom and that the emirates are subordinate to it. Furthermore, they said this assured the best functioning of government in the country. According to these people, the amir does possess general administrative authority over the branches in his region and also executive authority on matters which are related to general welfare of citizens and cut across government departments. Thus, his authority is widespread for local matters and, in fact, is often policy-making when it comes to planning, depending on his relationship with the various ministries or ministers. One or two of those interviewed (for example, Dr. Saleh Al-Malik), said they hoped that in the new regulations the omara would be given executive authority over the region allowing government to become less centralized and more efficient on local matters.

19. Participate in the development of regional budget and the budgets for projects for various ministries. There seems to be some disagreement over this issue among those interviewed. Quite often, the ministers stated

91

that the omara were consulted and encouraged to participate in budget planning or to submit budgets to the ministries. Several of the branch representatives also said that this was so. However, it appears that in some cases, the amir's budget was considered strongly by relevant ministries and in other's it was put aside. In all cases, it is the Ministry who is deemed to be the final authority for budget prioritizing in conjunction with the Ministry of Finance. A few of those interviewed expressed the need for local budgets: Dr. Abdul Rahman Al Shohail, for instance expressed a preference for a "program budget" for the district as a whole. Mr. Mohammed Saeed Farsi talked about the need for additional sources of revenue, e.g. from corporations or/and citizens (fines, fees, duties, levies, etc.).

In summary, these are the major opinions of the roles of the omara and the emirates as expressed by those interviewed. The subtlety of the differences expressed in each area can be gleaned by reading the dissertation itself. In addition, there are many minor points mentioned by only one or two persons which are not cited here. A summary table of each individual's opinions on the nineteen points above can be found on the last pages of this paper. (See Table One). It should be emphasized that an "X" on the table means that a statement in favor of the role was made. Where no "X" exists, it means the issue was not discussed, not that the opinion was negative.

Table 1

Statement cited that Amir or Emirate holds this role

	1	2	3	4	5	6	7	8	9	10	11	12	13	14	15	16	17	18	19
MINISTRY OF INTERIOR OFFICIALS																			
Prince Ahmed bin Abdul Aziz, Vice Minister of the Interior	X	X	X	X	X	X		X	X	X	X				X		X	X	
Dr Ibrahim Al Awaji, Deputy Minister of the Interior	X	X	X	X	X	X	X	X	X	X		X	X		X	X	X	X	
Prince Bandar Bin Abdul Aziz, Deputy Minister of the Provincial Department	X	X		X	X	X	X	X	X	X	X	X							
Mohammed Al Duraiby, Deputy Minister of Security Affairs, Ministry of the Interior		X			X	X		X		X					X			X	
OMARA																			
Prince Salman Ibn Abdul Aziz, Amir Mantikat Riyadh	X	X	X	X	X	X	X	X	X	X	X				X		X	X	
Prince Abdul Mohsen Ibn Jalawi, Amir of the Eastern Province	X				X	X				X	X			X				X	
Abdul Rahman Al Sudeiry, Amir Al Jawf	X				X	X	X			X	X								
Prince Majed Ibn Abdul Aziz, Amir Mantikat Makkah	X	X	X		X	X	X	X	X	X	X				X			X	
Prince Saud Ibn Mohsen Ibn Abdul Aziz, Vice Govenor of Makkah Province	X	X	X		X	X	X	X		X	X		X		X			X	

93

Statement cited that Amir or Emirate holds this role

	1	2	3	4	5	6	7	8	9	10	11	12	13	14	15	16	17	18	19
BRANCH MINISTRY AND MUNICIPAL REPRESENTATIVES																			
Dr. Abdul Kareem Al-Kowaileet, Director General of Water and Regional Affairs		X			X	X		X										X	X
Dr. Abbas H. Marzuky, Director General of Health Affairs		X			X	X		X							X			X	X
Dr. Mohammed Saleh Al-Fawaz, Director of Education in Abha					X	X		X	X				X						X
Mr. Abdul Aziz Al-Hamdan Al-Judaiee, Director of Agriculture and Water, Branch in Mantikat Al-Riyadh					X	X	X	X	X					X					
Dr. Saif Al-Deen Al Shashakly, Director General of Health Affairs in the Eastern Province				X										X				X	
Municipal Mayor of Al Jawf						X	X	X											
Mr. Mohammed Abdullah Osrah, Director of Roads Administration In Jeddah		X	X		X	X		X			X								
Dr. Abdul Rahman Abu Milhah, Director of Roads in Asir Province		X			X	X		X	X										
Dr. Abdul Qader Koshak, Mayor of Makkah	X		X		X	X					X							X	X

Table 1 continued . . .

94

Statement cited that Amir or Emirate holds this role

	1	2	3	4	5	6	7	8	9	10	11	12	13	14	15	16	17	18	19
Prince Khalid Al Faisal. Amir Muntikat Asir				X	X	X	X	X	X		X	X		X				X	
MINISTERS																			
Hisham Nazer, Minister of Planning	X				X	X	X	X		X					X		X	X	
Dr. Abdul Aziz al Knoweiter, Minister of Education		X		X	X	X	X		X	X			X		X		X		
Abdul Wahab Abdul Wasea, Minister of Pilgrimage and Endowments		X		X	X	X	X	X					X		X			X	
Dr. Hussain Al Jazairy, Minister of Health	X				X						X			X			X		
Dr. Ghazi al Qusaiby, Minister of Industry and Electricity						X	X	X	X								X		
His Excellency Sheikh Hussain Mansouri, Minister of Communications		X	X			X	X	X	X						X				
Dr. Alawi Kayyal, Minister of Post, Telephone and Telegraph					X	X	X	X	X						X				
Dr. Saleh al Malik, Deputy Minister of Municipal and Rural Affairs	X				X	X	X	X	X		X						X	X	

Table 1 continued . . . .

95

Statement cited that Amir or Emirate holds this role

	1	2	3	4	5	6	7	8	9	10	11	12	13	14	15	16	17	18	19
Dr. Abdullah Al Zaid, Director General of Education in the Western Province	X	X	X	X	X					X							X		
Mr. Hani Abu Ghazalah, Acting Director General for Municipal and Rural Affairs in the Southern Province	X			X	X			X	X		X							X	
Mr. AbdulRahman Al-Shohail, Director General for Municipal and Rural Affairs in the Eastern Province				X	X	X	X	X	X		X				X				
Mr. Mohammed Saeed Farsi, Municipal Mayor of Jeddah					X	X			X										X
Mr. Hasan Mugharbil, Director General for Municipal and Rural Affairs in the Western Province	X	X		X	X		X	X											
Mr. Assad Jamjoom, Director General for Water in the Western Province					X			X	X		X					X			X

SAUDI ARABIAN MUNICIPALITIES: HISTORY, ORGANIZATION AND STRUCTURE

by Aidros Abdullah Srour Al Sabban, Ph.D.

The municipalities in Saudi Arabia are among the oldest divisions of governmental administration. They existed even before the unification of the Kingdom, especially in the western area and specifically in the cities of Makkah, Al-Medinah, and Jiddah. This paper focuses on the establishment and organization of municipalities since the time of King Abd al-Aziz Ibn Saud. It presents an account of the early organization of municipal authority and the subsequent division of functions between local, regional and central government as well as the growing complexity of structure up to the 1980s. A description is given of the historical development of regulations pertaining to the municipalities, beginning with the Basic Regulations of 1926, and continuing with the Municipal Ordinance of 1936, the establishment of the position of Deputy Minister of Interior for Municipal Affairs in 1960, and the reorganization regulations after the 1975 establishment of the Ministry of Municipal and Rural Affairs. In addition, organizational structure, financial structure and duties and functions of various important positions and offices are described, with particular emphasis on those of the present period.

THE ESTABLISHMENT STAGE

At the time of its establishment under King Abd al-Aziz, the main objectives of the government were to have one nation, united geographically and politically, and to provide better conditions for its people to live in greater peace and safety. At that time, the kingdom consisted of a number of areas, each different in terms of the people, their lifestyles, level of education, and degree of communication with other nations in the area and around the world.[1]

In January, 1926, the year in which all the regions became one nation, there were five municipalities: Makkah, Al-Medinah, Jiddah, and Yanbu and Al-Wejeh.[2] All these municipalities are in the western region (Al Hejaz) which was once under Turkish domination. For almost one year they acted according to the old regulation; however, on September 3, 1926, the government issued the Basic Regulations (Al Talim-at Al-Assasiah), and then in the following year the Ordinance of Municipal Administration (Nezam Da'irat Al-Baladiya).[3] By 1933, when Ar-Riyadh municipality was set up, five additional municipalities were established: Dheba, Katif, Taif, Al-Hassa, and Jazan.

On December 30, 1932, the government issued the Deputies Council Ordinance (Nizam Majlis Al-Wukala'). Article 17 of this law declared that the municipalities in the western region were to be under the authority of the Ministry of the Interior; others fell under the supervision of the regional governor (Amir). The Ministry at that time contained only a small department called "the Projects Administration" (Idarat Al-Masharia) which took care of social affairs alone.[4] Financially, the municipalities depended on their charges for services on a small grant from the government budget.

Before 1926, the existing Municipalities Administration was headed by a Municipal Mayor and an eight-member council chosen by a court in each city made up of notable local citizens. However, this system changed when the Saudi government issued its Basic Regulations in 1926 and the Municipality Administration Ordinance in 1927.[5]

In 1927, the government issued the Municipal Administration Ordinance containing twelve sections and sixty-two articles. This ordinance applied only to Makkah, the capital municipality. In 1936, this ordinance was modified by the addition of articles and became applicable to all cities; this event represented a major turning point in the history of Saudi municipalities.

THE MUNICIPAL ORDINANCE OF 1357 A.H./1936 A.D.

The Municipal Ordinance of 1357 A.H./1936 A.D. (An-Nizam Al-Aaam Lee, 'Amanat Al 'Aasima Wal-Baladiyat) is vital to the history of municipalities in Saudi Arabia because it stated the strategy, policy, and organization which the Saudi government felt would turn its cities into municipalities as modern as any of the period.

The ordinance contained sixteen sections in addition to an introductory eight articles which did the following: named the ordinance; contained definitions; outlined the duties in general; outlined organization and responsibility; provided for the board for the city; dealt with Makkah's report

98

to the Deputy General and administrative governors, described the position and duties of the Municipal Mayor and assistant, the Municipal Council, the Administrative Council, the municipal committee, and the municipal body. The first section (Article 9) explained the functions of the municipality. They were to:

(1) organize, clean, and light the city, (2) supervise public and private construction; price control; weights and standards; and the cleaning of bakeries, mills, etc., (3) construct and maintain roads and the sewage system, (4) map the city and determine and protect government lands, (5) construct parking lots and markets for wood, coal, etc., (6) supervise the cleaning of houses which would be used by pilgrims, (7) count and number buildings and houses and demolish the old dangerous ones, (8) monitor the sale of dangerous foodstuffs, (9) create jobs and take care of the handicapped, (10) supervise butchers, (11) build and operate cemetaries, (12) prepare fire-fighting equipment, (13) establish cities and provide equipment to dispose of the garbage outside city limits, and (14) care for animals.

The second section (Articles 10-13) stated that the Municiple Mayor was appointed by the king and served for a three-year renewable term. He was the final authority in municiple administration and was responsible for all its work; he was also the liaison with other government and private administrators.

The third section (Articles 14-20) specified the duties of the Municipal Mayor, his relation with the municipal and administrative councils, his financial limitations, his authority over employees, and who would make the final decision if he and the administrative council could not reach an agreement.

The fourth section (Articles 21-38) concerned the Municipal Council, its membership and eligibility, when it was to meet, how its officers were elected, and how membership was terminated. It stipulated that the results of "public election" were to be approved by the king. Each member was to serve a three-year renewable term. The Municipal Council was supposed to study any matters related to the municipality; decide what is necessary to improve its work; approve its annual budget; determine service charges; deal with matters from the Municipal Mayor; and study all ordinances, proposals, and contracts made by the municipality. The Council appointed its own administrative employees and could establish special committees of its membership. The Council had to remind the municipality if it ignores its decision; if this practice continues, the Council issues a report to the government. The members were to serve without salary.

99

Section five concerned the Municipal Mayor's assistants. It explained their duties: to assist the Municipal Mayor in his job and to do whatever was asked by him related to administrative functions and to supervise employees and report any problems to the Municipal Mayor. They were to attend the Administrative Council meetings as members.

The sixth section (Articles 40-42) concerned the Administrative Council. The members included the Municipal Mayor, his assistant, the Municipal Committee, the Chief Administrative Clerk, Financial Officer, and the Treasurer. The Municipal Mayor was the chairman. The Council's responsibilities were the formulation of municipal regulations, the preparation of the municipal budget proposal, and the examination of any matter referred by the Municipal Mayor.

The seventh section (Articles 43-47) dealt with the Municipal Committee. The members were to be elected according to election regulations. The Municipal Mayor was to be the Committee's chairman. The Committee's responsibilities were mainly financial and administrative auditing.

The eighth to fourteenth sections were concerned with the regulation of each department in the municipality.

The fifteenth section (Articles 68-73) dealt with the municipality's General Assembly, which was to meet only at the request of the governor. Its membership was to consist of the Municipal Council and the Administrative Council with the Municipal Mayor as chairman. Its decisions were to be sent to the governor. The General Assembly was required to meet (1) to study any matter about which the government had requested their ideas, (2) if there were a disagreement on any matter between the two councils or between the Municipal Mayor and the Administrative Council on the subject of regulations, or (3) if the Municipal Mayor requested a discussion of a major city matter. The last section (Articles 74-83) consisted of general regulations.

This ordinance was in effect for over forty years (1936-1977), but during that time some of its articles were modified and some were abandoned due to developments in the country and the government. Other articles became obsolete with the creation of new central or local government ministries and offices which specialized in certain municipal functions.

THE ESTABLISHMENT OF THE DEPUTY MINISTRY OF THE INTERIOR FOR MUNICIPAL AFFAIRS

At the central government level, the situation of the municipalities remained the same—with all municipalities in the western region under the Minister of the Interior, and under the governor's authority in the other regions. This situation continued until 1960, when the Ministry of the Interior was moved to the new capital, Ar-Riyadh, in the central region. At this time all municipalities in the kingdom came under the authority of the Department of Municipal Administration in the ministry. When this department was established in 1958, it provided social services only, as mentioned above. In 1960, the department started to control, supervise, and provide administrative, financial, and technical services.

In 1962, the Council of Ministers approved the Interior Minister's proposal to establish an independent central system in the ministry to deal with municipalities. This sub-ministry was named the Deputy Ministry of the Interior for Municipal Affairs.[7] Its formation marked the second major development in the history of Saudi Municipalities. The expansion of municipal services, the addition of new municipalities, the desire of government to provide more and better services, the general changes and development of the country, and the increase of the national income were some of the reasons behind the establishment of this new organization.

ORGANIZATIONAL STRUCTURE

Central Structure

During the first year of its existence, the Deputy Ministry contained only a few major departments. In Ar-Riyadh there were departments for finances, personnel, statistics and land; in Jiddah there was an office for city planning and one for technical administration. At the same time, all municipalities were linked to the deputy minister (see figure 1).

As time went on, the Deputy Ministry established more departments, sub-departments, and regional departments to meet the demands for more services. There were some limitations due to the lack of Saudi technicians and various budget constraints. But with the increases in the budget, the conclusion of contracts with foreign technicians, and sending Saudi students to technical institutes, these limitations decreased.

The establishment of new departments and the expansion of old ones have continued to the present day. A look at the Deputy Ministry's 1973

101

FIGURE 1

THE 1964 ORGANIZATION CHART OF THE DEPUTY MINISTRY OF THE INTERIOR FOR MUNICIPAL AFFAIRS

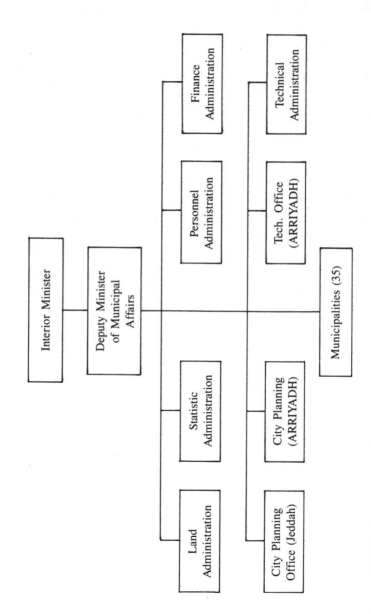

SOURCE: Mohammad T. Sadik, *Government and Administration Evolution in the Kingdom of Saudi Arabia* (Ar-Riyadh: Public Administration Institute, 1965), p. 250. [In Arabic.]

102

organization chart (see figure 2) illustrates its increasing development. All water administrations in the major cities have come under the Deputy Ministry and a sewage administration was created, either separately or in conjunction with the Water Administration. In 1963, offices for technical and city planning were established in Ar-Riyadh; later additional regional offices in addition to a general administration office were established in the Deputy Ministry to oversee the regional offices. In 1965, the Deputy Ministry set up the Technicians Assistant Institute to meet the need for assistants in municipalities and the water administrations. In 1966, the Health Environment General Administration was founded to supervise the Health Environment Departments in the municipalities (which became independent and more important). In 1967, the General Utility Administration was established to deal with water and sewage in places where there was no independent water and sewage authority. Basically, this administration supervises municipal utility departments. In addition, the municipalities provide electricity where there is not a private electric company.

The central departments act as bodies for direct and indirect supervision, guidance, research, coordination, monitoring, evaluation, and participation in emergency cases. In addition to the above mentioned departments, there are the recently established departments of land, law, city council inspection, and organization and programs. These departments' functions are discussed in detail below.

Regional Structure

At the regional level, the importance of municipalities also grew. They were established in most areas of the kingdom, their services were broadened and their influence on central government increased. The Deputy Ministry recognized the need to create four regional offices, each containing departments of utilities, engineering, survey, and city planning. Regional offices were located in the eastern, central, western, and southern regions of Saudi Arabia.

These regional offices were not actually regional administrative authorities as much as they were liaisons or centers of communication for technical matters. They participataed in municipality functions in some cases and actually performed part of the job in other cases, depending on the ability of the municipality and its size. They also supervised the local technical departments to ensure that they followed the same direction as general policy. This entire structure was changed with the establishment of the Ministry of Municipal and Rural Affairs.[8]

103

FIGURE 2

THE 1973 ORGANIZATION CHART OF THE DEPUTY MINISTRY
OF THE INTERIOR FOR MUNICIPAL AFFAIRS

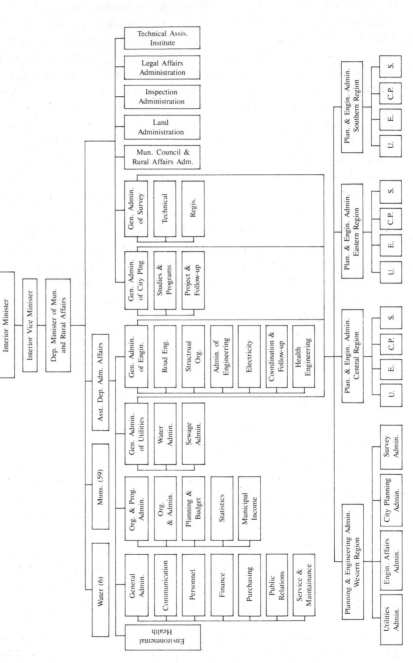

SOURCE: The Deputy Ministry of the Interior for Municipal Affairs, *The Municipal Services*, vol. 1, no. 1 (Ar-Riyadh: Public Relation Administration, 1973), p. 6. [In Arabic.]

104

Local Structure

The number of municipalities in the kingdom increased yearly, reaching 101 in 1975. At the local level, while all municipalities were linked to one central administration and they all operated under one set of ordinances and regulations, there were many differences in their structure and functions. For example, some municipalities had a city council, research unit, city planning department, etc., while others did not. Administratively, some municipalities had adequate personnel, finance, and public relations departments, while other municipalities contained only some or none of these departments. This situation still exists today.

The same is true regarding municipal activities. Reasons for this diversity include the following: (1) population levels range from only a few thousand to more than one-half million; (2) the status of the cities varies from industrial, agricultural, or commercial or a combination of these types; (3) the personality and activities of the Municipal Mayor of each city varies from those at the central level; (4) there are differences among the governors of small cities and how they evaluate their cities' circumstances; (5) a city's importance to the planners in the municipal central administration varies; (6) budgets and budget levels vary; (7) there is a difference in availability of technicians, staff, and administrators; (8)the experience and educational levels of local officers vary; (9) available equipment differs; and finally because: (10) municipalities have existed for differing lengths of time.

Financial Structure

Regardless of the late establishment of the Central Municipal Administration, municipal budgets were often as old as the municipality itself, going back to the 1930s or before. The old municipalities relied mainly on their own small grants from the central government, and grants from citizens (according to ordinance). The low level of income affected the quality and quantity of services. But this changed after the discovery of oil in Saudi Arabia. Government grants became the main source of local income, far surpassing small local income.

Some taxation was stopped by the government (e.g., the rent and pilgrimage taxes) and others remained at the same rate (e.g., the motor vehicle). Service charges did not increase and, in some cases, actually covered only 20 percent of real costs or less.

105

The first budget of the Deputy Ministry was 4.5 million Saudi riyals; it increased rapidly reaching over SR300 million in the tenth year just for the central administration of municipalities.[9] At the local level, the year the Deputy Ministry was begun, for example, the budget of the municipality of Makkah was about SR29 million; by 1972, it was about SR45 million.[10]

THE NEW STRUCTURE OF THE MINISTRY OF MUNICIPAL AND RURAL AFFAIRS

From the beginning through the middle of the 1970s, the Kingdom of Saudi Arabia experienced its first five-year development plan which resulted in tremendous social, physical, and economic developments. The second plan started in fiscal 1975/1976, the third one in 1980/81 and the fourth one in 1985/86. Accordingly, municipalities were given greater responsibilities and offered expanded services, resulting in an expansion of the entire municipal system at the central, regional, and local levels. The government realized then that it was necessary to reorganize the system and established the Ministry of Municipal and Rural Affairs (MOMARA) to replace the Deputy Ministry of the Interior for Municipal Affairs at the end of 1975.

The development plans had far ranging effects on the municipalities' activities. The various development plans contained many projects and programs relating to municipalities and every branch of government. The Real Estate Development Fund and the Industrial Development Fund were established to fund private buildings and industry by providing non-profit long-term loans for 80 percent of the cost in some cases. They also offered agricultural loans, and paid generous prices for private land used for public projects. All these changes resulted in increased building, and expansion of city area, as well as a rapid growth in the migration rate from the countryside to the city. Saudi Arabia's small population and the lack of manpower, both unskilled and professional, resulted in growing numbers of foreigners to fill the increasing number of jobs. With rapid increases in income, Saudis began expecting more modern lifestyles and the government started to provide more sophisticated services to its citizens.

All these elements, which were far from comprehensive, meant more people, houses and industry. These developments, in turn, led to a need for increased services such as city planning, water and sewage systems, building inspection, recreation areas, health services and other municipal services. Before the establishment of the MOMARA, government policy

106

had regulated every aspect of the municipalities; but now new situations and increased needs forced a change in the outdated administrative structure. The Ministry took the first step toward modernization by contracting with a foreign consultant, McKinsey International, to study and focus on decentralization in a new organizational structure. The result was a decentralized organization which extended more responsibilities to the municipalities and regional offices, leaving the central administration in charge of general municipal policy, planning, supervision and follow-up.

The remaining sections of this article focus on a description of this new system.

THE REORGANIZATION FRAMEWORK[11]

The reorganization focused on decentralization as the new approach for the MOMARA administrative policy. Briefly, the new organization is outlined below.

(1) The Ministry's central offices were originally structured into four main integrated deputy ministries to work primarily on the development of policy and overall program control instead of day-to-day work and detailed project implementation.

(2) A highly qualified planning and programming department was upgraded to make a fifth deputy ministry in 1983.

(3) The Deputy Minister for Municipal Affairs is in charge of municipal services and administrative matters.

(4) To achieve coordination and consistent standards and technical policies, all technical services are to be directed and controlled by one central official and office.

(5) More attention is given to projects of the Department of Rural Affairs so that rural areas will experience development similar to that in urban areas.

(6) Six highly qualified regional offices have the ability to support and coordinate the municipalities and make the best use of the available skilled manpower.

(7) Authority and responsibility are given to senior officials in the central administration department, so that regional and local levels can depend on their ability and qualifications.

After the completion of McKinsey International's study, the resulting proposal was reviewed and evaluated by the Ministry's officials and final-

107

ly authorized by the Higher Committee for Administrative Reform (see figure 3).[12]

FIGURE 3

THE 1978 ORGANIZATION CHART OF THE MINISTRY
OF MUNICIPAL AND RURAL AFFAIRS

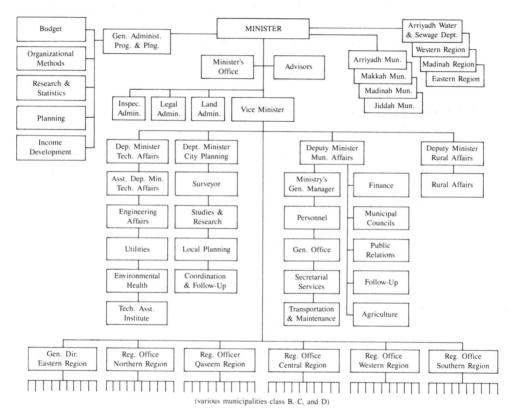

SOURCE: The Ministry of Municipal and Rural Affairs
Organization Structure Chart, 1978. [In Arabic.]

THE ORGANIZATIONAL STRUCTURE
The Minister

At the top of the Ministry's organization is the Minister who is responsible for all the Ministry's bodies, departments, and municipalities. He

108

is the final authority, the senior policy-maker, and the Ministry representative to the Council of Ministers (Cabinet), both in the kingdom and abroad. Some departments, the larger municipalities, the water and sewage departments, and regional offices are directly connected to him while others are managed by his deputies.

The Minister's Office

The Minister's Office is responsible for preparing documents for presentation to the Minister and documents issued by him. It prepares background material and supporting information for documents presented to the Minister. At the Minister's instructions, it issues any proposals or drafts concerning setting up special committees or conferences and schedules the Minister's meetings, interviews, public appearances and business trips. The office drafts a preliminary program of activities and reviews it with the Minister for approval.[13]

The Advisors

The advisors are a team of experts in different fields related to the Ministry's work. Their main responsibility is to reply to any request for advice (such as a legal interpretation) by the Minister or his office or the Ministry's departments. The Minister may also request their advice in making a decision or before the presentation of a new program, law, or regulation prepared by one of the Ministry's departments for the Council of Ministers.

The Inspection Administration

The Inspection Administration is responsible for investigating any violation of regulations, in the ministry or the municipalities, either by individuals or organizations. Its authority extends to administrative or financial affairs, but auditing is not included.

Investigation begins with a request from the Minister, Senior Official, or Municipal Mayor. The public request is screened by the Inspection Director who marks those with the highest priority. The second step is to undertake an investigation and prepare a detailed report to the Minister and include its recommendations for action.

While inspectors conduct the investigation, they also ensure that the regulations and formal procedures have been followed. The Administration contains two departments: The Administrative Inspection Department and the Financial Inspection Department.

The Legal Affairs Administration

The Legal Affairs Administration also reports to the Minister; its main jobs are to help any local or central department or administration to prepare contracts or review them before they are signed, to review any regulation before it is announced, to study ordinances and regulations to recommend necessary changes, to give legal advice when requested, and to help municipalities prepare documents to undertake legal action against a contractor.

The Land Administration asks for the participation of the Legal Affairs Administration in complicated land issues. The Inspection Administration refers its disciplinary reports to the Land Administration and asks for legal remedies or reviews of punishment.

Finally, the Administration maintains comprehensive and up-to-date information and files of all the laws, regulations, decrees, and instructions that control and direct the Ministry's work.

The Land Administration

The Land Administration's responsibility is to help in the organization of the new land departments in the regional offices and the large municipalities and to assess and develop the old ones. (All land issues should be resolved at the local level.[14]) The local land departments also seek advice about the updated rules and regulations from the central administration to follow in their day-to-day work, especially with regard to land sales, land grants, land needed for municipal and public projects, and conflicts over land ownership (by the public).

In special cases the administration cooperates with the Ministry of Justice on the issue of legality and land regulations. It also helps the Ministry resolve "issues for land grants and sales that come from the King and the Crown Prince. It ensures that any land disputes that are brought directly to the Central Ministry, either by aggrieved individuals or, for example by an Emir, are resolved."[15]

Two departments take care of these functions: the Legal Department and the Land Services Department.

THE DEPUTY MINISTRY OF PLANNING AND PROJECTS

"The Central Ministry had neither the local information to approve detailed plans and budgets for every municipality, nor the management system to control the process of achieving its targets and objectives."[16]

Thus, the establishment of the Deputy Ministry of Planning and Projects was primarily to strengthen management control at all levels, to improve planning and programming policy and strategy, and to increase and improve efficiency of the available manpower and resources. One of the results of this innovation has been that the future fiscal budgets will contain funds only for those projects and programs that can actually be implemented in that year. Therefore, general principles have been developed to guide the planning process.

(1) The Ministry activities should be systematically planned and controlled to meet all citizen needs in urban and rural areas.

(2) Plans should satisfy and stimulate development within the current budgeting regulations, which means focusing on and analyzing the projects in the current budget to include only those projects that are actually needed and can be implemented.[17]

(3) This Deputy Ministry is responsible for the overall control of Ministry plans; municipalities are responsible for program development; and regional offices will coordinate, assist, and review the local plans and functions.

The Deputy Ministry is responsible for allocating development resources wherever the ministry services reach, preparing the five-year development plans and then formulating yearly details and determining priority and urgent projects for the best use of resources. But its primary responsibility is to determine the objectives of the services and analyze performance and results to determine if there is any need for changes or new objectives. At the same time, it prepares a periodical report to the Minister which evaluates performance and explains management action needed to increase efficiency.

In addition, this Deputy Ministry organizes and reorganizes the new and old departments or municipalities, develops the organizational effectiveness of the existing organization structure for all levels, analyzes the data and studies any problems in order to implement new methods or alternative processes to reduce wasteful uses of manpower. It also prepares the central Ministry budget and helps regional offices with theirs. It gathers all budgets for negotiation and approval and analyzes the current budget expenses to determine any deviation from the original plan.

For the purposes of actual planning, research, and analysis, a monthly statistics and information report is sent from each department, office and

111

municipality to this Deputy Ministry for current use and for records. The Deputy Ministry also publishes a semi-annual report covering most of the activities of the MOMARA and the municipalities. To deal with all of the above tasks, the administration contains five separate departments: (1) the Planning Department, (2) the Budget Department, (3) the Organization and Methods Department, (4) the Statistics and Research Department, and (5) the Income Development Department.

THE DEPUTY MINISTRY OF MUNICIPAL AFFAIRS

This Deputy Ministry is responsible for all the administrative and financial affairs of the central Ministry and all its departments and administrations. It organizes and plans for manpower. It carries out its job through the following departments: Personnel, Finance, Public Relations, Maintenance and Transportation, Office Services, Municipal Council, Agriculture and Recreation, Follow-up, and General Office.

The Personnel Department

The main functions of the Personnel Department are to study the manpower system and programs in order to provide a strong basis for managing manpower resources, requirements, motivation, and training. The department contains three divisions:

(1) Manpower Planning: Because of the new decentralized system, the regional and local offices need more qualified personnel to assume their new responsibilities. This department concentrates on ensuring that skilled manpower is allocated according to development priorities; it determines manpower requirements for area programs and how to supply the needs.

(2) Personnel Management: This division has two functions: performance evaluation and career planning. Performance evaluation entails the study of each employee's performance and determination of areas in which he should develop his skills or the judgment that he is ready for promotion. Career planning evaluates an employee's overall career progress to date and indicates the career opportunities he should pursue. All information in an employee's file is evaluated before any decision is made regarding promotion, transfer, training, or allocation of special allowances.

(3) Training Programs and Priorities: This division coordinates with other divisions in the department and the Department of Planning and Programs.

Its job is to review the needs of the Ministry and the entire system for employee training. There are two programs. A long-term program meets the Ministry's requirements for additional skilled staff (engineers, architects, etc.). To this end, over 100 potential employees are sent abroad annually for a period of five years to obtain their B.S. degrees. To fulfill the need for technical assistants and surveyors, the government has established two more Technical Assistants Institutes. A short-term or in-service program is offered when and where necessary for a duration of approximately two weeks. This sort of program trains employees on new systems or deals with specific problems that exist in the area.

The Municipal Councils Department

The Municipal Councils Department has three main concerns: Municipal Council matters, vocational affairs, and commercial issues.[18] This Department assists the Municipal Councils in increasing their participation in developing the municipalities they serve. They deal with improving job efficiency, resolving problems, and setting the approach to be used in cooperation with muncipal departments. The Department also prepares and distributes guidelines "to the various vocational trade associations concerning membership, elections, efficiency of work. It issues guidelines on trade licenses, sets up interpretations to be applied by muncipalities in determining the fees that should be charged."[19]

It is important to remember, however, that most of the muncipalities still operate without a council or few members participate. Some cities have a special committe rather than a Municipal Council (e.g., Ar-Riyadh). The Council is the only government position to which some members are elected.

The Department of Financial Affairs

The Financial Affairs Department is structured into four sections according to tasks: accounting, auditing, tendering and contracts, and stores sections. The department is in charge of accounting and auditing procedures for all financial transactions in the Ministry and all its departments. It also deals with all concerns regarding contracting and purchasing for projects at both the local and regional levels which exceed their financial authority or capacity. In addition to auditing the regional and local financial projects, the department furnishes all municipalites, rural complexes, and

113

regional offices with equipment that has been purchased centrally and keeps a record of the Ministry's equipment and requirements. The Ministry is attempting to decentralize its financial authority, in accordance with the general financial policy of the government, so that it can devote more time to financial planning and comprehensive control at the central level.

The Public Relations Department

The Public Relations Deparment deals with two aspects of communication: one within the MOMARA and one with the public. Concerning the MOMARA, the Department's task is to collect information and report it to the Minister and top officials regarding what concerns the public — problems, requests, suggestions, and complaints. Then it disseminates pertinent information through means of the mass media.

With regard to the public, the department collects information about the Ministry's events, plans, activities, official visits, public appearances of the Minister and top officials, meetings, objectives of Ministry programs, and the proper use of facilities and services provided by it. All this information is then furnished to the public via the media. As an adjunct, the department prepares the Ministry's publications and distributes them to various departments, municipalities, government agencies, general public and reseach institutions.

THE DEPUTY MINISTRY OF TECHNICAL AFFAIRS

The Deputy Ministry was formerly the General Administration of Engineering Affairs and was changed at the establishment of the MOMARA. Added to its responsibilites were departments of Utilities, Environmental Protection, and the Technical Assistant Institutes. The primary functions of this Deputy Ministry are to set standards, provide techncial assistance, and follow up on project programs. In particular, there is an Engineering Department containing subdepartments which formalize standards and provide technical assistance to municipal regional offices dealing with roads and public buildings, parks, recreational facilities and public lavatories, etc. In other words, the Engineering department oversees the municipal offices by collecting information, evaluating their work and following up. These central functions are considered office or lab work (in contrast to field work), but the department does participate in local affairs if the experience and quality of the central official is required.

The Utilities Department has similar basic functions. Its responsibilities are limited to disruptions of water services and sewage and storm drains. Electricity is provided by the private sector in some cities and by this department in others; but recently, joint public and private companies are assuming the responsibility for providing electricity throughout the kingdom.

Wherever there are local water and sewage departments this administration's participation is limited unless it is asked to provide assistance. Because of a lack of specialists in this field, the central department exerts broader influence over the regional local departments (e.g., with project design).

The Environmental Protection Department formalizes standards, provides technical assistance, and conducts follow up studies. Specifically, it handles the licensing of food production, insecticide spraying, water purification, sewage bacteria, waste management (collection and disposal), and other related matters. There is a central laboratory which performs testing and research. A special assignment of this department is to participate in special situations (i.e., the annual pilgrimage). It is also active in emergencies such as the quarantining of contagious diseases.

In addition to engineers and professionals, specialists are required to perform most of these jobs. To this end, the Ministry utilizes the Technical Assistants Institute which trains and provides the needed personnel for the Ministry's regional offices and municipalities.

Technical Assistants Institute

Semi-skilled technicians assist engineers in performing their jobs; they conduct inspections to ensure that all municipal standards and regulations have been followed. The first Institute was established in 1965 in Ar-Riyadh to supply the municipalities with their needed technicians. It began with two departments but, by 1980/81, it contained seven departments, namely: Land Survey, Architectural Design, Hydrology, Hygienic Surveillance, Construction, Water and Road Building. Students must complete two years of academic work to graduate. In 1981, MOMARA had three institutes – the original one in Ar-Riyadh and two newer ones in the eastern and southern regions. By 1987, more than 2000 students had graduated from these three institutes, majoring in the fields of survey, construction, design, water, roads and highways.

115

THE DEPUTY MINISTRY OF CITY PLANNING

Prior to the establishment of the MOMARA, the Deputy Ministry of City Planning was called City Planning Department. The main tasks of the Deputy Ministry include: setting physical planning standards, providing technical assistance and following up projects. Specifically, the department and its sections set planning and performance standards for the regional and local departments and monitor them to make sure they are applied properly. It also directs the local offices in devising and implementing plans through development control and building permits. It advises them on analytical techniques to assess community development needs, to forecast growth patterns, and to evaluate plan options.

Through its various departments, the Deputy Ministry aids local and regional offices in resolving any planning problems beyond the capabilities of the local or regional units. It notifies these branches of the results, findings, and recommendations of studies. It also clarifies requests concerning standards and maintains records and information regarding city planning.

With regard to follow-up, the Deputy Ministry monitors the execution of local physical planning projects to ensure that they meet standards and the development requirements of the areas. "The Deputy Ministry of Physical Planning develops a comprehensive central register of planning consultants presently working with the Ministry and prospective consultants wishing to undertake planning work in the kingdom."[20] Therefore, the Deputy Ministry is organized into four departments: (1) the Department of Research and Studies, (2) the Department of Local Planning, (3) the Department of Follow-Up and Coordination, and (4) the Department of Surveying.

THE DEPUTY MINISTRY OF RURAL AFFAIRS

One of the basic principles of the Saudi government is to provide services to all its citizens, both rural and urban, without differentiation, according to the guidelines set by the development plans. Recently, greater attention has been directed towards rural affairs. The management of rural affairs has been more comprehensively organized, including many projects and programs aimed at raising the quality and standard of life for rural citizens.[21]

MOMARA established a deputy ministry to focus on rural responsibilities.

It conducts basic research and policy analyses, assesses rural development needs, and operates the new rural complexes. To accomplish these goals, the deputy ministry cooperates with other departments in the Ministry and with other ministries. According to the By-Laws of Rural Affairs, the Deputy Ministry is organized as described below:

(1) It is headed by the Deputy Ministry who is responsible for directing the organization, recommending policies and procedures for managing rural development funds, and coordinating rural programs with the various ministries so that they all reflect the agreed upon development priorities.

(2) The Rural Affairs General Administration and its sub-department constitute the main central official agency for rural affairs. They concentrate on collecting basic information about rural areas—population, social and economic surveys, and existing services. They prepare program proposals for each area according to its needs and the recommendations of local or regional officials. They also supervise budgets and control special rural development funds, monitor their projects at other departments, and coordinate them with the activities of other ministries.

(3) The Regional Rural Affairs Office is under the General Directorate of Municipal and Rural Affairs in each region. These offices act as liaison between the serviced area and the central official. They determine proposal priority and supervise and monitor project implementation and performance of the rural complexes.

(4) The Rural Complexes are the rural equivalents of the urban municipalities. The complex provides all municipal services needed in villages. The regional office performs any tasks or duties that the complex is incapable of completing.

THE GENERAL DIRECTORATES OF MUNICIPAL AND RURAL AFFAIRS (REGIONAL OFFICES)

With the new organization, regional offices assumed new designs, functions, and responsibilities and took the name of the General Directorates of Municipal and Rural Affairs. The Ministry established six regional offices (Central, Eastern, Western, Qassem, Northern, and Southern) which report and are responsible to the Minister. They were established to assume management and control and administrative responsibilities for the regions which had previously been the responsibility of the Ministry. Each office is headed by a Director-General who is accountable for the development processes in addition to the administration of municipalities and rural complexes within his boundaries (except for Class A municipalities; see discussion below). (See figure 4.)

FIGURE 4

THE ORGANIZATION CHART OF THE GENERAL DIRECTORATE
OF MUNICIPAL AND RURAL AFFAIRS
(Regional Offices)

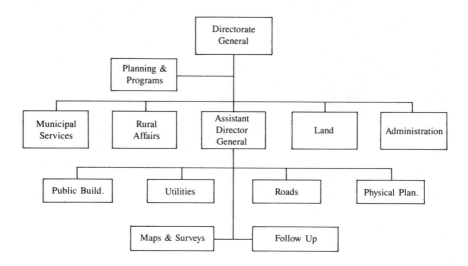

SOURCE: The Ministry of Municipal and Rural Affairs, *The Ordinances, the Regulations, and the Roles*, no. 5 (Ar-Riyadh: Public Relation Administration, 1980), p. 144.

The major tasks and responsibilities include:

(1) Developing Policies and Guidelines: The Director General and his staff gather the plans of the municipalities and rural complexes and review them. Then he devises a general plan for the region, in coopertion with the local units. The Directorate also guides local officials in analyzing data and understanding general development policy. According to the needs of the various areas, the Directorates determine the services to be provided to the rural areas.

(2) Technical and Physical Support: These offices supervise and direct the technical and physical work of the municipalities and participate when local capabilities are not equal to a task. They aid in locating consultants

118

for projects and sometimes perform the consultative duties themselves. They also prepare municipalities for greater future independence.

(3) Administrative Services: Regional offices take care of all administrative affairs of their areas (both municipal and rural) without having to depend on the Ministry except for special approvals of specific aid. They assist in the preparation of budgets and developing staff in terms of recruitment, selection, promotion, and training.

(4) Land Administration: The regional offices are completely responsible for land administration matters, "including both the expropriation of lands for public projects management and disposition of free lands."[22] The Ministry has issued general rules and circulars which explain regional and muncipal limitations on authority.

ORGANIZATION OF MUNICIPALITIES

Due to the new decentralized system of MOMARA, greater authority and responsibility have been delegated to the municipalities. Increased duties necessitated the reorganization of the municipalities. Social and economic developments outlined in the five-year development plans led to increased need for services, both in quantity and quality, and many municipal functions have been undertaken such as water systems, and private building construction inspections. There is also a belief that local planning and problems are best handled at a local level.

In 1977, there were about 100 municipalities in Saudi Arabia serving populations ranging from over 700,000 to less than 10,000 inhabitants. The first step was to evaluate and classify these municipalities to determine the extent to which functions and responsibilities could be delegated and the consequent need for increased staff.

The result was a four-tier ranking of municipalites: A for large cities (over 300,000 population), B for towns (over 100,000 people), C for towns with +/−30,000 people, and D for small towns (+/−5,000 people). New organization structures were devised for each of these ranks.

Class A Municipality

The Class A municipality has no direct authority connection with regional or ministry officials except the Minister. But it does cooperate and coordinate many matters with the central ministry system, regional offices, and other municipalities. Thus, the Class A municipality is a highly indepen-

119

dent system; its Municipal Mayor and Municipal Council have complete authority to manage and control its own affairs and services according to the 1977 Ordinance, except for those matters which must be approved by the Minister, either administratively or financially. Its budget is also independent so, after it obtains the Minister's approval, municipal representatives negotiate directly with the Ministry of Finance.

There are five Class A municipalities—Makkah, Al-Madinah, Ar-Riyadh, Dammam and Jiddah—so designated because of their spiritual, political and/or commercial importance. Each city has a population over 300,000 people.

While Class A municipalities operate within the general policy guidelines and standards of the government and the Ministry, each also has a number of specific responsibilities, such as: (1) setting local policies and priorities for its services and developing its own approach to the provision of services, (2) preparation and approval of its master plan, (3) selection and supervision of consultants, (4) preparation of the annual budget (including staff requirements, operating budget and projects), and negotiation of it with the Ministry of Finance after approval by the MOMARA, (5) preparation, control and supervision (direct and indirect) of all the municipal ministry projects in the city, (6) selection of contractors and establishment of required payment procedures (after which the municipality sends payment to the ministry to be checked and transferred to the Ministry of Finance), (7) preparation of projects' design detail and specification of tenders, (8) all administrative affairs, (9) provision of all kinds of municipal services, and (10) all Land Administration tasks.

In accordance with the suggestions of the McKinsey International study, Class A municipalities receive a new proposed organizational structure as illustrated in Figure 5.

Financially, the Class A municipalities expend about one-half of the total budget of MOMARA (as these municipalities serve about 50 percent of the country's total population). The Municipal Mayor has the authority over day-to-day expenses, salaries, and small projects. He also has the authority to make direct purchases up to a value of SR100,000 for each individual case and up to SR2 million for tenders. The Ministry, in conjunction with the Minister of Finance, is seeking to delegate a high financial limit accordance with the philosophy of a decentralized system.

Class A municipalities receive substantial revenues from their services (compared to other municipal classes) because of their higher populations, greater numbers of automobiles and many private industries and commerical enterprises.

FIGURE 5

PROPOSED ORGANIZATION CHART FOR CLASS A MUNICIPALITY

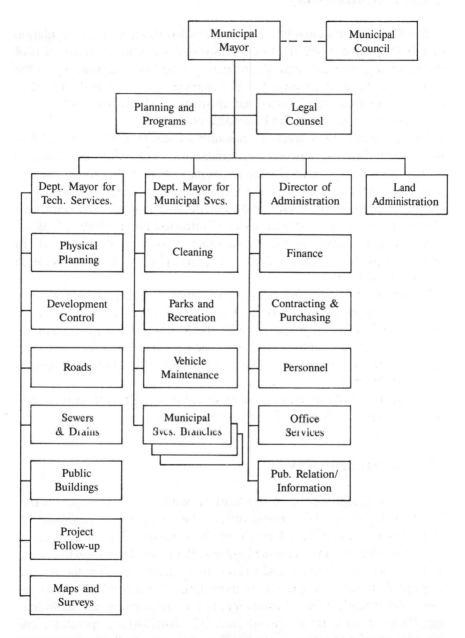

SOURCE: McKinsey International, Inc., *Mastering Orban Growth: A Blueprint for Management*, a report prepared for the Ministry of Municipal and Rural Affairs (New York, 1978), p. 41.

121

Class B Municipality

The Class B municipality refers to a town with an average population of 100,000 people. It reports to the regional office which assumes part of the technical, physical, and planning responsibilities, depending on the abilities of the municipality. It has complete autonomy with regard to municipal services and internal administration. The regional office acts as a supervisor, assistant, and coordinator.

The functions of the Class B municipality are similar to those of the Class A municipality but with certain limitations. Therefore, the Class B municipality is responsible for the following: (1) all land services with the help and cooperation of the Land Department in the regional office, (2) design and construction of small and medium-sized projects, (3) coordination of consultants and the implementation of infrastructure projects, (4) all required administrative works, (5) all other municipal services, and (6) preparation of city, technical, and development plans with the cooperation of the regional office.

Financially, it is responsible for the preparation of the annual budget which it provides to the regional office. The regional office includes it in the regional budget and negotiates it with the Ministry. The municipality is also responsible for daily financial procedures; it collects fees and fines up to SR100 but this income is very small, generally about one percent or less of its total.

A comparison of the organizational structure of a Class B municipality (see figure 6) with that of a Class A municipality reveals the differences.

Class C Municipality

The Class C municipality refers to towns with an average population of 30,000. It reports to the regional office which guides and supervises it. The Class C municipality depends on the regional office more because of its lack of technicians and skilled experts. While the differences in responsibilities relegated to Class B and Class C municipalities are few, the authority available to those of Class C is more limited and employee ranks are lower. Accordingly, Class C municipalities are responsible for the following: (1) all required municipal services, (2) distribution, operation, and fee collection for the water system, (3) participation in the preparation of plans and determination of the city's priorities, (4) carrying out small pro-

122

FIGURE 6

PROPOSED ORGANIZATION CHART FOR CLASS B MUNICIPALITY

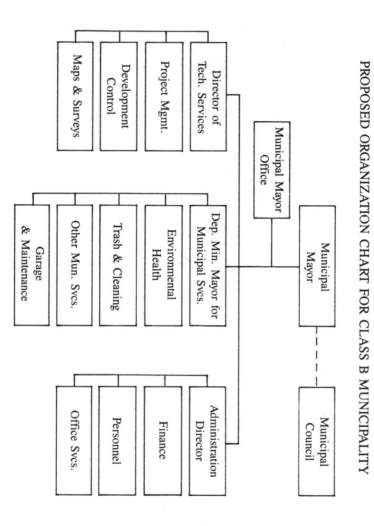

SOURCE: McKinsey International, Inc., *Mastering Urban Growth: A Blueprint for Management*, a report prepared for the Ministry of Municipal and Rural Affairs (New York, 1978), p. 44.

123

jects according to their capabilities (tasks beyond are the responsiblity of the regional office), (5) preparation of the budget, and (6) overseeing administrative affairs.

Financially, the municipality has authority over its own expenses (day-to-day expenses and small projects supervised by the regional office) within the limits of the approved budget. Its organizational structure (see figure 7) appears to be the same as that of Class B municipalities but employee ranks are lower and the level of services and responsibilities is lower.

FIGURE 7

PROPOSED ORGANIZATION CHART FOR CLASS C MUNICIPALITY

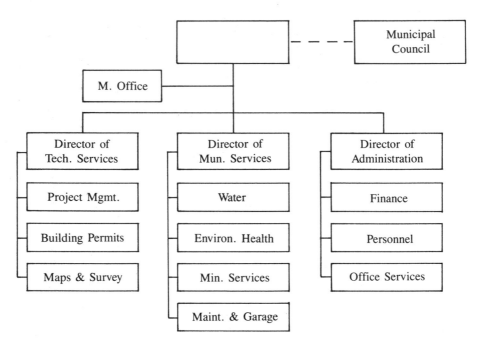

SOURCE: McKinsey International, Inc., *Mastering Urban Growth: A Blueprint for Management*, a report prepared for the Ministry of Municipal and Rural Affairs (New York, 1978), p. 45.

124

Class D Municipality

Class D Municipalities are those towns with an average population of 5,000. Most of the municipalities in this class were established in the 1970s; because of their smaller populations, they have proportionally smaller responsibilities. Most of their work and all of their research and planning are supervised by the regional office. Still, these municipalities participate to the limit of their capacities. Larger Class D municipalities employ an average of thirty to forty public workers. The responsibilities of this class of municipality include: (1) issuing permits and inspecting buildings, (2) designing and implementing projects under their control, (3) providing needed municipal services, and (4) performing internal administrative affairs (financial, personnel, and office services).

The organizational structure of Class D municipalities is very simple, merely a small department with different sections (see figure 8).

FIGURE 8

PROPOSED ORGANIZATION CHART FOR CLASS D MUNICIPALITY

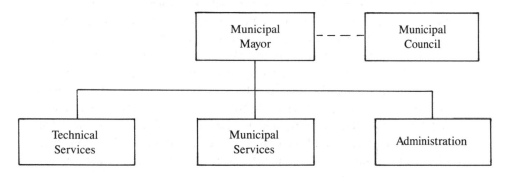

SOURCE: McKinsey International, Inc., *Mastering Urban Growth: A Blueprint for Management*, a report prepared for the Ministry of Municipal and Rural Affairs (New York, 1978), p. 46.

WATER AND SEWAGE DEPARTMENTS

Water affairs in Saudi Arabia are administered by two different ministries—the Ministry of Agriculture and Water and the MOMARA. The

125

Ministry of Agriculture and Water is responsible for water resources and their development, for the delivery of water to cities and villages, and for related services (e.g., dams, wells, desalination of sea water).

The MOMARA is responsible for the operation of water systems, the collection of fees, management and maintenance of water inside city limits, and sewage. The Ministry has divided these duties into two categories: (1) a municipality takes care of water affairs in its area as a municipal service, and (2) a city has its own water and sewage department. Water affairs departments in Makkah and Al-Madinah are of the first type and were established before 1940. In Dammam, on the other hand, water affairs are separated from the municipality.

Presently, at the end of the 1980s, there are four water and sewage departments: Ar-Riyadh, Western region, Eastern region and Al-Madinah. All departments report to the MOMARA directly, and each is directed by an appointed Board of Directors (recently the Governors or the Vice Governors serve as the Chairmen). The members are the Municipal Mayors, four ministry representatives from the ministries of Muncipal and Rural Affairs, Health, Agriculture, and Finance, and two other additional members. A full time General Director is responsible for the administration of each department, which carries out various functions and services.

Therefore, the Departments of Water and Sewage are responsible for developing projects for the cities they serve so that water and sewage networks reach every household. They strive to reduce maintenance problems of old systems, increase water resources, and (with the cooperation of the technical services departments in the Ministry) set standards for contractors to apply. In addition, they are responsible for operating and maintaining the existing water and sewage plants. They provide their customers with such needed services as water distribution and sewage disposal, system connection, and meter reading and fee collection. Each department has its own administrative and financial staff and has control and responsibility over administrative and financial affairs according to regulations.

Conclusion

In summary, the municipalities in Saudi Arabia have undergone radical change since the founding of the Kingdom in 1926. Their structure, organization and functions have shifted several times but major changes were made in 1960 with the creation of the Deputy Ministry of Interior for Municipal

126

Affairs (which led toward centralization of structure and function), and again after the establishment of the MOMARA and the initiation of the five-year development plans beginning in 1975 (which led to greater decentralization and local control.) By now, municipalities are ranked by population size and have quite a complex structure. Their functions have multiplied dramatically, particularly since 1975 in the great effort to modernize the Kingdom and to provide the best services available to their citizens.

Footnotes

1. E. Awaji, *Local Administration in Saudi Arabia,* The Saudi Arabia Local Administration Seminar, Riyadh, The Public Administration Institute, 1981, pp. 7-14. (in Arabic).
2. Deputy Ministry of the Interior for Municipal Affairs, *Municipal Services,* Riyadh, Government Publication, 1973, p. 44. (in Arabic).
3. Deputy Ministry of the Interior for Municipal Affairs, *Semiannual Report,* vol. 1, no. 2, 1967, p. 139. (in Arabic).
4. Abdul-Hameed A. Katib, "The Municipalities as the Important Factor in Developing Saudi Arabia," unpublished research, 1968. (in Arabic).
5. The Deputy Ministry of the Interior for Municipal Affairs, *Semiannual Report,* op. cit., p. 139.
6. Mohammed T. Sedeq, *The Evolution of the Government and Administration in Saudi Arabia,* Riyadh, The Public Administration Institute, 1965. (in Arabic).
7. Katib, op. cit., p. 4.
8. The Deputy Ministry of the Interior for Municipal Affairs, *Municipal Services,* Riyadh, Public Relations Department, 1973, pp. 3-16. (in Arabic).
9. Ibid., p. 36.
10. Ibid. p. 46., and the Deputy Ministry of the Interior for Municipal Affairs, *Semiannual Report,* (in Arabic).
11. The information in this section is derived from "The Organizational Structure of the Ministry of Municipal and Rural Affairs," (typed manuscript), Kingdom of Saudi Arabia, Ministry of Municipal and Rural Affairs.
12. The consulting company worked for two years in Saudi Arabia for the Ministry of Municipal and Rural Affairs.
13. "The Organization Structure of the Ministry of Municipal and Rural Affairs," pp. 8-9.
14. Ibid., p. 19.
15. Ibid., p. 15.
16. Ibid., p. 10.
17. Ibid., p. 11.
18. Ibid., p. 24.
19. Ibid., p. 24.
20. Ibid., p. 36.
21. Ibid., p. 38.
22. Ibid., p. 57.

CITIZEN PARTICIPATION IN THE SAUDI ARABIAN LOCAL GOVERNMENT

by Ahmed Hassan Dahlan

"The state, according to Islam, is nothing more than a combination of men working together as servants of God to carry out His will . . . In the working of the state all those (servants) will participate . . ."

Abul Al'a Mawdudi

"If there is a political revolution going on throughout the world, it is what might be called the participation explosion."

G. Almond

"We support mass participation in governance."

Fahd ibn Abd al-Aziz

I. Introduction

Very little research has been done on citizen participation either in Saudi Arabia or in the so-called advanced countries, the United States in particular. Wengert wrote regarding the U.S. case:

> It is probably not surprising that neither normative nor empirical theories applicable to the topic (of citizen participation) have been formulated. Little research on the subject has been undertaken, and even as speculative philosophy the ideology of participation has not been systematically organized or neatly structured.[1]

In Saudi Arabia, nearly all literature on the subject is very recent and quite tentative and exploratory. Little research has been done, and the issue on the whole has mostly been either neglected or treated inadequately even in recent studies by advanced students of public administration and political science. Nizar Samman, for example, in his unique work about the emarates, did not devote any effort to this issue.[2] Another writer, Muhammed Al Buraey, in his recent study about administrative development, also failed

129

to address this issue.[3] Although he included a chapter on man and development, he did not provide a framework or formulate any policy for citizen participation.

The few studies which have dealt with citizen participation are inadequate or incomplete. Al Rawaf, for instance, did not explain the Islamic foundations of citizen participation.[4] Al-Sabban in his unique and extensive study about the Saudi municipal system raised the issue of participation, but did not follow through with any discussion of its implications.

The primary purpose of this brief study is to call to the attention of Saudi researchers the need to devote more time and effort to the study of citizen participation because it plays a vital role in the development and welfare of Saudi society. A second purpose is to suggest some necessary elements to establish a broad public policy for developing constructive, Islamic public participation. In exploring the topic, several different aspects of participation will be covered. First, an analysis of the meaning of the term "citizen participation" will be made, both as found in social science literature and among a sample of Saudi students. Secondly, several arguments will be put forth regarding the importance of citizen participation, both for society and for individuals. Thirdly, a discussion will follow on the Saudi environment which affects and accounts for the amount and degree of citizen participation in government affairs. Historical, religious, educational, economic and institutional environmental elements will be explored. Particular attention will be made to the value system of Islam as it is seen to influence participation, and a framework for discussion and analysis given the values will be proposed. Also, Saudi motivation to participate and the inseparability of politics and religion in Saudi Arabia will be briefly discussed. The role such institutions as the mosque, the majlis and the mass media play in motivating and educating citizens to their public duties will be looked at. Finally, the process by which citizens engage in participation in their city and government affairs will be analyzed.

II. The Meaning Of Citizen Participation

The role of government everywhere has been growing so steadily that it is accepted that government, in one way or another, is involved in every aspect of citizens' lives, from birth to death. However, with its increasing role, government has found itself unable to perform alone its multifarious, multilateral functions. Nearly everywhere it urgently needs its citizens' cooperation and involvement since without citizen involvement governments ultimately enter into a state of dysfunction. What constitutes citizen involvement however, either what it is or what it should be, has hardly been agreed upon by political scientists. Wenger wrote:

Although the participation phenomenon may be worldwide, its meaning, role, function and importance vary from culture to culture and political system to political system. It also seems evident that the drive or reasons for seeking more participation vary, depending on the perspectives from which the subject is approached, the institutional, political, economic context, and the personal interests and points of view of those opposing as well as supporting participation. Similarly, the phrase "public participation" and "citizen involvement" have many meanings and connotations, depending on the situation to which applied and the ideology, motivations, and practical orientations of the users.[6]

Bearing in mind the preceding observation, what follows is the meaning of "citizen participation" as it is seen by first some Western scholars, and then by a sample of Saudi Arabian citizens. Weiner defines the concept as including:

Any voluntary action, successful or unsuccessful, organized or unorganized, episodic or continuous, employing legitimate or illegitimate methods intended to influence the choice of public policies, the administration of public affairs, or the choice of political leaders at any level of government, local or national.[7]

Verba used the concept to refer to "those legal acts by private citizens that are more or less directly aimed at influencing the selections of governmental personnel and/or the actions that they take."[8]

On the other hand, citizen participation, as understood by a sample of forty Saudi Arabian citizens was found to mean a number of different things, among them: giving advice and offering suggestions; holding jobs in a program and performing the work in a sincere and effective way; making decisions within an administrative or political framework; having an influence on decision-making; and assessing the activities and output of governmental institutions or any action that affects the public interest.[9] As one student observed, citizen participation is a very broad and general issue. It means action. It is the opposite to passiveness. In Islam, this activity may range from picking litter out of the street, to participating in the holy war at the risk of life and wealth. In other words, for the Saudis sampled, the rationale for participation is that it can affect outcome, on the local or national level. Citizens can participate by getting involved in program planning or decision making, in implementation or oversight, in financing or assessment. All can be positive contributions.

III. The Importance of Citizen Participation

Why should citizens participate? Simply, because there are many important advantages that can be achieved only through involvement. A partial listing includes:

1. Participation and legitimacy of Government

Mass participation is the most effective defense against tyranny . . . (And) governments which fail to accord the natural rights of political participation, are declared not to be legitimate. Mass participation, by making governmental policies more acceptable and enforceable, gives legitimacy to actions taken by the government. Participation in an activity . . . tends to increase the sense of legitimacy of its results.[10]

It can be argued that there is a direct relationship between how legitimate the government is on the one hand, and how and to what extent citizens participate on the other. The more citizen participation is constitutionalized and institutionalized, the closer the government is to legitimacy.

2. Participation and Equality

For more than 1400 years, since the Qu'ran was revealed to the Prophet Mohammed, social, economic and political *equality* has been one of Islam's principles and goals. Mohammed the Messenger was not only instructed to treat people equally regardless of their race, color or sex, but was also ordered to consult with them and have them participate in community decisions. Citizen participation in public activities, according to a recent writer, is one method that can help maintain a reasonable degree of equality. It tends to eliminate some of the social differences and enables citizens to enjoy more balanced lives.[11] In other words, participation serves to assure citizens that there is equal or reasonable distribution of the state's wealth. Citizens who participate tend to demand to be kept informed of the govern-

132

ment's income and expenditures and want reasons for government's policies, plans and programs clarified.

3. Participation, Human Dignity, and Satisfaction

From the human perspective, participation is considered both an enhancement of human dignity and a means to satisfying one's needs.[12] When an individual has a share in governing the affairs of his own community, it will contribute to his moral and intellectual development. On the contrary, if he is deprived of this legitimate share, it will lead him toward passiveness.[13] As Pennock summarized it:

> Participation gives the active citizen a feeling of power and efficacy and a sense of making a contribution that increases his own sense of dignity and of moral worth . . . It (also) satisfies his need to belong and to achieve personal identity by becoming an integral and valued part of a collective entity and enterprise . . . (On the other hand), men without power become apathetic and privatistic, or else rebellious.[14]

4. Participation As a Source of Information

A great deal of information is needed for any decision made or any policy drawn in local government if it is to be effective. Information should not depend on only the official point of view. Instead citizens should be used as a source and their knowledge, needs, demands, expectations and speculations used by officials. Wenger suggests that the reason people demand more participation is to improve information input into administrative decisions. He continues:

> Since government is designed to serve people, the views and preferences of people are necessary inputs to responsive decisions. Often, it is argued, the technician or bureaucratic specialist will make "bad" decisions when he decides *for* people instead of *with* them.[15]

5. Participation and the Government's Activities and Policies

For the purpose of illustration, as well as of analogy, let us take any ministry, organization or department and attempt to understand the difference in goal attainment when all of its members participate and when they do not. In the first case, the organization is likely to reach its goals

133

effectively and efficiently, but in the second case quite the contrary is probable. Indeed the organization may not attain any of its goals. This is very true on the provincial level as well as the local government level where a citizen is not only part of the community but also is greatly affected by the policies, programs and decisions made regarding his needs and welfare, i.e., municipal, recreational, hygenic, cultural, and so on. Moreover, local people, of a region or city, know best their own needs, capabilities, resources, and goals. King Abdulaziz emphasized this fact when he addressed the citizens of Makkah in 1924 when the city came under his control:

> Lands such as yours need great care in the administration of their affairs. We have a proverb familiar to everyone. 'The people of Mecca know best their valleys." You are better acquainted with your city than those who are far off from you. I do not see what is more desirable for you than that the responsibilities for affairs should be placed on your shoulders . . .[16]

In this regard, as Nasser summarizes it:

> Many efforts are underway in the Kingdom of Saudi Arabia to improve the level of living of its citizens. These efforts, however, cannot be fully effective unless the people are capable of participating in and sharing responsibility for many of the programs.[17]

In addition, in Saudi Arabia citizens are not only required to participate but they are considered a primary force among several which influence the government in the performance of its activities. In no country does government exist in a vacuum; it exists and survives only by, for and of the people. Government therefore, without real, truthful, planned participation of citizens cannot achieve its goals and policies and this, in turn, affects its legitimacy.[18] The extent to which interaction between the two groups exists in any given country can be determined by answering the following questions:

> Do citizens admit and share the government's ideology? Do citizens support the government's plans and programs? Do citizens respond to and interact with the government? Do they exercise assertiveness in dealing with the government or are they characterized by passiveness? Are they sincere or selfish? and, Are these citizens conscious and cognitive of their duties, roles and rights?[19]

134

6. Participation As Conflict Resolution

In many cases participation may reduce conflicts between concerned groups and foster more and mutual understanding. This is because it often exposes different members of a group to each other and educates them to different perspectives. It may also reduce personal biases and self-approbation. However, if a particular situation is characterized by a high degree of diversity, participation may contribute little to, or even intensify, conflicts. Wengert writes:

> . . . As conflicts rest upon misinformation, participation and involvement in town meeting situations provides opportunities for exchange of information and may induce modifications of values and opinions and increase confidence and trust . . . (but) where a diveristy of interests is clearly established, participation can contribute to conflict resolution *only* in highly structured situations with institutionalized procedures and a willingness to accept an acceptable decision (as in litigation.)[20]

7. Participation and Thrift

Another advantage that can be achieved through citizen participation is thrift. If the citizens and government pay more attention to the benefits of participation, draw a sincere and astute policy, and establish appropriate programs, not only will participation

> lead to a more accurate and clear direction for the most needed services, but it will also save money, efforts and time by reducing investigation to find out what kind and where the services should be established.[21]

A good example in Saudi Arabia of thrift due to participation has been the establishment of schools and building of roads in rural areas where local citizens have been more knowledgeable than the representatives of the central government about where best to establish such facilities.

8. Participation as a Right of Citizens

In addition to the wide scope of advantages that citizen participation encompasses, as previously mentioned, it has one more significant quality which makes it a far more important and more obvious imperative. That is, for a citizen, it is his or her *right* to participate in the affairs of the state.[22] As Abul A'La Mawdudi puts it:

> According to Islam, governments are representatives (*Khalifa*) of the Creator of the universe; this responsibility is not entrusted to any individual, family or particular class or group of people, but to the entire Muslim community . . . *Khilafa* (succession) is a collective gift of God in which the *right* of every individual Muslim is neither more nor less than the right of any other person . . . Under no circumstances does Islam permit an individual, a group or a party to deprive the common Muslims of their rights or usurp powers of the state.[23]

IV. The Environment of Citizen Participation

The phenomenon of citizen participation can not be studied in isolation from its environment. In order to consider the Saudi State as a mega-institute, a brief background of its recent political history is necessary. This will first be presented, and then the value system which prevails in this environment, both social and economic, and some Saudi institutions will be dealt with in relatively more detail.

Re-Birth of a Nation: A Historical Glance

Saudi Arabia acquired its political entity as it is known today only in 1926 when Abd al-Aziz ibn Saud took control of the Hijaz (the Western Province of the Arabian Peninsula), ending a long course of battles to consolidate a vast but torn and fragmented territory.[24] He started rebuilding the nation when he seized Riyadh (in the interior province of the Najed) in 1902. In 1916, Abd al-Aziz conquered Al Hasa (in the Eastern Province); in 1921 he added Hail (in the Northern Province); and Asir (in the Southern Province) was conquered in 1922.

In simple terms it can be said that via Abd al-Aziz ibn Saud, "an effective territorial state was superimposed upon the old tribal structure and had to a large extent, replaced it."[25] This history must be borne in mind when discussing the citizen participation issue in Saudi Arabia today. After the decline of the Islamic Empire in the 13th century, the Arabian Peninsula, (with the exception of the Hijaz) existed without any sort of state government. This condition negatively affected both past and present educational, economic and political institutions, and in turn hindered citizens

136

from establishing, developing or participating in any type of stable and sophisticated government of any notable size. However, as will be made clear in the discussion which follows, many necessary and important elements were present in tribal and local politics and religious practices that were later to develop into strong and positive forces of participation at the national level.

Ever since the country was reunited in 1926 under the Saudi government, citizen participation as an issue and practice has been making some strides towards institutionalism through traditional and often unique structures such as the mosque, the *majlis* and most recently the mass media. The degree, direction and pattern of participation has varied throughout the kingdom and many forces have affected it, but most particularly Islam and dramatic economic changes. These forces constitute the environment of participation and will be presented under following four headings: a) the value system; b) the education environment; c) the economic environment, and d) the institutional and structural environment.

A. The Value System

The value system that surrounds the environment of citizen participation in Saudi Arabia has a theological nature. For the Saudi people, Islam is the opulent source that dominates their thinking, feelings, and behavior. It touches every aspect of their lives: it motivates them, provides guidelines to citizens of their relationship with rulers and officials and provides them with a framework for their everyday actions.

A significant point in this regard is the inseparability of religion and politics in Saudi Arabia. In fact, politics and government are viewed as constituting only one sphere of religion. According to Islam, the concept of worship, for example, means not only praying, fasting, giving alms, and performing pilgrimage, but it includes administration of justice, governing according to the laws of God and acting on earth as the vicegerent of God.[26] Any activity, be it economic, political, administrative, or social, is considered to be religious practice. Hence, participation in local government, if it complies with Islamic principles is a type of worship. Put succinctly, participation equals worship.

In Islam, there are several different interrelated and interdependent values, beliefs and behaviors which may be identified as a framework from which to analyze and discuss citizen participation in the Kingdom (see figure 1.) The most important of the elements are: 1) The concomitancy of belief and deed, 2) the vicegerency principle and the concept of leadership 3) *Al-Shura* or mutual consultation, 4) mutual cooperation, 5) the duty of hearing and obedience, 6) the duty of enjoining rightful behaviors and beliefs and forbidding wrongful ones, 7) responsibility and accountability.[27]

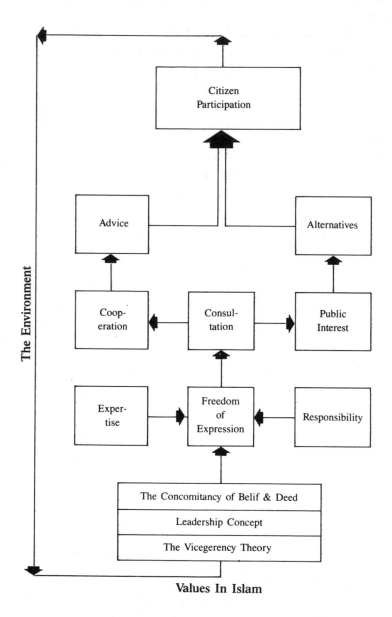

Values In Islam

138

1) The Concomitancy of Belief and Righteous Deeds

One of the most important principles in the Islamic Ideology is the necessity of concomitancy of the creed and deed. That is to say, neither one alone is considered adequate. In the Holy Book, the Qur'an (Koran), whenever the belief in God is mentioned, it is either preceded or followed by emphasis on the righteous deeds. Two verses from the Glorious Qu'ran will represent the idea of concomitancy:

> . . . Whoever expects
> to meet his Lord, let him
>
> Work righteousness, and
> In the worship of his Lord
> Admit no one as partner.
>
> (Qur'an 18:110)

> Shall we treat those
> Who believed and work deeds
> Of righteousness, the same
> As those who do mischief
> On earth? Shall we treat
> Those who guard against evil,
> The same as those who
> Turn aside from the right?
>
> (Qur'an 38:28)

Through religious education and acculturation, the citizen gradually comes to realize this principle in all of his actions and activities in local government. This belief is so strong that it should be regarded as basic part of the value system.

2) The Vicegerency Theory and the Concept of Leadership

Islam affirms that, under the sovereignty of God, man is the representative or *Khalifa* of God.[28] As Al Mawdudi explains it:

> According to the Qur'an, the vicegerency of God is not the exclusive birthright of any individual, clan or class of people; it is the collective right of all those who accept and admit God's absolute sovereighty

139

over themselves and adopt the Divine Code, conveyed through the Prophet, and the law above all laws and regulations.[29]

According to the Qur'an:

Behold, thy Lord said to the angels:
"I will make a vicegerent on earth."

(Qur'an 2:30)

Also, God said:

". . . We made you vicegerents
In the land . . ."

(Qur'an 10:14)

"To illustrates what this means," Al Mawdudi continues,

Let us take the case of an estate of yours which someone else has been appointed to administer on your behalf. Four conditions invariably obtain: First, the real ownership of the estate remains vested in you and not in the administrator; secondly, he administers your property directly in accordance with your instructions; thirdly, the administrator exercises his authority within the limits prescribed by you; and fourthly, in the administration of the trust he executes your will and fulfills your intentions and not his own. Any representative who does not fulfill these four conditions will be abusing his authority and breaking the covenant which was implied in the concept of representation.[30]

Following the argument to its logical implications, all individuals of an Islamic nation are successors or vicegerents. Every Muslim citizen should take a role in his or her community. A Muslim citizen has no choice or alternative but to participate, it is a duty that derives from the succession principle.

The preceeding discussion, though it emphasizes the equality between people does not negate the concept of leadership. In fact, the Qur'an and the tradition of the Messenger make it clear that there have to be some people who are to be charged with authority and accountability. The relationship between those who are to hold authority (leaders and officials) and the rest of the community (the citizens and the public) has been explained by various Muslim scholars, especially the companions of the Messenger. Omar Ibn Khetab, the second Right-Guided Caliph, for example, considered any Muslim leader, including himself, and anyone who is in charge of any Muslim's affairs to be a slave or servant to his people.[31] Other learned

140

Muslim scholars considered the ruler in Islam to be a) a representative, b) a vicegerent, or c) an employee.[32] Thus, any citizen who deals with an official at any level of government, including the mayor of a city or the governor (*amir*) of a province should have all or some of these concepts in mind. This in turn, should not imply the supremacy of a citizen over an official. All of them are equal, but the official has "public" responsibility and accountability.

3) *Al-Shura* Mutual Consultation

According to any Muslim, for a government to be legitimate, it must be Islamic. And in order to be Islamic, it has to be consultative. It is not only the central government that must be consultative, but every level of government has to enforce this Divine Rule. As Muhammad Asad puts it:

> (Mutual Consultation) is so comprehensive that it reaches out into almost every department of political life, and it is so self-expressive and un-equivocal that no attempt at arbitrary interpretation can change its purport.[33]

In regard to one method of consultation, Al-Mawdudi emphasized citizen participation as he wrote:

> The method recommended by the Holy Qur'an for running the affairs of the state is as follows: "And their business is (conducted) through consultation among themselves." (42:38). According to this principle it is the right of every Muslim either to have a direct say in the affairs of the state or to have a representative chosen by him and other Muslims to participate in the running of the state.[34]

In other words, mutual consultation is considered to be one of the most important forms of government advocated by the Prophet himself which has relevance to the issue of citizen participation. The predominant opinion among Muslim jurists is that the rulers and officials, including those in local government (the *amir*, mayor, etc.,) are obligated to consult their citizens on public matters and abide by the obligation. Citizens, moreover, must express their views on matters of concern to them, even if not asked to do so. In short, the Qur'an by expressing the concept of *Shura* deals precisely with the question of participation.[35]

141

4) Mutual Cooperation

One of the unique characteristics of a Muslim Society, and the Saudi Arabian one in particular, is the fact that the relationship between the rulers and the ruled, as well as between the citizens themselves, is in principle at least, based on cooperation and not on confrontation. God says:

Cooperate with one another
For virtue and heedfulness, and
Do not cooperate with one another
For the purpose of sin and aggression

(Qur'an 5:2)

The Messenger said "The Faithful are to one another like (parts of) a building—each strengthening the others."[36] Thus Asad states that mutual cooperation in all phases of life is a fundamental requirement of Islam and no state can be called an Islamic state unless it guides that cooperation by legislative means, and thereby enables its citizens to live up to the demands of Islam.[37]

5) The Duty of Hearing and Obedience

To hear and obey the leader and officials is another value whose use is suggested for analyzing the impact of Islam on citizen participation. God says:

Obey God and obey the Apostle,
And those charged
With authority among you.
If ye differ in anything
Among yourselves, refer it
To God and His Apostle . . .

(Qur'an 4:59)

In the tradition, narrated by the Companion "Ubadah Ibn As-Samit, it is said that:

The Prophet called us, and we pledged our allegiance to him. He imposed on us the duty to hear and obey in whatever pleases and displeases us, in hardship as well as in ease, whatever our personal preference, and (impressd on us) that we should not withdraw authority from those who have been entrusted with it, "unless you see as obvious

142

infidelity (*Kufr*) for which you have a clear proof from (the book of) God.[38]

From the preceding Qur'anic verse, Hadith, and the context of all the traditions pertaining to this point, some guidelines are self-evident: a) As long as an official adheres to Islamic law, all citizens owe him their allegiance. b) If the government or any one of its officials, issues regulations which contradict this Islamic law, the duty of obedience ceases to be operative with regard to these regulations, for the Messenger said: "No obedience is due in sinful matters: behold, obedience is due only in the way of righteousness."[39]

6) The Duty of Moral Belief and Behavior

As mentioned above, it is a duty of a Muslim citizen to hear and obey. However, this duty ceases when the government, at any level, deviates from Islamic laws, regulations and principles; or when it commits or intends to commit any action that is not in accordance with Islamic principles. According to the Glorious Qur'an, as Asad summarizes it, the citizen is duty bound to combat evil whenever he encounters it and to strive for justice whenever people disregard it.[40] The Qur'an and Hadith explain this duty very clearly:

Let there arise out of you
A bond of people
Inviting to all that is good,
Enjoining what is right,
And forbidding what is wrong;
They are the ones
To attain felicity.

(Qur'an 3:104)

By Him in whose hand I repose!
You must enjoin right and forbid wrong,
Or else God will certainly send down chastisement
Upon you; then you will call to Him, but He
Will not respond to you.

(Prophetic Hadith)[41]

The highest kind of Jihad (holy war) is to speak up for truth
in the face of an aggressive governor (or government.)

(Prophetic Hadith)[42]

143

If any of you see something evil, he should set it right by his hand; if he is unable to do so, then by his tongue; and if he is unable to do even that, then within his heart—but this is the weakest form of faith.

(Prophetic Hadith)[43]

So, in brief, it is the duty and right of the citizen to participate in all governmental activities, and public affairs. Raising one's voice against manifest wrong, for example, is considered one of the foremost duties of a Muslim, and particularly so when the action occurs on the part of a governmental officials.[44]

7) Responsibility and Accountability

The Apostle of God said:
Behold, every one of you is a shepherd, and every one is responsible for his flock. Thus, the imam who has been placed over his people is a shepherd, and is responsible for his flock; and the woman is a shepherdess over her husband's household and his children, and is responsible for them; and the servant is a shepherd over his master's property, and is responsible for it. Behold, every one of you is a shepherd and every one is responsible for his flock.[45]

The above quote serves as a source to demonstrate that according to Islam, every Muslim is responsible for several duties and has to be accountable for his or her actions. Just as the government is responsible for enforcing Islamic law in all its transactions, and has to be held accountable for its practices, so every citizen is charged with different responsibilities and he or she must account for his or her actions.

Motivations and Goals

So far, we have discussed some of the most important values and beliefs in Islam which constitute a framework of accountability for activities of citizens in local government in Saudi Arabia. These values can be interrelated with various motives and goals also found in Islam which further affect citizen participation. A few are listed below. In theory, every Muslim citizen should feel the influence of such common Islamic goals and motives, but in practice their influence may or may not be strong upon the individual.

144

1. Equality *per se* is one of a Muslim citizen's goals, and he is motivated to participate in local affairs by the desire to attain the highest level of equality, whether economic, political or social.
2. The citizen is motivated to participate more and more, because participation contributes to his satisfaction and enhances his human dignity.
3. Citizens are motivated to participation in order to provide their input for more responsive policies and programs relevant to their communities.
4. Local government provides a wide range of services to its citizens; thus, it touches every aspect of its citizens' lives. Therefore, local citizens feel a strong desire to participate in governing and administering their own affairs.
5. Another incentive that motivates a citizen to participate is that participation is both a duty and a right.

In this regard Wenger writes:

> Demands for more public participation may be motivated by a desire to alter the power structure and thus weaken "the establishment" or they may simply seek better information inputs and more responsive public service.[46]

In addition to the preceding immediate, short-term and long-term goals of participation, there are goals regarding eternity. All true Muslim citizens of Saudi Arabia believe in the life hereafter. Thus they take for granted that they will be held accountable for all of their beliefs and deeds, including all of their affairs in local government, on the Day of Judgment. God says:

> . . . Those who
> Obey God and His Apostle
> Will be admitted to gardens
> With rivers flowing beneath,
> To abide therein (forever)
> And that will be
> The Supreme achievement.
>
> But those who disobey
> God and His Apostle
> And transgress his limits
> Will be admitted
> To a fire, to abide therein

145

And they shall have
A Humiliating punishment.

(Qur'an 4:12-4:14)

B. The Educational Environment

Two main points will be discussed here. First, a quick glance at the educational history of the Arabian Peninsula will be provided. This will be followed by a brief discussion on how education affects citizen participation.

The first word and order revealed to the Prophet in 610 A.D. was to "Read," and the concept of speculation was emphasized several times in the Qur'an. With the spread of Islam, one of the greatest empires history has ever known was established (633-1250 A.D.) providing the world with one of the greatest civilizations ever, rich in scholarship, in the sciences and the arts. Nevertheless, the 13th century witnessed the decline of that Islamic Empire and the education of the Arab people in particular. All extant political, economic, social and educational institutions experienced severe setbacks, and in many areas of the former empire scholarship and Islamic institutions died out altogether.

The Arabian Peninsula ceased to be the center of Islamic political and cultural power, starting from 657 A.D., when the capital of the Islamic Empire was moved from Medina to Damascus and subsequently to Baghdad.[47] In fact, between 1250 and 1800, Arabia experienced an era similar to the "dark ages" in Europe. As Shaker summarizes it:

> . . . Evidence indicates that the people of central Arabia had brought alive once again the pre-Islamic era from which they were rescued by the call of Islam a thousand years ago. Yet, the two periods, the pre-Islamic and the [pre-Saudi] were considerably different in certain respects. . . . While before Islam the Arab had a primitive though well organized civilization, with a literature of outstanding merit, the decadence of Arabian Islam . . . appears to have been accompanied by unrelieved moral and intellectual stagnation.[48]

In 1926, the Arabian Peninsula took a new direction when Abd al-Aziz Ibn Saud finished reunifying the vast and torn territory, from the east coast of the Arabian Gulf to the west coast on the Red Sea. Only by that year, when a Directorate of Education was established, was formal education introduced. However, as Shaker explains it:

146

. . . the progress of education . . . was very slow at all educational levels. In 1948, there were only 182 primary schools with enrollment of 21,409 pupils. By 1952 the number had risen to 301 schools with an enrollment of 39,920. In 1962 the Unesco estimate of the percentage of Saudi illiterates of 15 years of age and above was 98%[49]

In the early 1960s, dramatic change began to take place in the Saudi educational system. But despite substantial expansion in education, illiteracy remained high (45% for adults of both sexes) and the level of education very low. Education was still facing serious deficiencies and problems.[50]

Through the 1970s and 1980s the government began to pay increasingly greater attention to the quality of education, and the building of school facilities through the development plans. As a result, literacy rates increased sharply. By the middle of the 1980s the enrollment of Saudi students at all levels exceeded 1.5 million.[51] In 1987 more than 2 million students were recorded as having taken the final exams.

The second main point regarding the educational environment of citizen participation is the relationship between the extent a citizen participates and the level of his education. The needs and demands, background and expectations, and desires and capabilities of educated and uneducated citizens to participate in government affairs are, by all means, not identical. The more an individual is educated, the more sophisticated his demands are, and also the more willing and qualified he is to participate. According to the Holy Qur'an:

. . . God will
Rise up, to (suitable) ranks
(And degrees), those of you
Who believe and who have
Been granted (mystic) knowledge.

(Qur'an 58:11)

An educated citizen knows better what is going on in his (or her) local government. He is aware of the value system he belongs to and the environment he operates in. He is conscious and perceptive of his duties, roles, and rights—including his right to participate.

C. The Economic Environment

The history of the economic environment in modern Saudi Arabia is

147

composed of two main periods; one prior to and one following the discovery of oil. Oil was discovered in 1918, but was first exported in commercial quantities in 1938, enabling the Saudi government to start building a modern economy and to transfer technology from the Western world.

The price and production of oil increased steadily during the 1970s, and even more rapidly after the oil embargo of 1973. As a result, so did national income. In 1975 the Saudi gross national product (GNP) was $39.7 billion, with an average per capita income for Saudi citizens of $4,420—higher than more than 120 world nations including Britain, Spain, Italy, Greece, Brazil and Venezuela.

In 1981-82 the already rising price of oil skyrocketed to more than $30.00 per barrel, with production exceeding 10 million barrels per day (BPD). As a result the Saudi GNP reached $126.8 billion, and per capita income rose to $13,072—exceeding even the highly industrialized countries of Germany, France, Japan and the U.S.A.

In conjunction with the rising national income, the Kingdom undertook a series of Five-year Development Plans designed to transform the country economically and socially. Hundreds of billions of riyals were committed to the establishment of a sophisticated infrastructure. Probably the most valuable outcome of this wealth and planning has been a corresponding increase in the number of educated Saudi citizens.

By 1983, however, the price of oil had decreased to $8 per barrel, and production to 2 million BPD, so that revenues declined to 50% of the 1982 figures with a corresponding decline in the economy. Today, at the onset of the 1990s, citizen input and cooperation are needed more than ever before in order to manage the new situation.

D. The Institutional and Structural Environment

There are a few different types of institutions, some traditional and others more recent, through which Saudi citizens participate. These will be catagorized into five types as follows:

1) The Mosque, 2) The open *Majlis,* 3) the Municipal Council,
4) The Neighborhood Councils, and 5) Mass Media

1) The Mosque and its Indispensible Role

Unlike the church and its increasingly weak effect on people's lives in the West, the Mosque in Muslim societies still plays a vital role in many aspects of Muslims' thinking and activities. Many groups of Muslim citizens, not necessarily the same ones every time, meet five times a day to perform their prayers wherever they are: in their governmental offices, schools, markets, etc. (For Muslims, any clean, dryland can be considered a mosque.) In addition to the daily prayers, there is a weekly congregational prayer. This Friday prayer includes a sermon for about thirty minutes prior to the practice of prayer.

In the Friday prayer speeches on a variety of topics and subjects can be addressed. The topic may cover social, economic, or political affairs and relate to the past, the present or the future. In addition to what pertains to Muslim belief and worship, for example, international politics and local policies can be discussed. Sometimes prayer is combined with famous historical event and, in fact, on January 8, 1926 Abd Al-Aziz Ibn Saud was declared King after the Friday congregational prayer in the Holy Mosque of Mecca.[52]

Recently, King Fahd advised the Imams of the thirty thousand mosques in the Kingdom to address the problem of the Middle East, Jerusalem, and the Muslim struggle against Zionism. The Afghanistan problem and the fight against Russian imperialism has been a common topic in recent years. Also, on May 28, 1987 (Shawwal 1, 1407H), the first day of the Muslim feast of the 'Eid, the Imam of the Holy Mosque of Makkah, warned that the weakness of Muslims today is the result of amoral behavior on the part of most leaders who claim they are followers of Islam.[53]

However the Mosque at present has not been playing as vital a role as it is supposed to or as it has done in the past. This fact has led the Saudi government to reconsider the current situation of the mosque. According to the Saudi Minister of Information, steps are being taken to improve the current situation so that mosques will resume their position as centers for religious and scientific illumination, as schools for Islamic law, and as institutes to prepare citizens for *Jihad,* or Holy War against imperialism and injustice.[54]

2) The Open *Majlis* and The Access Theory

The open *Majlis* or Council is another institution through which Saudi citizens participate in local government affairs. Besides being traditional and unique in the Arab world, "this institution" as Lipsky observed, by "incorporating the process of consultation and discussion . . . is quite

149

effective in reflecting the varied interests of the community."[55]; As Al-Rawaf tells us:

> At the present . . ., the open Majlis . . . remains the keystone of the political system in Saudi Arabia . . . The system of the open Majlis has been institutionalized, consisting today of formal and informal meetings between (officials) and the masses.[56]

There are two forms of the open *Majlis,* formal and informal. The King and many princes hold informal *Majalis* at which citizens come forward to request personal demands or to give advice or suggestions concerning local public policy or improvement of public services.[57] In addition formal *Majalis* are held by the Minister of the Interior, the Governors of all the provinces and by the King himself. The King holds an official *Majlis* every Monday while the other top officials hold their *Majalis* daily. All of these political leaders meet with the *Ulama,* (men learned in religious matters), the tribal sheikhs and many other citizens.[58] In regard to the theory of citizen access to power, Weiner wrote:

> In no political system do people have equal access to power . . . Those who participate have different degrees of resources. The variable of organization, (education), information, status, wealth, and social affinity to those whom they are trying to influence all affect the success of political participation in having access to political power.[59]

To clarify the significance of the open *Majlis* in context of the Saudi local government, Al Rawaf states that:

> All the formal *Majalis* were instituted by a royal decree issued in 1952 by King Abdul Aziz stating that every subject has the *right of access* to his ruler . . . or (even to) the king himself. This decree has actually created an open door policy through which *any citizen* can go directly to any government official in his open Majlis or in his work office . . . Abdul Aziz (himself, for example,) welcomed any citizen of the country in his Majlis, provided assistance to those who asked for it, and received petitions of complaint against the government.[60]

However, as some students of the social sciences have observed, the open *Majlis* is an inefficient method for citizen participation.[61] Therefore it needs immediate improvement and reform.

3) The Municipal Councils

The municipal councils are another type of institution through which citizens participate in the affairs of their localities. These councils' origin and history can be dated back to 1926 when the Organic Instructions of the Hijaz Kingdom (the constitution) was written. According to this constitution, these municipal councils could be established only through elections. Their authority, function and membership are as follows:

> The General Municipal Councils have full right to examine everything in connection with the municipalities and to pass resolutions to ensure their good administration and order . . . The period of validity of membership of the General Municipal Councils is three years, after which *new elections* must take place . . .[62]
>
> (The Constitution: Articles 68,74)

4) Neighborhood Councils

Recently, in April 1983, the Mayor of Holy Makkah instructed the heads of the nine sub-municipalities of Makkah to form Neighborhood Councils, each in his own vicinity. Each council is to include educated citizens to help the sub-municipality's head to administer and improve the affairs of their neighborhood.[63] At present there are no details available about the progress of this new institution for citizen participation. However it is expected that citizens will get involved and contribute much to many aspects of affairs regarding their neighborhoods. This initiative on the part of the Mayor of Holy Makkah should be followed by other cities and towns in the Kingdom.

5) Mass Media

Journalism is a recent institution in Saudi Arabia which serves as a vehicle for citizen participation. Through several daily newspapers and weekly magazines in the Kingdom, citizens convey their needs and demands, suggestions and advice, and constructive criticism to top officials both at the central and local levels of government. When a citizen writes to a newspaper and his letter is published, usually the concerned officials or their public relations agents will respond. Meanwhile, the public is kept informed and sometimes other citizens are encouraged to participate either by advocating, elaborating or evaluating an issue. Thus, journalism has become a very effective institution through which citizens may get involved in the public affairs of their localities.

V. PROCESS

The process of citizens' involvement in various local government activities, taking into consideration the environmental factors presented earlier, will be discussed under two headings: A) Methods of citizen participation and B) Problems and constraints.

A. Methods of Citizen Participation

The scope of citizen participation may involve, in one way or another, all the activities of local government. In Saudi Arabia there are many ways and means, which vary in the range of their effectiveness, through which a citizen may become active, if he so chooses. Some of the most important include:

1. Elections: In this regard Weiner tells us that "the establishment of new electoral procedures and institutions . . . have historically been the ways in which political participation has been institutionalized."[64] In the case of the local government in Saudi Arabia, the Municipal Councils, according to the chairman of Makkah Municipal Council, can be established only through free elections by the people of the city.[65] In these elections, each vocational group in the city would elect among themselves a representative who would look after their affairs in the city and represent them before the local government.

2. Compliance with Laws and Regulations: This mechanism is related to the obedience principle mentioned earlier. According to Al-Sabban, "citizen participation is evident when people help the government to achieve its goals by observing the regulations . . ."[66]

3. Financing Programs: This mechanism is very pertinent to the cooperation principle discussed above. According to Al Sabban, participation of citizens "is evident . . . when they help finance special programs."[67] Some of these programs play a strategic role in the progress of the society. The birth and development of King Abdul Aziz University in Jeddah is a good example. The idea of establishing this university was born in 1964, and three years later it was opened, on the initiative of a number of citizens living in the region.

4. Contact: There are different modes through which contact between citizens and officials can be established. Verba, Nie and Kim observed four modes of participation, of which one is "communal" and involves contact with government officials either personally or through groups. A second mode is "particularized" and involves individual contact on personal matters. In the authors' words, they are:

(Communal contacts involve) individual contacts by citizens with government officials where the subject of that contact is some general social issue (and) . . . activities involving group or organizational attempts to deal with some social issue.

The particularized contact activity involves contacting officials on personal matters where the citizen as individual, or perhaps with a few family members, contacts government officials on a particularized problem—that is, one limited to himself or his family.[68]

Verba, Nie and Kim emphasize that these two modes, while they put low pressure on leaders, convey to them a great deal of information.[69] In the case of Saudi Arabia, Lipsky asserts that "contacts between the government and the people are maintained . . ." through such types of activities.[70] Bearing in mind the two types Verba mentioned, several approaches can be seen to exist in Saudi Arabia:

(a) The direct contact: This involves contact between a citizen and an official concerning a compliant or a suggestion regarding local public policy. It may involve a personal meeting in the open majlis or in a business office, or mailing a letter or telegram directly to an official.

(b) Contact through influencial citizens: This is a common route used both by individuals and groups in Saudi Arabia. An influencial person, perhaps a businessman, a prince or a religious man is contacted and he in turn takes the issue discussed to the appropriate official.

(c) Contact through the mass media: Increasingly in Saudi Arabia complaints and questions about local problems are presented through the newspapers or special broadcasting programs. Here citizens often question officials directly. To date quite a wide variety of issues have been brought forward in this way, encouraging a response from viewers, readers and listeners so that public opinion can be assessed. This mechanism has generally demonstrated its usefulness and dynamism to officials and the public.

5. Sharing Education: Educating another person produces, eventually a participating citizen. Sharing educational skills is very advantageous especially in a society with a high percentage of illiteracy. This educational process may start with one's family members in the process of educating them about their city's affairs, history, capability, problems, policies and plans.

6. Citizens oversight of officials' actions: It is the duty of citizens not only to assist the leaders and official of their localties, but also to evaluate and assess them and their actions. This duty of oversight derives, in part, from two principles mentioned earlier regarding the value system, namely: a) enjoining what is right and forbidding what is wrong and b) public responsibility. In order to enjoin or forbid a given behavior, a citizen has to watch and oversee public officials' actions. If he does not, he is not carrying out his duties as a good Muslim. Also, it is his duty to prevent and fight corruption in the government. In this regard, the Saudi Arabian Minister of Interior, Prince Naif, has encouraged citizens to refuse to accept bribes and to help abolish bribery everywhere.[71]

B. Problems and Constraints

There are some problems and constraints that hinder citizen participation. Some of these are due to citizens themselves and some stem from conditions beyond their control.

1. Lack of participation: There is an imbalance of participation in Saudi Arabia. While some citizens are extremely active, others are not active at all. As Al Sabban summarizes it:

   It is true that a small segment of people would be happy if the government shopped for groceries for them even though they do not need this service . . . Others feel that the government is strong and wealthy so government officials should do everhting on their own. And still others feel an unwillingness to deal with the municipality because of the slow rotation process which exists.[72]

2. Lack of knowledge: Citizens often lack knowledge of how, when and where to participate. For example, when there is an election for the

154

Municipal Council, voter participation is limited due to citizens lack of knowledge.[73]

3. Lack of cooperation of some officials: Sometimes, this lack of cooperation is because an official is already over burdened with his duties. However, sometimes, it is due to unwillingness to provide information. Some consider discussion of issues with citizens as interference in the official's business.

4. The inadequacy of citizen participation institutions: Participation through the institutions discussed earlier varies greatly with individuals. There is at present no government policy or planning for public participation.

5. Lack of expertise: Many citizens want to be able to tell the government their opinions on various issues, even if as ordinary citizens they do not qualify as experts on the issue.[74]

VI. Conclusion, Evaluation and Recommendations

Islam, as previously discussed, provides general, broad and encouraging principles for citizen participation. Since Saudi Arabia claims to be the center of Islam, its government, including local governments should be the first to realize, respect and practice Islamic principles. Despite the fact that the Saudi government has encouraged and supported public participation, it is indisputable that a government policy on the issue is lacking, and that many citizens simply do not get involved in local or national government affairs. Some basic recommendations for the construction and development of public policy for public participation are:

1. The Organic Instructions of the Kingdom should be reviewed in order to update its mechanisms and make it appropriate for today.

2. A similar review of structures and procedures within the local governments and within the institutions of citizen participation needs to be undertaken.

3. For the citizen to participate effectively, he or she ought to be kept informed adequately of all regulations, procedures, plans and problems of his or her locality. Therefore, he should have access to all reports and information concerning his city or neighborhood. This requires the establishment of "information centers" at all governmental agencies.

4 Since municipalities are the keystone in the local governments, it is necessary that these municipalities "take the first step in determining

155

the goals of participation, drawing guidelines, guiding, counseling, and telling the people what their responsibilities are and listening to their needs."[75]

5. The new institution of the Neighborhood Council should receive all necessary support, administratively and financially, from the local government and local citizens.

6. At present, the Municipal Councils have no budget or funds, nor expert administrators to help them achieve their goals.[76] Therefore, in order to facilitate these councils to fulfill their responsibilities and function adequately the government should provide these councils with independent and sufficient funds.

Footnotes

1. Norman Wengert, "Citizen participation: Practice in Search of a Theory," *Natural Resources Journal*, Vol. 16 (January, 1976), p. 23

2. See Nizar Samman, 'Saudi Arabia and The Role of Emirates In Regional Development," Ph.D. dissertation, Claremont Graduate School, 1982.

3. See Muhammad Al-Buraey, "Administrative Development: An Islamic Perspective. The Possible Role of the Islamists in Development of the Muslim World", Ph.D. dissertation, The University of North Carolina at Chapel Hill, 1981.

4. See Othman Y. Al-Rawaf, "The Concept of the Five Crises In Political Development — Relevance to the Kingdom of Saudi Arabia," Ph.D. dissertation, Duke University, 1980.

5. See Aidros Al Sabban, "The Municipal System In the Kingdom of Saudi Arabia," Ph.D. dissertation, Claremont Graduate School, 1982.

6. Norman Wengert, op. cit., p. 23

7. Myron Weiner, "Political Participation: Crisis of the Political Process." In *Crises and Sequences in Political Development.* Edited by Leonard Bender, et. al., Princeton University Press, 1971, p. 164.

8. Sidney Verba, et al., *Participation and Political Equality: A Seven Nation Comparison,* the University of Chicago Press; 1978; p. 1.

9. A sample of 40 Saudi Arabian students in the United States was seleced; 90% of them were graduate students who were working either on their Master or Ph.D. degrees. Each student provided one or more segment for this definition. Adding to their ideas, the writer of this paper came up with this definition of citizen participation.

10. Othman Y. Al-Rawaf, op. cit., pp. 300-301.

11. Ali M. Al-Saflan, "The Essence of Tribal Leaders' Participation, Responsibilities and Decisions in Some Local Government Activities in Saudi Arabia: A Case Study of the Ghamid and Zahran Tribes," Ph.D. Dissertation, Claremont Graduate School, 1981, p. 48.

12. Al-Rawaf, op. cit., pp. 301-302.

13. J. Roland Pennock, *Democratic Political Theoru,* Princeton University Press, 1979, p. 443.
14. Ibid. pp. 443-444.
15. Wengert, op. cit., p. 26.
16. George Rentyz, "The Saudi Monarchy," in *King Faisal and the Modernization of Saudi Arabis,* Willard Beling, ed., Westview Press, Inc., Boulder, 1980, p. 27.
17. Saleh A. Nasser, "The Importance of Community Development In The Development of the Southwest Region of Saudi Arabia," Ph.D. dissertation, Michigan State University, 1976.
18. Ahmed H. Dahlan, *Dirasa fi alSiyasia al Dakhiliya Li'l-Mamlaka al-Arabiya al-Saudiya* (A Study of Internal Politics of the Kingdom of Saudi Arabia), Dar Al Shoruq, Jeddah, 1985, third edition, pp. 87-92.
19. Ibid., pp. 90-91.
20. Wengert, op. cit., pp. 26-27.
21. Al-Saflan, op. cit., p. 49
22. Abul A'La Mawdudi, *Human Rights in Islam,* Islamic Foundation, London, 1980, second edition, p. 33.
23. Ibid., pp. 33-34.
24. The present officia name, Kingdom of Saudi Arabia, was given in 1932 when a group of notables drew up a petition to King Abdul Aziz suggesting to change the name of the "Kingdom of the Hijaz and of Najed and Its Independencies" to the present name. (This incident is a good illustration of the Saudi citizen participation and their sound influence on public affairs.)
25. George Lipsky, "Saudi Arabia-Its People, Its Society, Its Culture"; HRAF Press, New Haven; 1959, p. 16.
26. Muhammed Al-Buraey, op. cit., p. 129-130.
27. It is beyod the scope of this paper to expain those principles in detail; our purpose is only to shed some light.
28. Abul Al'a Mawdudi, op. cit., p. 10.
29. Abul Al'a Mawdudi, *First Principles of the ISLAMIC State,* ISLAMIC Publications Ltd., Lahore (Pakistan), 1978, Fifth Edition, p. 25.
30. Abul Al'a Mawdudi, Human Rights in ISLAM, p. 10.
31. Thus, this Muslim leader (Ibn Al Khetab) – (633-643 A.D.) preceded Max Weber and other Western scholars on the concept of public servant.
32. Ahmed Dahaln, op. cit., pp. 35-39.
33. Muhammad Asad, *The Principles of State and Government in ISLAM,* Dar Al Andalus, Gibraltar (Britain), 1980, Second Edition, p. 44.
34. Abul Al'a Mawdudi, *Human Rights in ISLAM,* p. 34.
35. Othman Al Rawaf, op. cit., p. 13.
36. Sehih Al Bukhari, translated by Muhammad Muhsin Khan (Islamic University, Al-Medina Al Munawwara), Kazi Publications, Chicago Ill., 1977, third edition, Vol. III, p. 374.
37. Muhammad Asad, op. cit., p. 89.
38. Ibid., p. 79.
39. Ibid., pp. 76-80.
40. Ibid., p. 81

41. Ibid., p. 81.
42. Abu Daud At-Tirmidhi and Ibn Majah, on the authority of Abu Said Al-Khadri.
43. Sahih Muslim, on the authority of Abu Said Al-Khadri.
44. Muhammad Asad, op. cit., p. 77
45. Sahih Al-Bukhari, op. cit.
46. Wengert, op. cit. p. 23.
47. Fatina Amin Shaker, "Modernization of the Developing Nations: The Case of Saudi Arabia," Ph.D. dissertation, Purdue University, 1972, p. 99.
48. Ibid., p. 100.
49. Ibid., p. 256.
50. Abdullah Al-Ibrahim, "Regional and Urban Development in Saudi Arabia," Ph.D., University of Colorado, 1982, p. 67.
51. Hussein Mansour, "National Manpower and the Post-Infrastructure Period", Gulf Institute for Human Resources Development, Jubail, Saudi Arabia, Nov., 1986, pp. 11-16.
52. Ahmed Tawati, "The Civil Service of Saudi Arabia: Problems and Prospects", Ph.D. dissertation, West Virginia University, 1976, pp. 70-71.
53. Al Riyadh Daily Newspaper, no. 6915, May 30, 1987 (Shawwal 3, 1407).
54. Al Nadwa Daily, Makkah, no. 7329, April 16, 1983.
55. Lipsky, op. cit., p. 105.
56. Al-Rawaf, op. cit., p. 363.
57. See Time, May 22, 1978, p. 46.
58. Al-Rawaf, op. cit., p. 363.
59. Weiner, op. cit., p. 196.
60. Al-Rawaf, op. cit., pp. 363-364.
61. Shaker, op. cit., pp. 310-311.
62. Solaiman A. Solaim, "Constitutional and Judicial Organization in Saudi Arabia," Ph.D. dissertation, Johns Hopkins University, 1970, p. 182.
63. Al Nadwa Daily, Makkah, April, 1983.
64. Weiner, op. cit., p. 193.
65. Al Nadwa Daily, Makkah, No. 7318, April 3, 1983. See also Al-Sabban, op. cit., pp. 127-128.
66. Al Sabban, op. cit., p. 126.
67. Ibid., pp. 126-127.
68. Verba, Nie and Kim, "Participation and Political Equality, op. cit., p. 54.
69. Verba, Nie and Kim, op. cit., p. 54.
70. Lipsky, op. cit., p. 93.
71. Ashraq Al-Awsat (newspaper), No. 1567, March 14, 1983, (5,29,1403 H.), London.
72. Al Sabban, op. cit., pp. 128, 135.
73. Ibid., p. 128.
74. Charles Lindblom, The Policy Making Process, Prentice Hall Inc., New Jersey, 1980, p. 12.
75. Al Sabban, op. cit., p. 128.
76. Al Nadwa Daily, Makkah, No. 7318, April 3, 1983.

THE ESSENCE OF TRIBAL LEADERS' PARTICIPATION, RESPONSIBILITIES AND DECISIONS IN SOME LOCAL GOVERNMENT ACTIVITIES IN SAUDI ARABIA: A CASE STUDY OF THE GHAMID AND ZAHRAN TRIBES

Ph.D. dissertation by Ali Mashhoor Al-Seflan, Claremont Graduate School: 1980.

Review by Constance B. Joy

The main focus of this dissertation is the examination of the role of tribal leaders in their communities in Saudi Arabia. Particular emphasis is placed on delineating the positive effects of leader participation, both for central and local government and for the people of the tribes. This study was done in the late 1970s and is unique in that it first presents conceptual and descriptive materials on Saudi legal, tribal, and government structure and systems, and then goes on to document the functioning of these systems as they operate among the Ghamid and Zahran tribes in the Al Baha area of Southwestern Saudi Arabia. As a result of findings made by the author, recommendations for improvement of tribal-government interaction in local affairs are suggested.

Evidence and information for this study were gathered from literature and various documents on Saudi Arabia, and through a case study analysis involving interviews, observation and personal experience of the author. The study is useful particularly for three kinds of readers: those interested in a clear and simple statement of Saudi legal, political and tribal structure and systems; those interested in public administration issues in Saudi Arabia, especially in interactive negotiations between government officials and citizens; and those interested in tribal societies in transition.

In the first part of this study, important concepts and information from four different areas are presented as having particular relevance for analyzing the activities of tribal leaders. These are: public administration theory; the Saudi constitution and legal system; the Saudi political system; and finally, the Saudi tribal system.

From the area of public administration theory, Al-Seflan feels that shared decision-making, participation and responsibility are key concepts which go a long way towards explaining leaders' roles. In Saudi Arabia there has been a long history of respect for the position of *sheikh* and *'amdah* as leaders and this has not changed in recent years despite the installation of central government in 1926. Tribes in Arabia have functioned for centuries as groups in which the leader shared decisions with his own people and at times with other tribes. Participation, accountability and responsibility were all encouraged within the rules of tribal custom and the precepts of Islam. With the beginning of modern national and regional government, traditional features of tribal government were, and are still, being gradually adapted to wider communities beyond the tribe, according to Al-Seflan. All citizens are being encouraged to participate in activities at different levels of government, to look beyond the interests of their tribes and to share their opinions and activities with officials. Citizens and government officials alike are being encouraged to utilize the tribal leader as a person of power and position through whom information can be shared, conflict and problems can be efficiently resolved and nationalism can be promoted.

According to Al-Seflan, shared decision-making in government affairs is increasing advocated by both public administrators and theoreticians. It is of great advantage to share knowledge, information and skills and moreover, it is likely to result in greater efficiency of service and wider public support in favor of whatever decisions are made. At the time of his study, Al-Seflan saw several indicators that shared decision-making was being officially promoted in the Kingdom: the establishment of the Institute for Public Administration in 1961 in essence mandated the training of administrative skills so that a larger section of the citizenry would have the education and qualifiation necessary to participate in government affairs; the declaration of the "Regions Ordinances" in 1939 and 1963 allowed regional governments to share in decisions regarding their areas with the central government; and the existence of tribal committees permitted tribal members to jointly decide on particular types of community affairs.

Citizen participation in community life is also advocated by Al-Seflan as being helpful, desirable and functional for government. It tends to promote democracy and eliminate social differences among citizens. It helps decision-makers gather information on community activities more efficiently, tends to establish good relationships between officials and citizens and

160

reduces conflict. In the long run, both people and government benefit, and this is true even if citizens are not highly educated or motivated so that communication is more difficult. In Saudi Arabia, Al-Seflan noted that the trend to promote citizen participation was increasing with the decentralization of government decision-making and the encouragement of tribal and community leaders to express their views.

Responsibility is another important concept in Al-Seflan's view. What it means basically is that citizens are responsible for participating in public life and governments are responsible for fulfilling their mandated duties to their citizens. As governments become increasingly complex, the demand for their services becomes greater. Both governments and the citizens they represent have heavier responsibilities. In Saudi Arabia, responsibility is rooted in Islam, but also in citizen interest to demand that their governments function effetively and smoothly. Citizens have both an obligation and a duty to report information to officials and leaders and to share in decions about community affairs, enforcement of laws and regulations.

In order to understand the role of tribal leaders it is also necessary to have a basic understanding of the legal, political and tribal structures in which they function. Both the legal and political structure find their basis in Islam in Saudi Arabia.

Islamic law, or *shari'ah*, is rooted in the Koran as the primary source and in the *sunna* (the Prophet Mohammed's words and deeds), *'ijma'* (a consensus or agreement between religious leaders or *ulema* as to what is law when no solution is found in the Koran or *sunna*), and *qiyas* (or legal analogous solutions). In addition to Islamic law, there exist *al 'urf*, or customary law, and statutory or written law. *Al 'urf* involves traditional solutions when there is no conflict with Islamic law. The enforcement of this sort of law falls particularly within the jurisdiction of tribal chiefs in the case of minor or petty issues and saves government officials much time and effort—although as Al-Seflan explains it, it is the responsibility of leaders to report all legal violations and any sort of law enforcement to local authorities. Statutory law can be said to form the consitution of the country, and consists primarily of the 1926 Constitution of the Hejaz, the legal regulations of 1958 delineating the formation and duties of the Council of Ministers, and King Faisal's "Basic Law" of 1962, which set in motion the development of new regulations governing banks, social welfare, vehicle codes, the civil service, etc. In the case of an infringement of the law, the determination must first be made as to whether or not precept of Islam has been violated in which case punishment falls under *shari'ah* if the in-

161

fringement is minor it may be resolved through the agreement of the tribal leader in consultation with religious leaders. As cases become more serious, however, plaintiff and defendant must go to court and official governing bodies (which the tribe is not) must be informed. Al-Seflan describes the appeal system and the three levels of courts in Saudi Arabia, culminating in the Judicial Supervisory Committee at the top.

The political system and structure also help explain the role tribal leaders play. Al-Seflan explains in some detail the authorities, responsibilities and relationships between the king, the crown prince, the Council of Ministries, the ministers, the ministries, the governors, the deputy governors and the district *amirs*—the primary administrators of central and local government. From a theoretical point of view, tribal leaders may have contact with any one of these persons and/or the organizations they represent. From a practical point of view however, leaders deal mainly with local administrators.

Finally, Al-Seflan selects concepts from tribal structure and systems. His study provides a very clear and quite thorough discussion of the relationships between tribe, sub-tribe, clan, kinship and family. He delineates the major tribes of pre-Islamic times and names the major tribes of the southwest region, his area of focus. According to Al-Seflan the tribe functions mainly as a social unit in Saudi Arabia, its political and economic functions having been largely taken over by the central government. Leaders still give orders to their people and solve conflicts and disputes, but they must always consider the legal limitations of their power. Tribes are generally divided into two tyeps of social communities, the city dwellers (*al-hadhar*) and the desert nomads (*al-badw*) or bedouin. Tribes (*qabilah*) divide into clans (*firqah*) defined as groups of extended families with a shared sense of community headed by a respected leader called a *sheikh*. In general, tribal families tend to engage in agriculture and animal husbandry and distinguish themselves from city dwellers who tend to identify more with families than with tribe and are likely to engage in trade and manufacturing activities. The life of tribal people can be particularly difficult, especially for nomadic desert dwellers and the government of Saudi Arabia has been trying to encourage settlement into towns with limited success. This is because the government recognizes their responsibility to ease the hardships of life for the bedouin and the need for training and manpower development. At the same time, the nomads are reluctant to give up the freedom of what they view as a superior lifestyle.

In the second part of his study, Al-Seflan describes the Ghamid and Zahran tribes in terms of where they dwell, major economic activities and tribal structure, and then proceeds to document, at an empirical level, the involvement that leaders of these tribes have in government and community affairs.

The Ghamid and Zahran, he says, live in those areas of the southwest of Saudi Arabia known as the Tihama Plain, the Asarah Highland and the high plateau above these. Al Baha is their major city and the seat of government and other larger cities they inhabit include Baljurashi, Al Makhwa, Al Mandiq and Al 'Atawela. Eighty-five percent of the people of this region live in rural areas and fifteen per cent are urban dwellers. Agriculture and animal husbandry are the major occupation, although declining. At the time of the study, in 1975, sixty-three percent of workers were engaged in these activities, down from seventy-four percent in 1966, according to sources cited in the study. In the cities the main occupations were in services (13 % in 1975 up from 9 % in 1966), commerce (9 %, up from 7⅛), and construction (7 %, up from 4 %). Most activities involved supporting local demands with local goods, except where transport to outside major cities was no problem.

The Ghamid tribe includes ten subtribes in the villages (among them the bani-Abdullah, Bani al-Jurashi, Bani Dhabyan and Bani Khath'am), and nine sub-tribes among the nomads (including the Bani Kabeer, Bani Rafa'ah and Bani Talib). The Zahran tribe forms twenty eight subtribes and clans, among them the Bani Hasin, Daws, Bani Basheer and Bani 'omar. From the point of view of national government, these tribes come under the jurisdiction of the governor (*hakem*) of the province who is nominated by the Minister of Interior, appointed by the King and technically the ruler of the region and representative of the central government. Below him are the deputy governor and district *amir* who report to him. In addition, there exist central government agencies such as branches of the Ministry of Finance, Ministry of Agriculture, Interior, etc., and their agents which carry out policies at the local level and report back to the Central government. Only beginning in the mid 1980s were tribal leaders officially appointed. Although *sheikhs* of the major tribes have the right to contact the governor or his deputy when needed, they are encouraged to contact concerned parties of agencies first. Subtribes or clans must report to the district *amir*.

Al-Seflan found that tribal leaders were involved in several types of activities in order to represent their people to the government or vice-versa and maintain and enforce law and security.

a. *education* Leaders were involved in selecting school sites, encouraging youth to go to school, visiting schools and meeting teachers, and

163

informing regional authorities about needs so that recommendations could be made to the regional education office. Education is free in the kingdom and each student is eligible for a monthly allowance to support him through the college level. The number of schools and the percentage of both girls and boys going to school increased dramatically from 1970 to 1980, both in the Al Baha area and the throughout the kingdom. In part, this was due to the cooperation between leaders and officials and the recognition of the importance of education for development.

b. *agricultural development* Most agricultural development plans came from the central government and involved developing dams, roads and granting agricultural loans. Tribal laders helped avoid delays and conflicts by explaining these projects to their people. They also encouraged them to go to training centers to be taught about new methods of farming and new crops. They reported information on local weather and crop conditions to the regional agricultural office and they worked with local and national agencies to inform them to farmers' desires concerning farming policies, road construction, etc. Finally tribal leaders were able to assist both government, etc. Finally tribal leaders were able to assist both government and farmers by identifying which persons were needy and would really benefit from agricultural loans.

c. *assistance in legal decisions* Tribal leaders assisted local authorities to solve disputes both among their own people and between neighboring tribes. Generally, mediation was in accordance with local tribal custom and the local judge merely approved the result when the leader presented the agreement to local authorities. This sort of activity saved government authorities a great deal of time and effort and demonstrates the support for the power and position that traditional leaders still have in Arabia.

d. *transportation and communication improvement* During the years just prior to Al-Seflan's study (as indeed during the after), literally thousands of miles of asphalted roads were laid in the kingdom and hundreds of miles in the Al Baha area, along with numerous miles of agricultural roads. In addition, telephone, mail service and telecommunication systems were brought into the area for the first time. Tribal leaders played a very important role in explaining the projects to their people who sometimes were very uneducated, and in addition helped them to seek government compensation for loss of property where roads or development sites were built on private land. Where groups

164

held opposing ideas on whether or where to build a road, they helped to solve disputes.

e. *welfare and social assistance* The central and local government of the Kingdom has established numerous social welfare programs from 1965 to the present: vocational training centers, assistance programs for the disabled, elderly and needy, and social programs. Tribal leaders were seen to be especially helpful in identifying who would be eligible for such programs and encouraging training among their youth.

f. *investigation of citizenship privileges* Every year Saudi Arabia has thousands of pilgrims coming for pilgrimage to the holy cities of Mecca and Medina. They are welcomed in to perform their religious duties but they are not entitled to stay longer than the length of their pilgrimage visa, normally a month. Many others enter the Kingdomm on business contracts. Needless to say, with the increasing wealth of the Kingdom, many are anxious to find work and overstay their visa rights illegally. An important task of leaders is to help authorities identify anyone whose visa has expired in their local areas.

On the whole, Al-Seflan found that tribal leaders were a great help to both local and central government as well as to their communities. The fact that government authorities were willing to work with them indicates the desire of the government to maintain a traditional Islamic society and at the same time help the people to learn about new and modern methods which will ease their lives, when not a threat or danger to their basic values. Also the government's policy seems to indicate concern with promoting democratic principles and protecting the rights of individuals.

Despite the many advantages of leader participation, responsibility and shared decision making, Al-Seflan also found several disadvantages in their participation in government affairs, among them: lack of education; inherited position; favoritism and nepotism; resistance to change and counsel from younger persons; personal greed and desire for prestige sometimes created barrers to community development; refusal to cooperate with officials; violation of rules and regulations as an act of defiance when the official government process of follow-up and approval for petitions was not clear; sometimes leaders of differing tribes could not reach agreement; sometimes they were uninformed about their peoples' needs and therefore were unable to help authorities accurately assess local needs for schools, health facilities, etc.

Al-Seflan suggests that the government could implement several programs that would help overcome some of these disadvantages. For instance, the

165

government could require a certain level of education for anyone to be eligible for local leadership and encourage present leaders to join in local education programs which are free of charge. It could initiate training programs to familiarize leaders with major government regulations of interest to them and to aquaint them with the limits of their authority. Furthermore, it should institute fixed fees for the types of services commonly rendered by leaders and harshly penalize leaders who overcharge or ask for bribes. It should intercede when conflicts between leader and tribe get out of hand. The regional governor should make sure that all local authorities respect and appreciate the roles of tribal leaders and pay attention to their ideas and recommendations. Finally, the government could assist tribal leader to keep records on their people, such as recording births, deaths etc.

All in all, Al-Seflan's study represents a major effort in the field of tribal studies and local government. He has managed to gather data where little empirical information exists, and to relate it to important concepts and ideas regarding public administration. He has argued convincingly that the role of the traditional leader in Arabia serves in numerous ways to facilitate interaction between citizens and the government, as well as to encourage democracy in the Kingdom. Furthermore, he has provided the reader with an invaluable discussion of the political system in Saudi Arabia along with several charts clearly delineating lines of authority. Finally, he has explained how Islam and the legal system and tribal structure can be seen to influence and regulate the leader's role.

PART III:

WOMEN'S DEVELOPMENT IN SAUDI ARABIA

INTRODUCTION:

The women's movement in Saudi society has quietly achieved successful steps toward progress and development. As in many other Islamic countries, this movement has distinctive roots, principles, and concerns. Islamic principles and practices of Muslim leaders, including the Prophet, provide an "idealistic approach" to the position and treatment of women in society. Islam recognizes woman as an equal partner to man and grants her equal rights within a defined context. There are a few exceptions as in inheritance matters. In Islamic countries many believe that women, due partially to emotional and biological reasons, should not be encouraged to reign over state affairs (to be president or prime minister).

Even in most western societies women have not risen to these posts. The history of the United States, for example, tells us that since its independence not a single female has been elected president.

The tradition of society is a force that should be taken into consideration when preparing any development plan or program. Tradition, paradoxically, embodies both positive and negative aspects. At any rate, distinction should be made between religion and tradition. Tradition should be respected when it conforms with religion. If not, as in the case of some societal behavior, then tradition must be evaluated and reconsidered.

Before the 1950s, ignorance, combined with some traditional values, was responsible for denying most females in Saudi Arabia their rights to education and to work.

By the end of 1980s and beginning of 1990s, female students, at all levels, have increased dramatically. However, tradition still plays a major role in restricting and protecting women in the light of public interest. For example, tradition discourages women from working as waitresses, plumbers, bus drivers, gas station attendants, janitorial workers, and similar jobs. These *low profile jobs*, many believe, should not be opened for the gentle sex, rather they should *be restricted to men*. Saudi women's traditional place in society allows limited job opportunities for the educated female. As a response to the growing resource of educated women, the Saudi government has proposed establishing certain industries strictly for them and probably the 1990s will witness steady development in this direction. In brief, as women's participation in the workforce increases, there are certain fields and occupations that they should be encouraged to join.

In Part III Nura Al-Saad, in her article *"THE ROLE OF WOMEN IN GENERAL DEVELOPMENT PLANNING IN SAUDI ARABIA,"* warns first of all of the misinterpretation of Islamic principles. She emphasizes the need for continuing education programs and for training to ready women for an active participatory role and to prepare them for the opportunities available to them in the work force.

She believes that through education woman can be reinstated to her historic role of equality with man. Education can enhance women's awareness of the problems yet to be overcome and direct them on a path to increased participation in the planning and decision-making processes. Women are seeking training in new kinds of jobs and a more active role in the developing Saudi society. However, there are some obstacles that hinder this goal: some traditional values (not religious), i.e., the forced dependence of women on men for transportation and the transaction of certain official business.

The development plans have value, dimension, and intensity; however, the emergence of women in roles of authority needs more combined efforts of both men and women participating in the future development plans, especially in fields that directly affect women and children, e.g., education, gynecology, obstetrics, pediatric medicine, child development, and home economics.

On similar lines, but a different level, Dr. Aisha A. Al-Husseiny, in her article *"FEMALE ADMINISTRATIVE LEADERSHIP IN HIGHER EDUCATION IN SAUDI ARABIA: PREPARATION AND DEVELOPMENT"* presents the results and analysis of research conducted in the Western Province in 1985. The findings of her study both support and contradict many prior assumptions about why women participate in the education field, and how they and their male counterparts perceive their participation.

Dr. Al-Husseiny details the findings in the areas of motivations to work, job authority and tasks, job training, job difficulties and impediments, and job selection. It is worthwhile to note how the Saudi segregated educational system has actually created job opportunities for women, and how those women see the evolution of their position for the future of education, on which society greatly depends. Finally, Dr. Al-Husseiny offers a number of thoughtful recommendations based on the findings, calling for greater participation of women in the planning process, especially in areas of most concern to women.

The reexamination of social and traditional values, especially those pertinent to women participating in the work force, is now under way in Saudi Arabia. This reexamination is influenced by a deep-seated loyalty to Islamic values, by Western examples, and by the need for mobilizing a needed but idle human resource. Islamic history is full of shining examples of women participating in, and contributing to, different aspects of public life. Hopefully, the current Women's Movement in Saudi Arabia would proceed on similar lines.

THE ROLE OF WOMEN IN GENERAL DEVELOPMENT PLANNING IN SAUDI ARABIA

by Noura Khaled Alsaad*

"Development in Saudi Arabia is for every single person regardless of sex. For a woman to participate in setting the social and educational policy, this participation does not depend on gender but rather on the qualifications each person possesses. . . We should not underestimate the capability of the Saudi woman. She is a citizen that must have equal rights as well as duties. The door must remain open for her to play this role."

Hisham Nazher, 1980

In the late 1950s great changes have occurred in Saudi Arabia with regard to the status and participation of women in the fields of education and employment. Government schools for girls were established for the first time in October, 1959, and since then educational levels have increased. Women have begun to work outside their homes in small numbers. By and large, these changes are the result of the enormous impact of the economic boom in Saudi Arabia since the discovery of oil and of the response of the government with Five Year Development plans. The First (1970), Second (1975), and Third (1980) Development Plans all detailed policies, programs and projects related to women in such areas as social development, training, manpower, education, health and nutrition. Yet, despite such advances, women did not play an integral part in the country's development. The first two Development Plans did not envision female participation in any significant numbers in educational, economic, social or labor force activities. They were founded on the premise that women are not full and active members of the working and policy making community in Saudi Arabia.

Given these facts, the purpose of this study was to conduct research to solicit the opinion of Saudi women regarding both their own participation

---

*Based on the author's M.A. Thesis, University of Minnesota, 1982

173

and their vision of women's integration into the nation's future. This pioneering research involved four basic stages: literature review; sample selection and questionnaire construction and distribution; analysis and intepretation of findings; recommendations.

Literature Review

According to the literature clearly the guideing principle and the organizing structure of Saudi society stem from the teachings and tenets of Islam. However, it is of utmost importance that these teachings be used in a positive way to promote what is best in humankind and for societal growth rather than to restrict and inhibit. Islamic teachings should be based on their religious truth and not colored by the interpretation of individuals of any particular era. Until the end of 1950s, education was denied to women in Saudi Arabia based on what many believe to be the misinterpretation of Islamic teachings. Closest attention must be paid to preclude society from improperly ascribing similar inferior positions to women today.

Innumerable studies have shown links between education and development. Many have focused on the situation of women in the Muslim world. By and large, these studies show that in the Muslim countries in general there exist low levels of economic actvity, low literacy, and low school enrollment for women at all levels of society. These statistics reflect part misinterpretation of Islamic teachings regarding education and work for women. They also show that these countries still have strong traditional customs which restrict women.

Attitudes toward the education of girls in a traditional society like that of Saudi Arabia may be seen in the types of roles assigned to women, such as being good housewives and mothers. Hammad speculated that "perhaps this can explain why the public education of girls started as late as 1960, while the public education of boys began as far back as the 1930's".[1] As Parssinen stated, "the traditional conviction that female education was considered not merely unnecessary and superfluous, but positively wrong" is a common misperception of certain scholars of the Middle East.[2] The author agrees with Parssinen when she indicated that the historical development of prejudice against female education in Saudi Arabia, or elsewhere in the Arab world, owes its genesis to cultural attitudes and cannot be attributed to Islam. For example, when public schools for girls were established for the first time in 1960, despite the fact that the government delegated this sensitive assignment to a conservative group of religious leaders governed by 'Ulama, there were some cases of opposition. The most famous of these occurred in Buraidah, where some ignorant elements claimed that the planned establishment of a school for girls would produce demoralization and destroy the foundation of the family. A public demonstration erupted and government troops were dispatched to restore order.[3]

Now those people encourage their daughters and wives to finish their education to be good housewives and mothers, while some others realize that society needs educated women as it needs educated men.

The literature review has shown that changing attitudes is a critical element in changing female participation in development and work roles. In countries where women perceive work in a positive manner, there tend to be more women employed. At present, societal attitudes towards women's education and work in Saudi Arabia are undergoing rapid changes. These changes have led to major expansion of women's education. Between 1960 and 1985, the number of girls' schools has increased significantly, from 15 elementary schools with 5,180 students in 1960 to 6,608 primary and secondary schools with 851,201 students in 1985.[4] Girls colleges have been set up in large cities, and women's sections in the main universities. The enrollment in the colleges and universities reached 13,206 in 1980 and 35,382 in 1985.[5]

Yet, despite the rapidly expanding plans for involving women in higher education, some traditional and societal roles still influence both the philosophy of educational planning and the school curriculum. Many subjects reflecting the wife-mother role are taught.

At the same time, development has opened up new opportunities for women to work, and the actual number working continues to rise. In 1975 only 27,000 Saudi women were in the labor force. A decade later their numbers had increased by more than 340%, to 120,000. By the end of the Fourth Development Plan (1985-1990), 50,000 more women are expected to join the work force, not only in the traditionally acceptable fields of female education and health care, but increasingly as computer specialists and as managers for women's personnel matters in the civil service. In 1983, the Institute of Public Administration inaugurated a separate training facility to prepare women for more productive participation in the public sector.

As the nation develops, women's participation in the work force will continue to increase. Women have begun to consider non-traditional forms of work, particularly in the areas of new technical skills. The nation has recently filled many non-traditional jobs, previously held by foreigners, with Saudi women. Women's work and participation will continue to receive greater attention and be regarded in more realistic ways by the decision-makers of future development plans. However, to achieve adequate work participation by women, their involvement in planning and decision-making is essential in order that their needs, attitudes and orientation can be taken into account.

Methodology and Sample

In 1981, open-ended questionnaires were sent to a sample of Saudi women asking their opinions of women's role and participation in development. The questionnaire was divided into three basic areas focusing on women's attitudes toward work, family, and development.

The sample was drawn from a pool of 499 Saudi women working in Jeddah. An attempt was made to balance out occupations. Hence, in occupations where the numbers were particularly small, almost all employed women were chosen, but where they were larger, a random selection was made. Employers included universities, schools, hospitals, newspapers, and government departments of foreign affairs, social work, broadcasting and communications. An initial sample of 155 was selected, then 120 questionnaires were distributed and 76 completed questionnaires returned as usable. The responses were analyzed in terms of content and percentages. Associations were made between background and various attitudes expressed by the respondents.

Findings

The findings of the study were grouped into six major areas as follows:

1. *Attitudes towards work and job satisfaction and preference:* Women gave several reasons for working. By far the most overwhelming reason was to serve others (86%). The second most common reason was for self-fulfillment (48%). And the least common was for economic reasons (27%). Ninety-five percent of the women respondents said their families encouraged them to work. In all occupations seventy-five percent of single women said they would continue working after marriage and only thirteen percent planned on quitting once they had children. Among doctors and social workers none planned to quit. At least eighty percent of the respondents were satisfied

176

with their jobs for various reasons including serving their clients and use of their skills. Women who had lower levels of education appeared to be more satisfied with their jobs. The main reason for dissatisfaction was lack of needed authority in the work situation. Almost sixty-one percent of the respondents admitted that they desire jobs which are currently unavailable in Saudi Arabia, either for themselves or for others, but only half of them specified particular jobs. The most commonly mentioned jobs were in decor and design, government office jobs, airline and travel, and customs service jobs.

2. *Work related problems and solutions:* Thirty percent of the respondents stated that they had no problems. Among the others the most common complaints were lack of adequate transportation (31%), lack of authority in the work place (18%) and work desegregation by gender (18%). A few others complained about long work hours and little recognition from men. Solutions included improved transportation (especially for teachers), promotion of more authority for women and cooperation among co-workers.

3. *Work and family constraints:* When asked whether it was difficult for women who have children to work, fifty percent said yes and fifty percent said no. Some agreed that a dual role was difficult to handle and others said it was not. When asked for suggestions to overcome any difficulties, the most common responses were provision of child care facilities at the work site or in the community, flexible hours, and improved transportation.

4. *Social role of Saudi women:* In regard to the role of Islam, 75% of the respondents disagreed when given the following statement: "Islam as a religion discourages women from participating in educational or social and economic development." Eighty percent said that Islam gives women their rights and sixty-two percent stated that there were role models for female participation in Islamic history. Eighty-five percent said they felt positive about women's role in educational and social development and over sixty percent felt that society should give women increased opportunities. Seventy-five percent believe that the mass media have little or no influence in promoting women's role and suggested that media play an increasing role. When asked what social changes were having the greatest impact on women's affairs, eighty-three percent said expansion of women's education generally and sixty-nine percent said recent government policies to increase the number of Saudi women to replace non-Saudi female workers.

5. *Opinions about eduction:* Eighty-four percent of respondents felt that the time was now right to pass laws requiring compulsory education in the Kingdom. Of the 6% who disagreed the main reason given was that

some communities were not yet ready for the elaborate changes in laws and regulations that would be needed. When asked about school curriculum, eighty-seven percent said that changes were needed. But when asked to specify these, over half said that the current situation should be evaluated first. Among those who gave suggestions, the most common was the addition of physical education and foreign languages. Younger respondents tended to give more suggestions than older ones. Sixty-four percent of respondents felt that continuing education in all fields should be available to Saudi women. Administrative training was the most desired as well as clerical and secretarial work. Many other areas were mentioned also such as computer training, hair dressing, travel agency work, radio announcing and language training. Both age and education affected the responses to the question. The youngest and most educated respondents made the largest number of suggestions. The Girl's Education Presidency was felt to be the institution most responsible for providing these programs, although universities and women's institutes were cited as well.

6. *Work and the Development Plan:* Most respondents had many suggestions for improving their job output. Fifty-nine percent suggested continuing in-service education and improved resources to enhance understanding of work and improve performance. The second most common suggestion (53%) was to provide flexibility in work conditions. Others were to increase autonomy and freedom at work (36%), provide public evaluation of work (36%) and provide better technological resources (31%). When asked which kinds of jobs they felt would assure women's participation in future development in the Kingdom, the most commonly cited were teaching (70%), medical services (67%), social work (60%) counseling and research (46%) and administration (40%). Others less commonly mentioned were broadcasting, literary work and journalism, sewing, designing, decorating and foreign affairs.

Implications of the Study and Recommendations

The results of this study are limited to the sample only and caution should be used in generalizing to the population at large. In particular, it should be noted that the respondents were all educated working women in a country where a low percentage of women work. Therefore their opinions may not reflect the opinions of the majority of Saudi women but they may be common among working women. However, some implications which might be derived are the following:

178

— The fact that the most commonly cited reason for working was to serve others rather than economic reasons, as is common in most other studies on women's work, suggests that women are aware of society's need for qualified workers. This is regardless of their occupation or martial status.

— Women are generally satisfied with their jobs although they are excluded from planning and the decision making process, a primary cause of job dissatisfaction. Transportation and lack of authority are the main complaints. Until women are allowed to drive, transportation will continue to be a problem causing inefficiency in the workplace. A job without adequate authority is no real job at all. Increased participation in the labor force by women should really be a program of transfer of authority. As long as women are not encouraged to transact business in all official departments without the assistance of a male relative, the need for an adequate solution or as some suggest, separate but equal facilities for women, is obvious.

— Although there is a great awareness of women's contributions by male family members, a certain paradox arises, because of lack of respect in the work place. The resolution of their problem will not occur overnight. The acceptance of the new, ative role of women requires true understanding, and serious respect from all members of society.

— Saudi women's awareness of alternative jobs and their desire to have them as well as their recognized needs for in-service training suggests future development plans ought to allow for new kinds of jobs for women and provision of adequate training for them.

— The literature review and the study both suggest that teaching and medical jobs are those most highly valued by women. It remains for society to elevate the status of other occupations to a level of comparable worth to increase the number of workers in these fields.

— Despite significant progress in development in the Kingdom, women's educational opportunities lag behind other areas of development. In the near future, compulsory education and curriculum changes should rank high on the agenda in response to women's desires and needs.

— The mass media has a responsibility to support and encourage women's new role in society and Saudi women themselves should recognize the urgency of their full participation in the mass media as well as their need to participate in development plans.

179

— An awareness of female role models in Islamic history is acknowledged by the respondents. The researcher believes that the practice of true Islamic principles will reinstate women to their historic role of equality and provide them the opportunity to exercise their rights and duties in conjunction with men.

Recommendations

Based on the study, several recommendations can be made, particularly for the attention of government agencies and the heads of educational institutions or any agencies where women work. Some of these follows:

1. Draw up specific development plans to integrate women in the current and future Development Plan.
2. Provide for the participation of women in planning committees.
3. Provide technical, vocational and in-service training for women.
4. Encourage participation of women in professional conventions, and symposia, . . . , etc.
5. Conduct research about working women's situations in order to recognize their problems and respond constructively.
6. Increase child care facilities and provisions.
7. Facilitate a more active role for women in the media.

The central concern should be that women themselves become more aware of their expanded role so that they will continue to participate and to work in the development plan which needs the involvement of both men and women for its success.

Footnotes

1. Hammad, Mohammed A. *"The Educational System and Planning for Manpower Development in Saudi Arabia"*, Ph.D. dissertation, Indiana University, 1973, p. 58. Also: See El-Sanabary, Nagat Morsi. *A Comparative Study of the Disparities of Education Opportunities for Girls in the Arab States.* Ph.D. dissertation, Berkely, University of California, 1973, p. 217.
2. Cathereine Parssinen. The Changing Role of Women; *King Faisal and the Modernization of Saudi Arabia,* Willard Belling, Ed., New York: Harper and Row, 1980, p. 145.
3. Ibid., p. 159.
4. Kingdom of Saudi Arabia. Ministry of Education, Girls' Education, 1981, p. 48. Also see: Kingdom of Saudi Arabia, Ministry of Education, Educational Development, Statistics on Education in the Kingdom, 1984-85.
5. Kingdom of Saudi Arabia, Ministry of Education, op. cit. Also: see Mansor, Hussein, National Workforce and the Post-Infrastructure Phase, The Gulf Institute for Human Resource Management, 1986, p. 13.

FEMALE ADMINISTRATIVE LEADERSHIP IN HIGHER EDUCATION IN SAUDI ARABIA: PREPARATION AND DEVELOPMENT*

by Aisha A. Al-Husseiny, Ph.D.

"Saudi women have made tremendous strides and shown that they are capable of facing the challenges required in managing and running the female sector of the educational system. . . . However, they should participate in the planning process regarding the amelioration of the conditions of the working woman, because they are more capable of understanding their own situations and needs than men."

Aisha A. Al-Husseiny, Ph.D.

Introduction

Public education was opened to girls in Saudi Arabia in 1959. The impact of this has been enormous: the past high illiteracy rates among females are gradually being eradicated, and a large number of jobs have opened up for educated women interested in teaching and educational administration. As of 1987, close to 55,000 Saudi women were working in the educational fields in the Kingdom. The continuing increase in the number of schools and in job positions provided by schools has, at the same time, dramatized an important issue in need of attention: adequate training for teachers and administrators.

Saudi Arabia is a society which, by law, stipulated sex segregation in the work place and at all institutes of education. Paradoxically, this has meant that as schools have expanded, women have found jobs which might not have been available to them in countries with coeducational school systems—jobs as heads of institutes and in top level administrative positions,

---

*Based on the author's Ph.D. dissertation (in Arabic), Al-Azhar University, Cairo, 1985.

running school programs. Women alone shoulder the responsibility for administering much of what goes on in the female sector of the educational system.

However, with their increasing responsibilities has come the realization that, as a group, they have been left behind their male counterparts. This is true particularly as regards training and prepraation. The development plans have given opportunities to men which far outstrip those given to women. This fact has several serious implications. First, Saudi women have difficulty performing well at jobs they are not adequately trained for, as anyone would. Secondly, their lack of training has multiple downward effects on their employees, their students, their schools and ultimately upon society as a whole, since education is the cornerstone for societal change. Thirldy, due to these two factors, both individuals and the government must quickly assume the responsibility to implement more programs to improve the quality of female leadership in the school systems in Saudi Arabia.

RESEARCH GOALS

In 1985, research was conducted in the Western Province of Saudi Arabia with the following intent and rationale:

a. to identify the characteristics and ambitions of women working in the field of educational administration, and to find out their incentives for working in a society where a high percentage of woman does not.
b. to identify authority and tasks these women have in their jobs compared to what they feel they should have.
c. to investigate what negative factors, if any, they feel might inhibit them from carrying out their jobs as well as possible, and also what difficulties and challenges they face.
d. to find out what training and preparation women have had for their positions in educational administration, as well as what further programs for leadership training they feel are necessary.
e. to identify how job selection and hiring occurs for women in these positions.

METHODOLOGY

In order to conduct the research, a sample of 105 women and 150 men,

184

all leaders in the field of administration in higher education, were delivered questionnaires by hand. The women sampled were, on the whole, directors of girls sections, vice-deans (the highest possible university rank for women), heads of departments, and directors of different administrations. The men held positions as university presidents, vice-presidents, deans of collegs, vice-deans, heads of departments and directors of administration. Questionnaires were distributed in the following way throughout the university and college system in the Western Province:

	Women (sent)	Men (returned)
King Abdul Aziz Univerity (in Jeddah & Medina)	38	57
Um al Qura University (in Mecca & Taif)	44	38
Girls Colleges (in Jeddah, Mecca, Medina)	23	15
TOTALS	105	110

The response rate for women was 95.2%, and for men 73.3%, resulting in a final sample of 100 women and 110 men.

The men were given a questionnaire which was different from that given to women, but the large majority of questions on them were the same. Where they differed was mainly that women were sometimes asked to report their experiences, while men were asked what experiences they thought women had. The questions on the questionnaires were all closed ended, although many of those responding often felt free to write comments on the side. Some of these comments are reported in the findings and recommendations. Most questions did not have mutually exclusive answers and so were not open to statistical manipulations. Findings are reported in terms of total frequencies and percentages.

Findings

The findings of the research can be reported in relationship to five major areas of interest: motivations to work, job authority and tasks, job training, job difficulties, job selection.

185

1. Motivations to Work

Before this research was begun, it was hypothesized that Saudi women in the educational administrative field worked primarily for economic reasons, just as studies have shown most women do all over the world. It was also hypothesized that the jobs which women held gave them the chance to realize their ambitions, or they would not continue to work. The first of these hypotheses was not supported by the research, and the second only partially so.

When asked to select one or more responses to the question, "What are the reasons that motivated Saudi women to work?", 30% of answers from female respondents and 18% from males cited participation in public life. 15% of females said it was to achieve a social position, and only 10% to increase family income. Males were more likely to list family income (15.5%) than females, and nearly matched women on listing to achieve a social position. The frequency of both female (4%) and male (4.2%) citation of independence as a reason to work was very low.

There are several possible explanations for these findings. First, the respondents were most likely from middle or upper income families, since they all received grade school eduation in the years when there were few schools in the Kingdom, and now all hold advanced degrees. Their families must have been interested in the education of their children for quite a while. Secondly, Saudi economic development has been rapid since the 1970s, and few Saudi women work because they must for economic reasons. Thirdly, comments written on the questionnaires suggested that many women worked because they regarded it a religious or national duty, since they constituted the educated female elite of the country, or to attain a more well-rounded personality. A few men made the comment that society will benefit from allowing the full participation of women in the work force.

As regards working in order to fulfill ambitions, the study yielded mixed results. When women were asked, "Do you agree that Saudi women have been given the chance to realize their ambitions?", 26% said "yes," 73% said "more or less," and only 1% said "no." It is speculated that the basically positive emphasis of these responses was because the particular women interviewed had all risen to high levels of administrative leadership within a short period of time.

Of the 26% who answered "yes," they most often cited personal or social reasons for their ambitions having been fulfilled. Jobs gave them the chance for a new experience (28.8% of responses), for self-realization (25.4%), and for social position (17.5%). A few responses cited economic reasons, these being present and future security (9.6%) and financial independence (7.4%).

Of the 74% who answered "no" or "more or less," the most commonly cited reason for ambitions not being fulfilled was because women felt the work opportunities open to them were limited (52% of the females). It had been hypothesized that the few fields available for women to work in Saudi Arabia would minimize work ambitions. This hypothesis can not really be said to be supported by these data, since only 1% of the sample said "no" to chances for having ambitions realized. Still the majority of the respondents felt some limits on their opportunities. It seems that for these women at least, the positive outweighed the negative, and that while feeling that their ambitions may have been curtailed, they were still at least "more or less" satisfied. The second most common reason for not having ambitions fulfilled (21%) was limitations on opportunities to gain promotions to high level positions. In addition, 17.7% of responses indicated that family responsibilities took priority, or that the people in charge did not value women's work. 13.4% cited that male coworkers did not value women's work.

2. Job Authority and Tasks

Prior to conducting the study it was hypothesized that, on the whole, Saudi female administrators have the authority needed to fulfiill the duties required by their jobs. It was also hypothesized that Saudi men hinder the work progress of these female administrators and tend to minimize their authority. Regarding tasks, it was felt that the female sample would be more likely to be engaged in supervision activities than in policy-making, planning and development activities. The data gathered from the questioinnaires only partially support the three hypotheses.

Both men and women responded that Saudi women have "adequate authority to accomplish their leadership responsibilities." When asked if this was so, 19% of the female sample and 26.4% of the men said "yes," 54% of the women and 62.7% of the men said "more or less," and 27% of women and 10% of men said "no."

Both men and women were given questionnaires asking them to check off one or more of nine possible areas of "authority that *should* be given to women." In addition, female respondents were asked to list administrative tasks that they *actually performed*. It is worthwhile to compare the results of the two tables (see chart 1).

187

Chart 1

AUTHORITY AND TASKS

What authority "should" be given?		What tasks do you do?	
Men (f=516)	Women (f=459)	Women (f=506)	Authority or Task
11.3%	11.0%		1. executive authority
11.6%	9.1%	14.6%	2. organization
		6.7%	3. coordinate between different departments of administration
10.9%	9.9%	10.1%	4. planning and public policy development
		10.9%	5. supervision of work
8.3%	8.1%	10.9%	6. directing subordinates
		15.6%	7. follow-up work in the department
10.7%	10.1%	4.7%	8. selecting new female employees
6.3%	6.6%	3.0%	9. hiring new female employees
8.7%	8.7%	9.3%	10. evaluate employees work
8.1%	8.5%	8.5%	11. give rewards or incentives
7.8%	6.8%	4.9%	12. authority to give penalties

188

When asked what women *should* do, responses from both men and women ranged fairly evenly across the nine categories. However, there were slightly more responses indicating women should have authority over office and policy activities (such as executive administration, organization planning, policy development and directing), and fewer responses indicating authority over personnel matters (hiring, incentives and rewards, control, and employee evaluation). Selection of new employees was an exception.

Interestingly, there was high agreement between percentage responses of both men and women. For instance 56% of women and 47% of men indicated women should have executive authority, whereas only 34% of women and 26% of men selected hiring as an area for female authority. In a sense it might be said that the hypothesis that Saudi men minimize women's authority is supported since, in this sample at least, they are more likely to think that women should be engaged in some kinds of activities (mostly office administration and planning) rather than others (mostly personnel). On the other hand, it is clear that women have the same expectations regarding their own authority as men do. Therefore, Saudi women might also be said to minimize female authority in the same way that men do.

Indications given by women of tasks actually performed suggested women do a wide variety of activities, and not just supervision work as hypothesized. Indeed, as many responses indicated involvement with planning and policy making (10.1%) as supervision (10.9%). The highest frequency of responses were in follow-up work (15.6%) and organizational activities (14.6%). The low frequencies citing performance of tasks such as hiring, giving penalties, selecting new employees, and coordinating between different sections of the administration indicate that men are doing these activities instead. Thus, when it comes to actual tasks done, there seems to be support for the hypothesis that in actual performance, men are minimizing women's authority: they are not granting as much authority as they say should be given (see also section on challenges and difficulties below, for supporting data).

It is clear that women are more likely to perform some kinds of tasks than others, but not necessarily those hypothesized. It is also clear that women feel they are not involved enough in policy decisions.

When looking at differences between what authority men and women think *should* be given to women, and what female administrators actually do, there are few unexpected findings. The percentage of responses indicating a task was practiced, generally agreed that authority should be given.

Disagreements were highest in the areas where both agreed women *should* have the least authority. Only 15% of women were actually engaged in hiring, whereas 32% of men and 30% of women said they should have this authority. Only 4.7% of responses stated selecting new female employees was a task done, and just 4.9% said they gave penalties. In contrast, approximately 10% and 7% of respective responses indicated they should have these authorities.

3. Job Training

It was conjectured prior to the study that Saudi women in positions of administrative leadership were not as well qualified and trained as Saudi men in comparable positions. It was also thought that women most commonly received "on the job" training, rather than other types of preparation. Furthermore, it was supposed that both the women and men sampled would endorse further training for women in these leadership positions. All of these hypotheses were supported by the study.

When asked if Saudi women held their present positions of administrative leadership after having had adequate training and qualifications, only 50% of female respondents and 30% of male respondents said "yes." The rest said "no." The minority saying "yes" were asked to state what they thought were the most common means of female training. Both males and females answered most frequently that training was received through programs within the country, through delegation of authority, and through self-development by reading. Only half as many responses cited training abroad or attending academic conferences. The responses were so low as to confirm that these kinds of opportunities for training are lacking for Saudi women. In essence, this supported the hypothesis that, for women, most training is "on the job." Females were asked specifically whether or not they felt the "on the job" training they received was enough. Only 13% said "yes"; 87% said "no."

The overwhelming majority—indeed nearly the entire sample-felt women in these positions should receive more training before being promoted to higher positions: 95% of the female and 99% of the male respondents said so. The great majority felt that training should take place in their own work sectors; in other words at the university or collegs, and most women expressed willingness to allot time to attend training programs.

When asked to rank in order of significance a selection of training programs they would like to have women receive, the top five rankings were as follows, on Chart 2:

Chart 2

PERCEIVED RANKING FOR TRAINING PROGRAMS

Male	Rank Female	Programs for Developing
1st	2nd	Leadership capability
3rd	1st	Capability to solve problems/make decisions
2nd	3rd	Increased efficiency, effectiveness
4th	4th	Planning and public policy skills
5th	5th	Skills to solve human relations problems

Lower ranking choices included computer usage and time optimization. Obviously, the results of this study showed firm consensus among both males and females for the need and desire for more training programs across a wide variety of areas.

4. Job Difficulties and Impediments

As indicated earlier, Saudi women have only recently entered the work force. They have clearly made tremendous strides and shown that they are capable of facing the challenges entailed in managing and running the female sector of the educational system. If the results of this study can be generalized, those presented in the first two sections show that, on the whole, women who work in the field of educational administration feel positive about working and have a sense that they are realizing their ambitions. However, it is clear that women were also aware that they faced many challenges and difficulties in their jobs. They felt there were several factors impeding steady work progress aside from lack of training mentioned above. In this survey men, (but not women), were asked outright the simple question, "Do you believe Saudi female educational administrators face challenges and difficulties?" 89% of men answered "yes".

On the questionnaires, both male and female respondents were asked to identify those challenges and difficulties they felt Saudi female educational administrators faced in their positions. The women were also asked to rank these from being the most to the least difficult. The results are presented below. Statistics for respondents are given in terms of percentages stating an item was a problem. Weighted ranks are also shown.

Chart 3

PERCEIVED CHALLENGES FACING WOMEN

Rank	Female %	Males %	Difficulty
1.	74.2	44.5	They are not delegated enough authority
2.	61.8	60.9	Lack of training programs to prepare them for leadership
3.	60.8	47.3	There is no actual participation in drawing up public policy
4.	54.3	53.6	Lack of knowledge of rules and regulations
5.	49.6	50	Difficulties in communicating and coordinating with superiors
6.	34.7	33	Lack of acknowledgement of work by male coworkers
7.	21.7	24.5	Females do not accept male leadership
8.	13.4	22.7	Fear and hesitation to express opinion
9.	10	37.2	Other

The first five items can be identified as administrative challenges, and the last three as social and psychological challenges. The majority of women felt that the first five were challenges, but not the last three. More men rated the first five as challenges than the last three, but the majority cited only lack of training programs, lack of knowledge of rules, and difficulties in communicating with superiors. For women, lack of training, not having

192

enough authority, and not participating in drawing up public policy show up as the top ranked challenges (ranking were weighted for women only). The most striking differences between male and female opinion occurred regarding the issues of authority (74% of women, but only 44% of men, thought women were not given enough authority), and participation in policy planning (60% of women, but only 47% of men thought there was no actual female participation). It is worth noting that 50% of both women and men cite difficulties in coordinating with supervisors as a problem.

Female respondents were asked what they felt were negative factors which inhitibed Saudi female administrators from developing their administrative capabilities in their positions of leadership. A list of items was given, and the respondents were able to tick as many as they felt appropriate. Of 466 responses, the most commonly checked items were lack of knowledge of rules and regulations (13.1% of responses) and lack of experience of administrative affairs (12.7%). These results jibe with those given on chart 3, where 54% of women and 53% of men cited lack of knowledge of rules and regulations as a difficulty or challenge. Probable reasons for these results are the general weakness in technical and scientific training in general, and lack of preparation for leadership in particular among Saudi female administrators. Other factors which respondents felt were negative impingements were misuse of authority, and the fact that women in these positions were sometimes incapable of making decisions and of solving work problems. These results might indicate impressions regarding challenges cited above (for instance, perhaps they cannot make decisions or solve problems because they do not have the authority, or because they cannot coordinate well with superiors). Alternately, they might reflect their dual roles as working-women-managers as well as wife-mother-housekeepers.

5. Job Selection

How do Saudi female administrators get the jobs they have? It was hypothesized prior to the study that Saudization would be the primary criterion for selection of employees, but that other important variables such as proper qualifications and prior job experience would rank high as criteria as well. This hypothesis was supported. When asked, "What principles are followed to select women for higher administrative positions?", the following results were obtained (respondents could check as many answers as they wished):

193

Chart 4

CRITERIA USED TO
SELECT FEMALE ADMINISTRATORS

% frequency of response

Female f=238	Males f=269	Criteria Used
31.9	33.5	Need to fill positions with Saudi (Saudization)
17.2	19.7	Possession of adequate academic qualifications
16	13	Length of suitable experience
16.8	11.5	Trust by supervisor
5.9	10.4	Personal or family connection
9.7	10.8	Adequate job training
2.5	1.1	Other

Saudization was the most common response, constituting more than 30% of the frequency for both male and female responses, (80% of women and 81% of men). Length of suitable experience and trust were the next most common responses, with personal or family connection, and adequate training, coming in as close third catagory responses. The results indicate that once a Saudi is selected — and this is a goal of the Third and Fourth Development Plans — academic qualifications, trust and experience all come into play as interacting factors affecting hiring. In the past, academic qualifications, training and experience had little significance since few Saudi women had advanced degrees or any work experience. Trust and capability were judged on the basis of other factors. This is now changing, and most likely will continue to change as more training programs are implemented.

Male administrators sampled were asked to list characteristics they thought Saudi female administrators should have. The most common responses were that they should be able to solve work problems, make decisions, admit mistakes, be capable of planning, be innovative, and be fair.

RECOMMENDATIONS

Based on the results of this research conducted in the Western Province, the following major recommendations are suggested:

1. Higher level female educational administrators should participate in all planning activities with the decision makers regarding the amelioration of the conditions of working women, because they are more capable of understanding their own situations and needs than men.

2. It is important to increase female participation in the work force. However, job opportunities should be provided in a way that will ensure the public interest, and allow women contributing to development in the Kingdom to be in positions that are in conformity with Islamic Shari'ah principles and regional social traditions.

3. The Saudization of leading administrative positions for women in Higher Education should be gradual, and women should not occupy leading posts without prior experience in lower administrative positions.

4. More attention should be given to providing educational programs in administration in Saudi institutions of higher education. Master's and Ph.D. programs in the field of educational administration should be established for women in local universities.

5. Greater authority and responsibility should be delegated to women holding leading positions, to enable them to attain experience through practice.

6. Seminars and conferences should be held within the country to help women presently working. Invitations should be given to high level administrators to hold discussions and lectures. Senior government officials should be invited to assist in administrative problems through closed-circuit television.

7. Field studies should be conducted by research centers at the universities and girls colleges on the negative aspects and problems that adversely affect the efficiency of top female administrators and their staffs. There is a great need to determine the direct and indirect causes of negative factors and, once known, to devise training programs for women occupying leading positions in an attempt to remedy the situation. Both research and training programs should be developed and

195

conducted at women's universities and colleges, involving people best qualified to judge such programs.

8. The activities of the Institute of Public Administration (IPA) should be expanded to train female administrators at all levels on a par with the training of their male counterparts or peers. The training for women in the respective sectors should be in several stages in order to develop their skills, to increase their productivity and to support their progress and performance of duty in the best manner possible.

9. At the end of training, female administrators in higher education should be given the chance to use what they have learned in order to develop and improve their institutes, and planners and officials should facilitate their task.

CONCLUSION

Top level administrators in female institutions are important elements in the work force in Saudi Arabia, whose skills and capabilities should be utilized to their full potential. Efforts should be made to overcome difficulties which women face in their work, especially since the country is developing rapidly and needs input from all intelligent and capable workers, whether male or female. The path to successful development requires a scientific foundation from which valid recommendations for change in society can be made. Saudi social scientists should be encouraged to become involved in studying Saudi working women, and to help in making suggestions for training and other programs beneficial for the progress and development of women in the work place.

PART IV:

BUSINESS— GOVERNMENT RELATIONS & INDUSTRY

INTRODUCTION:

In his article, *"A COMPARATIVE ANALYSIS OF THE ROLE OF GOVERNMENT IN THE PRIVATE SECTOR IN DAHOMEY, SAUDI ARABIA, JAPAN, AND THE UNITED STATES,"* Khalid Al-Aiban briefly presents a useful cultural, historical, and social background of these countries as an essential step to introduce and understand their political economies and managerial systems.

The author presents some of the advantages of traditional systems and contrasts them to some of the disadvantages of the impersonal systems. In addition, he points out that some societies like Japan and Saudi Arabia have been successful in their efforts toward "modernization" while supporting "social continuity." On the other end of the spectrum, Western societies have abandoned many valid principles and traditions in their searches for equiality and freedom.

While government intervention in the business market varies from one state to another, and indeed between different arenas within the same state, Al-Aiban emphasizes the importance of government-business dialogue, and that both the public and private sectors should consult each other before making or undertaking any policy or project.

In this regard, the relationship between the government and the private sector in Japan provides a unique model. According to their cooperative model, the Japanese consider enterprises of the private sector only as divisions (branches) of the mega-corporation (the Japanese economy). On similar lines, the call of King Fahd of Saudi Arabia in the early 1980s for considering the public and private sectors as one sector should be evaluated. Many forces need to be taken into consideration in the evaluation of such an endeavor: the value system, authority structure, natural and financial resources, the international market, among others.

In *"A SYSTEM DYNAMICS MODEL FOR SAUDI ARABIAN INDUSTRIAL DEVELOPMENT"*, Dr. Hussein Murad Reda makes a strong argument for the application of this approach to the future development planning of Saudi Arabia's industrial economy.

Dr. Reda begins with a brief overview of the three general approaches to this type of study: (1) broad and descritive, (2) narrow or single variable, and (3) system dynamics modeling. His reasoning for application of the system dynamics approach cites advantages of "both quantification and complexity, (of) a broad focus, and the possibility of seeing the influence of single variables on others."

Following specific examples of how his approach would enhance development planning, Dr. Reda gives a prototype model of a workable system with detailed explanation of what it includes, and some of the possible scenarios it could foresee.

Dr. Reda concludes with strong reasoning for practical application of system dynamics modeling to Saudi Arabia's development planning. This is illustrated by graphic depictions of the results of the prototype model and how the results could be viewed and analyzed.

A COMPARATIVE ANALYSIS OF THE ROLE OF GOVERNMENT IN THE PRIVATE SECTOR IN ANCIENT DAHOMEY, SAUDI ARABIA, JAPAN, AND THE UNITED STATES

by Khalid M. Al-Aiban, Ph.D.

I. Introduction

Governmental involvement in the private sector is a complex issue because almost any public policy affects the competitive position of some businesses and industries in a positive fashion, without giving a similar advantage to other competing firms or industries. For example, in order to improve the incomes and well-being of some groups, it is often necessary to place taxes or restrictions on other groups. Persons who are hostile to those policies are likely to argue that the competitive market place, not the government, should determine the fortunes of persons, firms and industries.[1]

From one country to another we find great variation in the relative importance of various industries, differences in the relative sizes of business firms, and differences in historical background and culture.[2] So, it is not surprising that there is little consensus among countries regarding something so complex as the proper role of government in the private sector. However, in this paper I shall attempt to put forward a fairly simple framework for examining cross-national differences in public-private interactions. I will have to consider this issue quite broadly, because the circumstances and problems faced by various countries are so different that detailed comparisons tend to reveal little informative data. On the other hand, in order to place each country into a single framework, I shall emphasize the role of government in a single industry—agriculture. Agriculture is chosen because almost every economy, past and present, has contained some form of agricultural industry, while the same cannot be said about other industries.

The basis of my analytical framework is the recent work of Duran Bell.[3] This work has put forth an original theory of traditional societies as a contrast with capitalist forms of society. Of course, all societies have "traditions," or customs that are thought to be important and unique to the society. However, traditional society, according to Bell's model, is a characteristic of the social structure, or more exactly, it is a characteristic of a system of personal relation.[4] Bell argues that the structure of relationships among people constitutes a "social technology" that articulates a system of production.[5] People and their relationships with each other take on a central and independent importance in these systems that has been lost under the impact of capitalist forms of economic activity.

In contrast with traditional societies, the central relationships of capitalist societies are "impersonal." Capitalist societies are organized around a system of production in such a way that the "technology of production" and the relationships of persons to the means of production are likely to determine the relationships among people. Thus, under capitalism, the social structure and the status system are by-products of the system of production.[6]

Although capitalism tends systematically to destroy the basis for many traditional forms of personal relations, this tendency can be counteracted, at least in part, even in the face of advanced levels of economic development. For example, the often discussed Japanese management style with lifetime employment and cooperative task groups can be thought of as a carryover of traditional forms. The key factors here are: (a) cooperation versus competition among workers, (b) the importance of personal relationships to the company rather than the transformation of individual into impersonal **factors of production** and, (c) the unity of interests between workers and capitalists toward the growth of the cooperative, joint product.

Traditional systems tend to be politically centralized, and become more centralized when their social technologies are more fully developed. In contrast, capitalist systems tend to become less centralized as their productive technologies become more developed. In fact, it seems that the stability of the social technology of a traditional system — a system of status relations to which rights and responsibilities are attached — requires a super status at the top, like the head of a household, that is generally institutionalized in the form of monarchy or chieftainship.

Below the monarchy other status categories are defined, and the ideology of the system must always indicate the relative importance of each category to the system of social production. For example, persons who have responsibility for military defense are usually given high rank, as are those who are entrusted with the responsibility for the (usually religious) ideology. Beyond those categories it is difficult to state any general rule for the deter-

202

mination of the status categories. This is the case because there is no objective basis for the determination of the importance of various categories to social production.

In many cases the economic power of monarchies is derived from monopolistic control over foreign trade, and political power is based on the "generosity" with which the monarch redistributes wealth among the people. Of course the monarch has a higher standard of consumption than do other people, but this standard does not imply that the people have been cheated. On the contrary, the monarch is more important to the social product than his consumption implies — at least the accepted ideology of the system must say this. Other persons of high rank, while having a higher level of consumption than the average, are similarly underpaid relative to their actual importance. Bell's model of traditional systems makes it clear that the rewards to persons of rank is on the basis of "needs," and that work performed by each category must be on the basis of "ability;" where need and ability are determined in some part by biological factors, but more importantly by custom and ideology. Therefore, those persons who are able to make contributions that exceed their own needs deserve the respect and admiration of other, more dependent persons.

Capitalist systems differ greatly among themselves, but they tend to be much less centralized than traditional systems, with a much larger percentage of wealth earned directly by the people through a free enterprise system that is influenced, but not controlled, by the central government. Furthermore, a free enterprise system is one where a large number of independent persons or groups interact competitively — not cooperatively — and therefore each person or group has reason to be suspicious of a powerful monarch whose activity would necessarily have some effect on the competitive struggle among groups — to the disadvantage of some and the advantage of others. Within a capitalist system the monarch can be only a figurehead, symbolizing "the mythological unity" of a people long fragmented by the strident antagonism of social classes and the fierce competition of atomistic interest.[7]

On a purely theoretical level we may imagine a traditional system in which all incomes are controlled by a process of redistribution from the center, and at the other extreme a capitalist system in which government is limited to the enforcement of the laws that make a competitive market place possible, allowing all incomes to be derived from the "private sector." However, these are only theoretical extremes, and actual systems lie somewhere on a continuum in between.

There are many reasons for public involvemnt in the distribution of income in capitalist economies. We can place these reasons into two general categories. In one case there are **support activities** where governments provide a "safety net" in order to prevent poverty, or they may subsidize particular industries that are relatively unprofitable in the free market. In the United Kingdom for example, the government took over management and financial support of the coal mining companies when economic difficulties became so serious that the jobs of the workers, and the supply of coal, were threatened. The British have also developed a national health insurance system, with the hope that this would make health care available to all. In this way persons with low incomes can be made more secure, and businesses that are believed to be important to the society can be stabilized.

The second major type of government involvement in the private economy can be called **incentive activities.** These take place through grants, tax incentives and other related subsidies in order to encourage businesses and individuals to act for the national interest. Japan and South Korea are good examples of this type. South Korea followed the "Japan, Inc." model of development, but in their own special way. During the early 1960s President Park Chung Hee threatened the larger business leaders with arrest if they refused to come before him and join in a national campaign to develop the economy under his leadership; they enjoyed substantial benefits from cooperation. Furthermore, the National Bank of Korea offered high interest rates in order to put savings into government hands, putting the government in a financial position to direct the development of the economy.[8] Korea's goal was to redistribute income in order to encourage activities that would not take place without incentives.

These support and incentive activities of government within capitalist economies can be useful to the functioning of those systems, however both forms of activities represent deviations from pure **laissez faire.** In the case of pure **laissez faire** there are many independent and competing groups with conflicting interests, and the government is limited to simply setting the rules by which persons may compete in seeking their individual goals.[9]

In a traditional system, like Saudi Arabia, the government manages the economy by helping to assure that persons of the various ranks or categories provide the services that are expected of them, and it helps to assure that access to certain kinds of consumer goods is available to persons of the several ranks, in accordance with social expectations. This means that the *support* and *incentive activities* that are supplemental to the market mechanism in capitalist economies become the basis of the (non-domestic) economy itself in a traditional economy.

In this paper we shall focus on the manner in which government influences the economy by use of various monetary incentives and support activities. Although these activities represent only one side of government involvement, and may not be the most important aspect, monetary flows are generally easier to measure than some other forms of government activity. Secondly, monetary flows are affected by government activity in both traditional and capitalist systems, so that it is possible to place a wide range of social systems on a single continuum. For these reasons, this paper attempts a cross-cultural, or cross-national, study of the effect of government activity on the economy, using monetary incentives and monetary support activities as the measuring rod.

Admittedly, this way of looking at and evaluating government involvement has limitations. This is especially true of countries like Japan and South Korea, where the government is a direct participant in business decision-making on the strategic level. This form of direct involvement may reduce the need for financial incentives as a method of influencing private sector behavior. Also, the use of so-called monetary and fiscal policy has a powerful impact on the stability and growth of the economy as a whole, and sometimes these policies are not "neutral" in terms of their different effects on various enterprises and groups of citizens. However, these issues, although quite important, will not be considered in this paper.

I shall consider the manner in which the government may intervene into the economy, and how it selects particular types of monetary support and incentive activities. These issues will be examined by observation of policies and practices in ancient Dahomey, Saudi Arabia, Japan and the United States. These countries have been chosen for comparative analysis because they lie on a continuum between purely traditional (as defined by Bell's model of cooperative production) and purely capitalist. I shall attempt to enhance the analysis of governmental involvement with the economy by considering the concepts of "authority" and "market exchange." These concepts, taken from Charles Lindblom, are useful in understanding government involvement in the private sector of capitalist economies, especially the United States.

The states that have been chosen for discussion in this paper are all relatively powerful, with well-developed social economies, and they have been chosen in such a way that the more traditional societies are, in fact, more dominant in their social economies than the less traditional states.

205

However, these differences in government behavior will be shown to be only by-products of more fundamental differences in the social system. It should also be clear from the outset that traditional societies may differ widely in the technology of production. This is because the special feature of fully developed traditional systems is the existence of a social machinery (the "social technology") that guides the use of productive technology. In principle, any level of productive technology is consistent with the continuation of traditional social relation. The ancient Kingdom of Dahomey was not much more traditional than the contemporary Kingdom of Saudi Arabia, yet differences in the levels of productive technology are great, and rapidly increasing. Indeed, Saudi Arabia has been successful in demonstrating that modern economic development can be consistent with preservation of traditional social technologies.

Conversely, societies with advanced levels of productive technology may differ widely in their adherence to traditional values. The contrast between Japan and the United States is a case in point. As I shall demonstrate, Japan seems to be enjoying a competitive edge over the United States by virtue of having retained important elements of its traditional foundation.

DAHOMEY AS A SOCIAL SYSTEM: AUTHORITY AND DISTRIBUTION

Pre-colonial Dahomey was a small kingdom with a population of less than 200,000 and occupied part of the territory of modern Dahomey and Togo, just north of modern Nigeria. This area became the "slave coast" because of the Gap of Benin, an unusual gap in the thick tropical forest that made most of the west coast difficult to enter. Dahomey emerged from the turmoil created by the European slave trade in 1724 under its first king, Agaja, who ruled until 1740. It fell into ruins in 1818. Dahomey has been studied by many scholars[10] who have been fascinated by its unique traditional patterns of social organization. Anthropologists and ethnologists, like Melville J. Herskovits,[11] have described Dahomey as being exemplary of the high levels of culture and sophistication that existed prior to European contact. Pre-colonial Dahomey manifested excellence in technology and art, a complex political and social structure, and a rather profound and integrated world view.

Concepts like "business" and "government" are in many ways very modern, and do not adequately describe pre-colonial traditional structures.[12] "Government" and "business" describe very precise forms of social organization and economic activity which may not have been prevalent in ancient times. Nevertheless, it makes sense to think of "authority" types of relationships as being equivalent to what one may call "government" relationships. It should be noted from the outset that the main purpose of this focus on Dahomey is to see whether the ancient celebrated kingdom has any meaningful **organizational** similarities with contemporary Saudi Arabia.

In a traditional society, the way in which people are placed into production is determined by their social status; that is, social position is defined independently of a person's social contribution. Furthermore, in traditional systems, social status is determined and defined by a "social technology" that ranks persons relative to each other. That is to say, in traditional societies, rewards are a function of status, while in industrial societies rewards determine status. In a commodity system persons are not rewarded because they are important, rather they are important because they are rewarded.[13]

In ancient Dahomey the king was like a dominating father to all of the people under his control. The king controlled, and effectively limited, the supply of slaves to European traders from that area. From this trading monopoly most of the wealth of the country came into his hands. Assisting him were persons of rank who were appointed to high-level posts in state administration or military leadership, and the king was able to reward them for providing services to the state-level system of social production. Since "more important" people received greater rewards, and since distributions from the royal coffers were the primary source of income to most citizens, the distributions from government largely determined the distribution of income.[14]

According to Bell the determination of rank, or social status, within such a system is the function of an ideology that characterizes the relative importance of each class of persons to the production of society's joint product. This ideology is necessary because there is no scientific way of actually determining how valuable persons really are when production requires the cooperation of complementary activities. In a non-literate society, like Dahomey, the ideology would not be found in some document, and even in literate societies there may be little explicit recognition of the ideology as such. However, in most African societies, gender differences are basic to the domestic economy; differences in age are the principal source of rank within the male kinship group (patrilineage); and the inherited or achieved status of lineages provides the lineage elders with important positions in the state system.

207

It is a characteristic of traditional systems that persons whose rank justifies a particular social role are perceived to have the **ability** to perform that role, and that persons who lack that status are, by definition, inappropriate to the role. We can see this property of traditional systems simply by looking at traditional male and female roles in western industrial society. By definition women were qualified to be housewives, while housework was inappropriate for men. Similarly, certain persons are expected to receive certain benefits from the goods and services available, while such consumption by others would be considered wrong or absurd. For example, in Dahomey only the king was allowed to wear sandals, and it was illegal for others to do so. But certainly, if some ordinary person was found wearing sandals it would be as absurd as a woman wearing the clothing of a man in a western society.

There are hardly any general rules and criteria for the determination of status categories, nor are there any rules for determining the "abilities" and "proper rewards" for those categories. Bell uses the term "arbitrary" to refer to the manner in which these things are determined. However, once such a system is in place, differences in the amount distributed to persons of different rank become **expected** and are considered the natural and appropriate benefit to that type of person. In this way, an "arbitrary" allocation among persons becomes "socially necessary."

This form of traditional ideology is in rather sharp contrast to the capitalist ethos which says that persons should not be allowed access to social positions except through "achievement" within a competitive process, and that task allocations and the division of labor should be solely on the basis of productive efficiency. An example of this would be the guidelines of the U.S. Civil Service Commission which, since the Pendleton Act of 1883, has required that government jobs which are not political must be given on the basis of professional competence demonstrated through possession of formal qualification and, occasionally, through taking examinations. Thus, ideally, anyone can get a government job equal to their qualifications, and once in that position they assume the personality of the office.

The importance of redistribution under the control of the king was most apparent in Dahomey, because most of the redistribution process took place once each year over a several week period. A huge platform would be prepared with all types of valuables—imported goods such as brandy, silks, carpets and other luxuries—as well as cowrie shells (used as money). Europeans and notables from other kingdoms would arrive to pay homage, carrying gifts of enormous value. Such gifts were added to the spoils that could

208

then be redistributed. It was at this time that most persons received the money that they might need during the coming year.[15]

Polanyi emphasizes that the complete control exercised by the state in foreign trade was not allowed to extend into the traditional local economy. The social structure of the early state abounded in institutional devices that acted as safeguards, both to freedom and efficiency. The Dahomean countryside was teeming with big and small marketplaces, in village and bush, yet the choice of crops was directed by planning from the capital. Overseas trade was channeled through a bureaucratic network separate from the markets, through the intermediacy of the "port of trade." Arbitrary rule was barred through the formal separation of the central administration from activities originating in familial and local life, those cradles of tradition and freedom.[16]

The state determined the amounts of each crop that should be planted and in which locations, prohibited the production of certain crops altogether, and required that other crops be planted only for private consumption. Surpluses and deficits of various agricultural goods were avoided by state intervention.

The consumptive needs of the people, the number of people available for military campaigns, and the base on which taxes were to be levied were determined by an annual census that noted the numbers of workers in each occupation, the amount of goods stored in granaries, and the numbers of cattle and other animals. According to Polanyi,[17] no famine was ever reported to have taken place within this economy, although they were commonplace outside of it.

The monopolistic control of foreign trade and the strong guidance of the internal economy was not inconsistent with the preservation of liberty in commerce and freedom of individuals in village life. This was possible, perhaps, because the lives of the people were oriented by a traditional culture which was sufficiently well internalized to maintain orderly activity, even beyond the domain of state control. For example, work activity at the village level was influenced by the existence of a number of cooperative institutions: the **dokpwe** (reciprocal work team), the **so** (craft guild), and the **gbe** (mutual aid group). Every Dahomean man had to belong to a **dokpwe** and answer its call. And according to legend, even the king dared not fail to show homage to the **dokpwega** (head of the **dokpwe**). The **dokpwe** ensured that the fields of a villager were cultivated in the event of illness (and without cost if the villager were poor); it assisted persons whose lands were too extensive to be harvested by themselves (in return for a payment and a feast for the workers); it would assist a person who was indebted to his father; and it had special functions to perform at funerals. The **so,** or craft guilds, were also cooperative, and facilitated the production of blacksmiths, weavers and other occupations. These and other instruments of the social technology were important to the regulation and stabilization of work within Dahomey, and operated outside of the state sector.[18]

Dahomey represents a good example of what Bell calls "traditional." In particular, it was a society in which the needs and responsibilities of people were well defined "arbitrarily" by reference to age, sex and lineage.[19] Moreover, it was organized as a cooperative group at each level—the household, craft groups, the village and the state as a whole—and each cooperative group was dominated by a leader who had legitimated power over others. It was, to use the terms of Charles Lindblom, a system based on "authority relations," but we do not find Lindblom's dichotomy of authority versus market to be applicable here. We see in the case of Dahomey that the various authority-dominated institutions were located in quasi-independent sectors, so that domination by the state was consistent with freedom of other sectors to pursue their goals within the broad constraints laid down by the state. And authoritative domination within substate level authority structures may have been limited by custom, and by other cross-cutting institutions.[20]

However, of the four societies that I consider in this paper, Dahomey is certainly the most centralized in terms of direct state control over production and distribution. The development of this centralized and sophisticated state was prompted, in large part, by the pressures of European states that attempted to divide and conquer African societies in order to facilitate the acquisition of slaves. Each African group was expected to fall upon the other in a great slave hunt, and only the economically and militarily strong could hope to survive. There is evidence that the early kings of Dahomey were opposed to the slave trade despite the wealth that it represented for them,[21] and by developing a trading monopoly they were able to greatly reduce the supply of slaves.

On the other hand, Dahomey was a state for which the export of slaves played the same role for its economy that the export of oil does for Saudi Arabia today. The revenue from slaves was essential to the development of the strong and efficient central administration of Dahomey, and the existence of other aspects of international trade encouraged African producers to develop a finer division of labor and improved productive technologies.[22] Although the loss of population from the slave trade was costly for west

Africa in general, the evidence suggests that the drain of manpower was largely controlled by the powerful states of the area,[23] and that economic development in west Africa was stimulated by the slave trade.

In summary, we find that powerful traditional states derived their power from monopolies over foreign trade. Ancient Egypt displays this characteristic as well. The revenue from trade could be used to increase the military and administrative resources of the state, and it was important for maintaining the loyalty of the citizens, whose well-being depended on the success and stability of the state. Furthermore, we find that the state allocated positions of responsibility and reward among people on the basis of age and ancestry. This approach to task allocation and reward is comparable to traditional intra-household allocations within capitalist societies.

THE CASE OF SAUDI ARABIA: THE DOMINANCE OF AUTHORITY

Although Saudi Arabia has been pursuing a program of industrialization and infra-structural development it remains, rather proudly, a traditional society. As is common to almost all traditional societies, its value system emanates from a body of ideological precepts. In the case of Saudi Arabia, [Islam] constitutes the ideological factor that governs the authority of leadership and intra-societal relationships. As such, the ruling authorities derive their legitimacy and decision making by enforcing Islamic laws and regulations, and the Saudi political and social leaders are drawn and monitored with reference to religious values as prescribed by the Quran, and the deed and sayings of Prophet Mohammed. By the same token, the royal family and policy makers in Saudi Arabia work within the boundaries outlined by the Islamic rules and regulations of government. Moreover, by controlling the oil revenue, the Saudi government has control over most of the country's income and, like the Kingdom of Dahomey, is in a position to distribute that income in terms of its own goals. In principle, citizens in Saudi Arabia have an **ascribed value** to the system of cooperative production on which the Kingdom depends, and receive rewards that correspond with each individual's status. However, the issue of social status in Saudi Arabia is highly complex, and thus requires a brief explanation here.

During the unification process of Saudi Arabia initiated by King Abd al-Aziz, the founder of the kingdom, many tribal and prominent families came to his aid. Consequently, the King maintained a close relationship with these families as a sign of his appreciation for their unquestioned loyalty and support. However, it should be pointed out that the royal family and decision makers have sought to promote the concept of qualification as a prerequisite to the social status that citizens may acquire and enjoy. As a result, the status of Saudis is primarily determined by (1) the historical position of certain families and (2) qualifications.

In Saudi Arabia, public authority is a bureaucratic organization around the monarch. This bureaucracy has a decisive role in the economic system, and it plays a central role in the allocation of net public economic benefits among various social and geographical divisions in the country. The government also maintains a wide range of incentives that support private businesses deemed to be in the public interest.

Before the oil boom, the government bureaucracy was largely dependent on revenue obtained from fees paid by the pilgrimage to the holy places, because there was almost no other revenue from which the government could finance local expenditures or expand government activities. After the discovery of oil, however, a modern administration developed. The flow of oil revenue made possible the expansion of government services and, consequently, the emergence of a centralized administrative machinery to coordinate and control the various activities.

Over the years there has been, in Saudi Arabia, a positive correlation between the growth of government revenue on the one hand, and bureaucratic functions on the other.[24] Today the administration has exclusive jurisdiction in the preparation, implementation and control of government budgets, as opposed to the historical situation in which the royal family played a greater roles. The significance of government contribution to the economy as a whole is determined by the ratio of oil industry revenue to GNP. Since this ratio is so large, the administration has gained significant economic status. The government is also the principle distributor of rewards as an employer. In other words, the government administration has a monopolisitc power and authority in the distribution of economic resources. Persons who would have to act as simple rule followers in Western forms of bureaucracy may have greater latitude in the Saudi system. This can be explained by the fact that the Saudi government does not attempt to treat Saudi citizens as though they are undifferentiated and faceless. Indeed, the impersonalization of citizens, often praised as a high (Weberian) principle in capitalist systems, is avoided in this, and in other traditional systems of administration. Rather than attempting to be a relatively neutral force in the midst of competitive actors, where impersonal "bureaucracy" would

212

be desirable, the Saudi administration is an instrument for the management of a social technology to which its members belong; it manages "Saudi Incorporated," a corporation whose organizational chart displays the structure of a social technology for the society as a whole. At the apex of the administration is the Council of Ministers (cabinet) headed by the King, and contains a number of important "ministers" who serve as heads of various sections of the administration (see fig. 1). This cabinet assists the king in the management of specific domains such as education, housing, defense, industry, agriculture and natural resources.

In theory, the government of Saudi Arabia derives its legitimacy from Islam and Al-shari'ah law. However, the Kingdom has not fully developed a written constitution based on these Islamic sources, which set forth the basic principles of political and legal authority. The primary political institution is the Council of Ministers, whose political activity is a holistic process that contains both legislative and executive power. It is for this reason that the government bureaucracy is indeed an "administration."

There are influential interest groups in Saudi Arabia, but there is no political power structure outside of the monarchy[25] and Council of Ministers, with ultimate power undisputedly unified in the person of the King himself. Influential groups in Saudi Arabia interact and exert their influence within the monarchical framework, but hardly as autonomously powerful groups. Thus, Saudi Arabia has no political parties, nor any elected legislative body to shape political policy, although the King is assisted by a royal cabinet, which is equivalent to an executive staff in constitutional states.

It should be pointed out that the King can maintain his authority only so long as he upholds and applies the principles of Islamic law enshrined in the Qur'an and Al-shari'ah law. It is the royal family that selects the king from its ranks on the basis of seniority, from among brothers who are direct descendants of King Abd al-Aziz. An important element in the power of the royal family is the fact that they extensively participate in the bureaucratic machinery of the public sector by occupying important decision making positions. The role of the royal family is not limited to the public sector, but extends to the private sector as well. The government is thus in a position to provide profitable opportunities and incentives to the private sector since it is, after all, a major consumer of privately poroduced goods. This situation makes for a harmonious relationship between the public and private sectors within the kingdom.

It can be argued that the economic ideology of the decision makers in Saudi Arabia has changed very little since the reign of Abd al-Aziz, yet

Figure 1.

The Saudi Council of Ministers

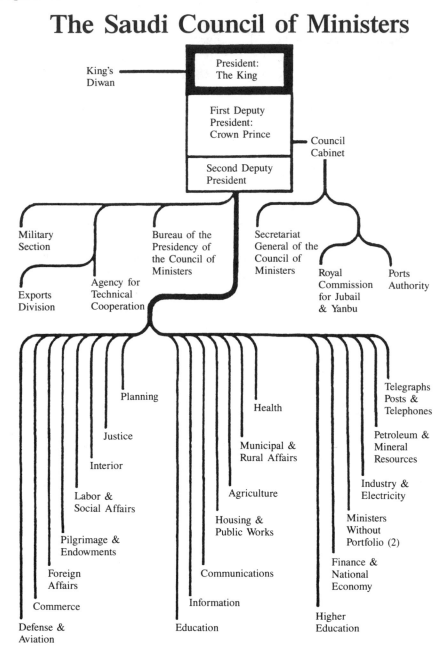

SOURCE: Fouad Al-Farsy, Saudi Arabia, 1986.

as we have already mentioned in this section, the role of government has changed considerably. In general, the goal of the government in Saudi Arabia has been to improve the economic conditions of the citizens, while at the same time retaining the country's traditional values and religious belief.

Historically, the method for achieving economic development and improvement in social conditions was to rely on individual initiative. The first King had little alternative but to rely on the private sector for growth because his revenue was inadequate to staff a government, let alone to undertake economic and social projects. This changed when oil revenues grew substantially.[26]

Before the 1970s, oil income increased slowly, and the government did not have revenues sufficient to finance the desired programs and projects. During these times, government economic decisions were largely those of determining priorities among alternative uses of limited resources. This situation dramatically changed in the early 1970s when oil exports expanded and revenues from royalty payments and taxes on foreign oil companies increased. A large portion of these revenues went toward industrialization in urban areas, with relatively little attention to the agricultural sector. Indeed, since the 1950s, long before the oil boom, the agricultural sector had grown at a slower rate than the rest of the economy;[27] so that by 1982 agriculture, including fisheries, contributed only one per cent to the gross domestic product. Also, agricultural employment had dropped from about 90 percent of the labor force before the 1950s, to less than 25 percent in the early 1980s, as the rural population sought better paying jobs in urban areas.

This situation has made the government take its redistributive commitments in agriculture seriously, resulting in subsidies and farm support program (see Table 1). The support for agriculture begins at the level of research and development. At the other end, the production process, the government purchases many farm products at prices well above the international markets. The Saudi Government's program of incentives consists of three elements: (1) subsidized purchase of machinery and equipment, (2) provision of inputs such as electricity, fertilizer and seed below cost, and (3) direct output subsidies, typically in the form of price floors.

215

TABLE 1
Main Subsidy Programs, 1982

Type of Subsidy	Terms of Subsidy	Agency Involved
Purchase of plant and equipment for dairy and poultry farms	30 per cent of cost	SAAB
Purchase of engines and pumps	50 per cent of cost	SAAB
Purchase of fish trawiers	Variable	SAAB
Air transport of imported cattle	100 per cent of cost	SAAB
Purchases on fertiliser	50 per cent of cost	MOAW
Purchase of animal feed	50 per cent of cost	SAAB
Potato Seed	First 5 tons free: SR1,000/ton up to 15 tons	MOAW
Electricity	SRO.05/k Wh	Ministry of Industry and Electricity
Wheat	Purchase price: SR3.5/kg	GSFMO[a]
Dates	Purchase price: SR0.25/kg	MOAW
Date palms planted	SR50 per tree	MOAW

Note: a. Reduced since 1982. The current program involves purchase prices from SR1.5 to SR2.5 per kg.
Acronyms: SAAB: Saudi Arabian Agricultural Bank: MOAW: Ministry of Agriculture and Water: GSFMO: Grain Silos and Flour Mills Corporation.
Source: *Third Development Plan*, Table 4.9.

By far the most important price support involves wheat. The Ministry of Agriculture purchases wheat from Saudi farmers and international markets. The price paid to farmers has been as high as SR.3.5 per kilogram, or about U.S. $1,000.00 per metric ton.[28] The government put the wheat price support program into effect in 1979. The farmers' response to the incentive has been overwhelming. The resulting surplus forced the government to lower support to SR 2,000.00 in 1984, with guarantees to maintain it until 1989.[29] The main channel for disbursing funds has been the Saudi Arabian Agricultural Bank, established in 1964 to provide subsidized loans to small farmers. In 1974-75, the value of loans made in that period nearly equalled the total credit given in the previous decade, as shown in Table 2.

216

TABLE 2
Agriculture Credits and Subsidies
(SR millions)

	Credits	Subsidies
1974/5	145	46
1975/6	269	134
1976/7	490	182
1977/8	586	237
1978/9	709	348
1979/80	1127	436
1980/1	2551	616
1981/2	2933	979
1982/3	4166	1321
1983/4	3496	1023
1984/5	2322	1378
1985/6	1551	—

Source: Saudi Arabian Monetary Agency, Annual Reports. The value of the Saudi Rial stood at 3.7 to the dollar in 1986.

The support programs for wheat have also had to deal with land distribution. Public land grants were originally aimed at settling Bedouins. However, the Public Lands Distribution Ordinance issued in 1968 had wider objectives.[30] This decree provided for the allocation of five to ten hectares (2.477 acres) of land to individuals free of charge. It also allowed land to companies and organizations, and up to 4,000 hectares for special projects. However, a number of projects exceed the latter limit. In 1985 five companies received 127,500 hectares.[31] The total area of land distributed to the corporate sector alone, much of it since 1981, exceeds the cropped area recorded in 1974. There has been a decided shift in favor of allocating progressively larger plots to the corporate sector, as is shown in Table 3.

217

TABLE 3
Land Distribution

	Individuals		Companies	
	# Plots	Hectares	# Plots	Hectares
1968-74	5711	34,884	0	0
1975	767	5,209	3	520
1976	189	1,091	3	1,200
1977	971	5,682	20	1,007
1978	4140	34,205	21	429
1979	1559	7,813	17	523
1980	6075	29,018	29	2,662
1981	1225	6,282	76	8,968
1982	2709	14,413	124	34,691
1983	8480	47,695	643	205,931
1984	9192	55,332	1225	171,697

Source: Saudi Arabian Monetary Agency, Annual Reports.

From the foregoing, it can be deduced that the role of government in providing agricultural support programs is quite pronounced in Saudi Arabia, and there is some basis for comparison with other countries. Rice growers in Japan, for example, enjoy similar, if not higher, government support. But there, the subsidy has been used to maintain **existing family farms** rather than **to spur growth**, as is the case in Saudi Arbia. These programs are quite costly to maintain relative to the resulting agricultural output. From a purely economic vantage point, the growth of agriculture that has resulted from these programs may not be sufficient to justify the expense. However, if we consider the principal objectives of the kingdom, the programs have very good benefit-cost ratios. For example, the wheat produced by the subsidies exceeds national requirements, making much of it available for grants of aid to poorer countries and as a trading good. As a result, the prestige of the kingdom is increased and patron-client relations can be established or strengthened. Secondly, the production of wheat makes the kingdom less dependent on other countries for essential products. In other words, the subsidy program is not the product of political pressure from special agricultural interests, as might be the case in a pluralistic democracy, but is the expression of a national purpose as propounded by the central government. Furthermore, these and other policies are made possible by state control over foreign trade—the reservoir of power that appears to be common to traditional systems.

THE CASE OF JAPAN: BALANCING TRADITIONAL VALUES WITH MODERNITY

Japan is an intriguing example of a country that has rather successfully mixed traditional values with modernity.[32] To be sure, there are differences between traditional Japan and modern Japan. By traditional Japan we mean the Japan of the feudal period known as the Tokugawa Era, covering the period from 1603 to 1868. Cultural developments leading to this period certainly played a crucial role in shaping Japanese culture as we know it now.

The examination of the Tokugawa society is vital to one's understanding of almost every aspect of the political economy and social development of modern Japan. The contemporary Japanese managerial system reveals imprints of the traditional values and ideology of the Era.

During the Tokugawa Era the Japanese class structure was well-defined and strongly imposed.[33] Below the imperial household and court nobles, four classes were established in the following descending order of status: warriors, farmers, artisans and merchants. In this period, Japan deliberately isolated herself from the rest of the world. The Tokugawa family resurrected Confucianism, made it their official philosophy, and used it as the ideological framework for an elaborate and rigidly controlled society.[34]

Traditional Japan placed greater emphasis on the strict regulation of society, and on conformity to prescribed behavior by members of different social classes and subclasses. By emphasizing outer conformity and the ritualistic embodiment of virtue in specific patterns of conduct, Confucianism provided the traditional Japanese with the external controls they required to form a well-regulated, peaceful society; a society that emphasized the correct observance of social relationships within an hierarchically structured society. For traditional Japan, Confucianism provided a "this-world-orientation" that rested on five dyadic social relationships: **affection** between father and son; respect and **royalty** between master and servant; **harmony** between husband and wife; **precedence** between older and younger brother; and **trust** between friends.[35] This explains why traditional Japan has often been characterized as a collectively oriented society with a strong system of authority, satisfying Bell's criteria of an hierarchically structured cooperative group.

It is important to realize that the modernization of Japan was accomplished without abandonment of traditional roots; there was considerable **social continuity**. As Haitani has noted, contemporary Japanese capitalism has more in common with Tokugawa Japan than with today's industrialized societies of the West.[36]

In his classic work, Abegglen has shown that the transformation of Japan took place with relatively fewer changes in social organization and social relations than would be expected from the western model of the growth of an industrial society.[37] In large part this can be explained by the fact that Japanese capitalism was not the result of the overthrow of the traditional, feudal elite by a revolutionary bourgeoisie as in the West. Rather, the traditional elite was paid quite well to relinquish its control over land, and these monies were then invested by the elite into new state sponsored industry—transforming the traditional elite into a capitalist elite.

Roles were assigned to each family by **ascription**, in accordance with the historical importance of each lineage group, as is typical of traditional systems. An individual's work was determined by the standing of the family to which he belonged, and the family's standing was reinforced by the extent of its participation in the affairs and productive activities of the community.[38]

Although the authority structure of traditional Japan was similar to that of pre-colonial Dahomey, there were some major differences. Most importantly, traditional Japan allowed for upward mobility on the basis of the individual's achievement, whereas in pre-colonial Dahomey social mobility was solely and exclusively the king's prerogative.

Indeed, it is this "achievement" motivation which has blended well with modern Japan's industrialization efforts within the context of traditional values outlined above. Unlike the free enterprise system of the United States, the Japanese system emphasizes a unique form of individualism which borders on collectivism, without lowering standards as has been the case in the collectivism of many socialist nations. This orientation has allowed the government in Japan to pay an important and direct role in the organization of the national economy.

In recent years, there have been suggestions that the relationship between government and business in Japan is best explained in terms of "Japan Incorporated."[39] This concept suggests that in relation to its industrial policy the Japanese economy is like a corporation with the government, through its famous Ministry of International Trade and Industry (MITI), serving as the corporate headquarters, and with the various business enterprises in the private sector serving as branches, or divisions, of the corporation. Some observers[40] have viewed the relationship between government and industry in Japan as that between hand and glove.

220

This is not to say that, in Japan, the private sector does not respond to domestic or international market forces. Rather, the point is that the intervention of government in guiding and directing the economy is far more pronounced than in the industrialized nations of the West.[41] Japanese businessmen take it for granted that there will be a continuous dialogue between business leaders and government officials, and that neither will make major policy decisions or undertake major projects without consulting the other. Consequently Japanese business, as a whole, does not object to its government's active role and involvement in business matters.[42]

One does not find in Japan the same adversary stance towards government that one would find among U.S. businessmen. Japanese are perhaps conditioned by cultural and historical influences, such as Confucian precepts, whose morality emphasizes that the interests of the state come before those of industry. For example the Samurai Warriors code, which embodied the Confusian morality of service to the nation, has been carried over from feudal times into the business life and civil service of contemporary Japan. Also, businessmen have come to accept the government's leadership, because that role was established in the beginning of Japan's industrialization, and because through the years since then the government has performed its duties and tasks with commendable and remarkable skill and efficiency. This is different from the United States where, historically, reaction to the oppressive policies of the colonial government of Great Britain tends to call for less government involvement in private affairs; and where "government" has, through the years, become associated with bureaucratic inertia, inefficiency, and waste of public resources. Although the Japanese government's involvement in the private sector is quite pronounced, it is also important to note that:[43] (1) the government's planning is **indicative**, rather than **authoritative** in terms of the nature of targets to be aimed for and guidelines to be followed; (2) government plans are not binding on the economic community and can be ignored or rejected; (3) much of the planning is piecemeal and ad hoc; (4) the blueprints are not all detailed and there is room for considerable improvisation and innovation; (5) many economic developments that have helped Japan prosper have come out of industry initiatives and business inputs into the planning process; and (6) planning, which is a key to understanding why there is substantial government involvement in Japan, is nevertheless part of what may be called Japan's success story.

For the most part government involvement in Japan is in the areas of trade and industry, rather than in the service sector. Consequently, Japan's manufacturing sector has grown more rapidly than the service sector.[44]

221

This is an important point because it says something about the structure of income distribution in Japan.

As shown in Table 4, the manufacturing sector has grown by 7 per cent annually throughout the sub-period indicated. The rapid growth of the manufacturing sector suggests that the economic transformation of Japan has been export and investment led, particularly over the period 1960 to 1973. Even today, Japan has continued to increase its export market share. Table 4 also shows that within manufacturing, growth in the traditional "heavy" and labor-intensive industries has declined steadily, so that it became very low by the 1980s. However, by contrast, the output of the advanced sectors, mainly in the electrical machinery area, continued to grow very rapidly. Employment composition shows a different pattern because of divergent movements in real gross domestic product (GDP) by sector. With productivity in the manufacturing sector growing so much faster than in the tertiary sector (6.9 per cent annually compared with 2.5 per cent), the share of total employment in manufacturing has fallen while that of services has increased.

The impressive performance of the manufacturing sector in Japan provides interesting comparisons with the agricultural sector in terms of income distribution implications. The share of agriculture in total output and employment fell steadily in the 1970s, although the pace of change was much less rapid than in the 1960s.[45] Redistributive adjustments during the 1960s were influenced by the agricultural Basic Law of 1961. This law enshrined the principle that agricultural income be maintained broadly in line with that of non-farm households. To achieve this, efforts were to be made to expand both productivity and the output of products other than rice.

During the high growth era of 1960 to 1973, rice prices were increased according to the increase in wages in the manufacturing sector, and according to input cost levels.[46] As real income rose rapidly and food tastes changed, consumers turned increasingly to livestock products, causing some switch to livestock rearing.[47] This led to greater imports of wheat, soybeans and maize, with the latter being used largely as feed for livestock.

In order to maintain parity between the growth of agricultural incomes and rapidly expanding incomes in the manufacturing sector, the Japanese government increased its rice support prices.[48] The introduction of machines in agriculture meant that non-agricultural employment could be obtained without people "leaving the land." This facilitated the part-time cultivation of rice fields.

222

TABLE 4
Structural Change 1970-1983
Annual Averages

	Average growth rates of real GDP			Average growth rates of employment			Average productivity growth	Average price change of gross output	Average deflater change	Shares (current price)		Shares of employment	
	$\frac{1973}{1970}$	$\frac{1980}{1973}$	$\frac{1983}{1980}$	$\frac{1973}{1970}$	$\frac{1980}{1973}$	$\frac{1983}{1980}$	$\frac{1973}{1970}$	$\frac{1973}{1970}$	$\frac{1983}{1973}$	1970	1983	1970	1983
*Primary sector	5.2	-1.8	0.7	-5.9	-2.1	-2.5	3.6	5.9	5.3	5.9	3.2	19.6	11.5
*Manufacturing sector	10.2	5.9	7.0	1.7	-0.7	0.9	6.9	4.7	2.0	34.7	29.1	26.7	24.4
Advanced industries	22.9	15.0	19.4	2.3	0.7	3.7	15.7	-0.3	-5.3	4.3	4.7	3.3	3.6
Other processing industries	7.9	6.2	5.6	2.1	-0.7	0.9	6.1	4.0	2.9	9.6	0.2	7.5	6.9
"Heavy" industries	13.0	4.6	1.5	0.6	-1.0	-1.1	6.4	6.4	1.6	8.5	5.7	2.4	2.0
Labour-intensive industries	7.8	3.6	0.7	-0.8	-1.6	0.0	5.0	5.2	3.8	5.6	4.5	5.8	4.4
Other	7.2	1.8	3.0	3.0	-0.5	0.6	2.7	6.4	4.8	6.8	6.1	7.7	7.4
*Construction	9.0	0.9	-2.2	5.9	2.0	-0.7	-0.3	7.3	6.6	7.5	7.6	8.1	9.5
*Electricity and gas	4.5	3.6	5.8	4.8	0.9	1.3	2.4	10.4	9.7	2.0	3.1	0.5	0.6
*Service sector	9.1	4.3	2.9	2.8	2.3	2.4	2.5	9.8	6.3	42.1	46.4	37.4	45.1
Retail and wholesale trade	10.7	4.3	1.4	1.2	2.0	1.3	3.4	5.3	4.1	13.9	11.7	16.2	17.7
Financial and real estate	12.6	5.4	5.7	4.4	2.7	3.2	3.7	7.6	5.7	12.3	16.2	3.1	4.1
Transport & comm.	5.7	4.4	0.6	2.5	1.2	0.1	2.6	7.5	6.8	6.6	6.6	5.5	5.7
Other services	5.5	2.7	2.5	4.4	3.0	4.2	-0.3	7.9	9.3	9.3	11.9	12.6	17.6
*Government	3.5	4.3	2.7	3.1	1.8	0.8	1.8	8.6	9.3	6.1	8.3	5.8	6.5

Source: OECD Economic Survey, 1984/85.

As a whole, Japanese agriculture has remained highly protected. In the view of the Japanese government such substantial agricultural protection is made necessary by the extreme shortage of farmland, given the very mountainous conditions. The mechanism and source of agricultural suprot varies among products. In the case of rice, imports are virtually excluded and the price of rice to consumers is subsidized, so that the wholesale price of rice is less than the government purchase price, as shown in Table 5.

TABLE 5
Price Ratios for Agricultural Products

A. OVERALL COMPARISONS

		1960	1965	1970	1975	1980
Polished rice	(P/B)	1.58	2.07	2.73	2.51	3.10
	(W/B)	1.65	1.77	2.47	1.97	2.79
Wheat	(P/B)	1.50	1.82	2.33	2.31	3.63
	(W/B)	1.42	1.33	1.32	0.74	1.23
Darky	(P/B)	1.53	1.71	2.57	2.59	4.08
	(W/B)	1.41	1.22	1.38	0.72	1.28
Soybean	(P/B)	1.50	1.45	2.19	1.73	3.85
Beef	(W/B)	2.23	2.71	2.54	3.46	2.75
Pork	(W/B)	1.53	1.19	1.16	1.34	1.00
Chicken	(W/B)	1.26	1.22	1.12	1.17	1.08
Eggs	(W/B)	1.01	0.89	0.93	0.94	1.43

Note: W = Wholesale price
     P = Price paid to Japanese producers
     B = Border prices

B. STATE TRADING IN WHEAT
000 y, per ton; fiscal years

	1960	1965	1970	1975	1980	1985
Price of imported wheat[1]	26.1	27.3	27.4	53.8	47.0	44.4
Buying price of domestic wheat	35.8	45.2	57.2	102.2	178.4	184.9
Selling price of wheat (wholesale)	33.4	32.6	31.9	49.2	60.4	68.9

[1]*United States wheat; c.i.f. and includes commissions paid to trading companies.*
SOURCE: Ministry of Agriculture, Japan.

Table 5 shows that for products other than rice, imports are generally purchased by a state monopsonist, which can then resell in the domestic market and use the resulting profits to subsidize domestic output. For example, wheat is imported by the Japanese State Food Agency, and then generally resold domestically at substantially higher prices.[49] Then, the profits that result are used to subsidize the relatively few domestic wheat producers, thus minimizing the need for any contribution from the General Government Accounts.[50] Similar arrangements apply to beef, where the difference between controlled import prices and domestic prices becomes the trading profit of the Livstock Industry Promotion Corporation (LIPC), and is used to support the domestic beef industry and improve its infrastructure.

One of the more interesting consequences of diverting excess resources to agriculture has been the maintenance of the traditional family farm. In marked contrast to the experience in other countries, the average size of farms in Japan has hardly increased. Indeed, Japanese agricultural production is distinguished from that of other industrial countries by the extremely small size of farms. The average size is one hectare, compared with 24 hectares in a small mountainous country like Austria.

Another feature is that there has been a significant increase in part-time farmers. As is shown in Table 6, the number of "core" farmers (i.e., the sum of full-time farmers and part-time workers who are mainly engaged in farming) has fallen rather sharply. But, because there has been a steady increase in farm ownership by households whose principal activity is not agriculture, the total number of farm households has declined much less. As a result, non-agricultural income now provides about 80 per cent of the total income of farm households.

The part-time farmers employ more capital, but farm their land much less intensively than full-time farmers. The fact that they have other jobs may increase the opportunity cost of their labor, but the high support price of rice makes it profitable to continue to hold land as a source of supplementary income, and as a potential source of capital gains.

In Japan, the importance of traditional forms of relationships is demonstrated by its policies toward the corporate and agricultural sectors. In the corporate sector we find Japan Incorporated, where the state plays an important role in directing resources in terms of national goals. In fact, the notion of "Japan Incorporated" implies that the nation is a (traditional) **cooperative group**, where allocations of resources are determined by the interest of the group as a whole. In the agricultural sector Japan strives

TABLE 6
Japan's Adjustment in Agriculture
% Shares

	1960	1965	1970	1975	1980	1985
Primary sector productivity/Manufacturing productivity			31.8	37.4	24.7	23.1
Share of gross domestic product (current prices)			6.1	5.5	3.8	3.3
Proportion of labour force in agriculture	30.0	22.8	17.9	12.6	9.8	8.2
Total farm households (000s)	6057	5665	5342	4953	4661	4522
Full-time	2078	1219	831	616	623	596
Part-time, mainly engaged in farming	2036	2081	1802	1259	1002	731
Part-time, mainly engaged in other jobs	1942	2365	2709	3078	3036	3195
Proportion of population living in farm households	36.8	30.6	25.1	20.7	18.3	17.4
Total farm household Income (000 yen) (=A)	410	761	1393	3414	4515	5122
of which:						
Agricultural income	225	365	508	1146	952	990
Non-agricultural income	184	396	885	2268	3563	4132
Grants, subsidiers, etc.[1]	40	74	199	546	1079	1353
Household income of urban workers households (000 yen) (=B)	490	821	1385	2834	4210	4716
A/B	0.84	0.93	1.01	1.20	1.07	1.09
Average size of farm (hectare)	1.00	1.06	1.08	1.12	1.17	1.20
Arable land as % local land	16.1	15.9	15.3	14.7	14.5	14.5

to maintain ancient small-scale family formations. It does this by assuring that the social category (rank) called "farmer" is able to perform customary tasks and, most importantly, enjoy an income level that corresponds to "needs." By implication, farmers are of the same rank as non-farmers and, hence, deserve a "parity" income.

THE CASE OF THE UNITED STATES: THE DOMINANCE OF MARKET EXCHANGE

To determine the role of government involvement in the United States is a complex exercise. However, it should be clear that government involvement in the American economy is different in form and in scope from the other countries discussed above. Unlike Dahomey, Japan and Saudi Arabia, the United States does not have a strong traditional basis. Rather, its history begins as a movement in opposition to traditional forms of governmental and economic relations.

226

The economy of the United States is generally thought to be one where individuals (households) and firms make their own decisions with a minimum of direct government involvement. However, this view is probably more accurate as a statement of official ideology than a description of actual operational facts. With the passage of time, the American government has been forced by circumstance to become more involved. First, there are the extensive activities of the government in the general regulation of economic actvity, such as monetary and fiscal policies. These policies tend to be relatively neutral in their effects among persons and firms, but they have a significant effect on the economy as a whole. In fact, people now seem to believe that the government can, and should, attempt to stabilize the economy and reduce, if not eliminate the business cycle. Secondly, as the economy becomes more complex, government is called upon to lead the way. This is especially true for the large set of issues related to national defense. The defense "establishment" is now a large segment of the economy, and the government is the only official buyer of its services.

Although it is still true that the "free market" has greater weight in determining social well-being in the United States than in most other countries, the United States is not strictly "laissez faire" in its policies. Government does intervene, and affects the performance and success of some persons and firms relative to other competing persons and firms. It has been argued by some scholars that businessmen, or capitalists, play a dominant and determining role in the political and economic decision making of the government of the United States. For example, C. Wright Mills[51] has described the overlapping membership of the powerful cadres of government and economy. His arguments would suggest not only that there are differential effects of government among persons and firms in the United States, but that these differentials are in part a function of the greater political influence of big business interests.

Many liberal social scientists have countered the "power elite" concept of Mills with the argument that American society is composed of a large number of competing power groups, and that big business does not have a privileged role in the control of government's economic policy.[52] These observers tend to see capitalist business as being one power among many, along with unions, churches, ethnic organizations, and so on. Hence, instead of perceiving a dominant power group, they see a set of pluralistic interest groups, as if all the interest groups were equal, or potentially equal, or even intermittently equal in their influence upon policy.

However, it does not take much analysis to show that these interest groups

227

are not equal. For example, ethnic minorities in the ghettos may be an interest group seeking to free itself from the cycle of poverty, but they are not in any way equal to organized businesses or other political elites who have favorable conditions of access and opportunity in the political and economic processes. Consequently, it is easy to exaggerate the extent to which the United States government avoids involvement in the private sector. The approach of Charles Lindblom is particularly instructive in this regard. Lindblom suggests that what is necessary is a close examination of the exercise of power in the **market place** and in the **state.**

Commonly in the literature, we find a distinction of these two key institutions in a nation like the United States:[53] markets disperse power, politics concentrates it; markets emphasize voluntary exchanges, while politics justifies coercion; markets coordinate without central direction, while politics makes planning possible.

Lindblom argues and shows that each of these common distinctions is plausible, partly true, but yet seriously exaggerated.[54] Instead of sharp and easy distinctions and contrasts, Lindblom says there is a variety of patterned relationships, governed by two general (empirical) rules: **there are no markets except under the protection and patronage of political authority, and no form of authority that does not make use of market activity.**[55] Politics and markets are two continually connected and interacting forms of social control.

So, according to Lindblom, we must study complex wholes in order to understand the role of government in the American private sector and vice-versa. Lindblom specifically focuses on two regimes: polyarchal market regimes, or liberal democracy, and authoritarian planning regimes (socialist or communist societies). There is planning in the first of these, of course, and a variety of other kinds of political interaction in the economy. Conversely, there are markets in the second, in jobs and consumer goods, though not in investment and capital goods.

Under capitalism, wages are the by-product or side effect of the private sector (i.e. self-interested entrepreneurial activity). Wages fall for those workers whose skill may now be obsolete because of a particular capital intensive innovation, or for a whole town where a newly outmoded factory is forced to close, as has happened lately in the automobile industry.

In a planned economy, wages and other costs are calculated in advance and are centrally assigned. In polyarchal market societies like the United States, businessmen are in a good position to influence those policies that affect labor and industry. Lindblom observes that liberal capitalism is dominated by capitalists and: "polyarchy is tied to the market system not because it is democratic, but because it is not."[56]

This may sound like the familiar radical criticism of the liberal state from Marxists, but Lindblom is not a Marxist. He does not view the power of capital in polyarchal regimes as a defect, but as one of its virtues—the avoidance of authoritarian rule. Nor does Lindblom see the exercise of business power as domination, since it too is subject to democratic controls (though it is rarely effectively controlled) and, more importantly, it is exercised in a piecemeal fashion (incrementally) and thus cannot, by its very nature, pose a totalitarian threat. Yet still, Lindblom observes that business has a privileged position in that it has great discretionary powers within the market itself. This is so even if consumers may be assumed to have sovereignty, because businessmen are usually free to make decisions which are particularly crucial to the management of commerce and industry. Decisions about the organization of the work force, plant location, executive authority and income, technological innovation, and investment either are not controlled by consumers, or consumers have only the loosest and most indirect controls. These decisions are effectively the prerogatives of capital.

Also, business can obtain extensive favors from the political authorities because polyarchal governments have a deep interest in continued and increasing productivity. In order to induce businessmen to act in particular ways, government must often be prepared to provide them with extensive protection against both violence and economic risk. This explains the importance of subsidies, tariffs, tax rebates and government sponsored research in a number of essential public sector related activities which include military production, health, education and public safety. Indeed, this activity shows that there is a great deal of government involvement in the American private sector. The real question is one of specifying the **nature** of the involvement because, unquestionably, the involvement is there; and it is extensive in the form of subsidies, tax preferences and various types of regulations.

The point here is that businessmen themselves require government intervention, but only in areas of their own choosing, as in the case of protecting businessmen from what they may see as unfavorable foreign competition. A case in point is the recent American imposition of tariffs against selected Japanese goods.

Also, it should be noted that businessmen intervene directly in political life in order to influence governmental interventions into the economy—primarily with money in amounts larger than most other groups are able to muster. For example, as Lindblom points out, unions lag incredibly behind

229

in their ability to collect and allocate money for political purposes, while a considerable amount of corporate wealth is paid out each year for advertising and educational materials aimed at upholding generally the values of the free-enterprise system. As such, business does clearly play a far more effectual role in the American political system than in the other political systems which we have analyzed in this paper. In the other systems each government took a commanding role relative to the economy with the objective of having all classes of people work in the national interest, but in the United States the capitalist class has a dominant position relative to other classes and compels government to act in the interest of free enterprise.

The contrast between the American and the other political economies is clearly illustrated with a discussion of U.S. government policies toward the agricultural sector. As indicated earlier, market exchange mechanisms in the United States, driven by the private sector, seem to have a greater role than the authority arrangements of the government. In the following section the agricultural arena in the U.S. will be analyzed using market economy concepts. The ultimate task is to determine the extent of the role of government.

There are two concepts relating to the demand for farm products which are important. One is the price elasticity of demand, which is related to the slope of the demand curve at a given point in time. The other is the income elasticity of demand which is related to the effect of changes in the real income of consumers on the demand curve. There are many statistical studies available which provide estimates of both the price and income elasticities for farm products.[57] These studies indicate that the demand for fram products **at the farm level** is inelastic, so that a given percentage increase in the quantity will only clear the market with a relatively greater decrease in price. Total revenue is therefore lower from a larger quantity than from a smaller quantity of farm products.

It is worth noting, as was mentioned in the discussion of agricultural subsidies in Japan and Saudi Arabia, that demand for agricultural products tends to grow more slowly than for industrial products, or for services of various kinds. This obviously is a common phenomenon. The reason for the slower growth was aptly stated by the father of economics, Adam Smith, in 1776.[58] He noted that the demand for food is limited by the size of the human stomach.

Demand for food and textiles depends on the number of people to feed and clothe. On the other hand, the demand for manufactured goods and

230

for services seems to expand without limit as incomes grow.

While demand for agricultural products in the United States has been increasing more slowly than demand for manufactured goods and for services, the supply of agricultural products has kept pace with the growth of supply in the other sectors of the economy.[59] Indeed, continuous improvements in the levels of technology, invention, and innovation have taken place in the agricultural, as well as in the non-agricultural sectors.

The relatively greater demand, and consequent price increases, for non-agricultural products over time makes their production more profitable than the production of agricultural products. This is reflected in the differences in incomes of those who live on the farm and those who do not. The difference in resource prices, and in individual incomes, between agricultural and non-agricultural production activities provides incentives for resources to move out of agriculture and into manufacturing and service industries.

Even though the population of the United States has been growing rapidly during this century, the farm population has decreased from some 30.5 million persons in 1930, to 3.8 million in 1984.[60] Diversion of capital resources out of agriculture has not been so dramatic. There has been a consolidation of capital into larger farms, and these enterprises can compete very effectively with non-agricultural enterprises for the use of the capital.

From 1933 to 1974 the United States employed farm price support programs[61] which, after a two year lapse, were reinstated in 1977.[62] The administration of Franklin D. Roosevelt put in place a massive program of farm price supports, beginning with the Agricultural Adjustment Act of 1933. The thinking of the administration and Congress seemed to be that if prices of agricultural products could be raised relative to other prices, the incomes of the farmers would also increase relative to non-farm incomes.

Agricultural price supports in the United States are put into effect, for the most part, through a storage and loan program. For example, a feature of the wheat support program is a so-called deficiency rate, a sum of "X" cents per bushel added to the loan support rate. The primary effect is to increase wheat output as well as any surplus that may occur from the price support program. The government determines a support price level for a given product such as wheat. At harvest time, any farmer can place wheat in government-approved storage facilities and receive a loan from the government equal to the support price on each bushel stored. When the loan becomes due the farmer has the option of paying it off, or of letting the government have the stored wheat in repayment.[63]

231

Under this sort of program wheat farmers are given an incentive to store wheat, and to borrow from the government whenever the support price exceeds the market price. When the repayment is due, and if the market price is still below the support price, the farmer then lets the government have the wheat. If, however, the market price is above the support price, the farmer pays off the loan at the support price, redeems the wheat, and sells it at the market price. In effect, the government guarantees that the farmer can receive the support level price for the wheat.

The graph below is an illustration of how demand and supply affect the storage and loan program in terms of price supports by the government. On the graph, unless the market price exceeds P_1 when the loan is due, farmers will let the government have the wheat in repayment of the loans.

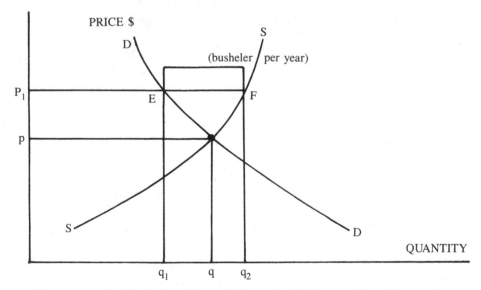

The support price P_1 is above the equilibrium price P. Buyers will purchse quantity q_1 at the support price, but farmers produce quantity q_2. The government purchases the surplus, making total payments to farmers equal to the area $q_1 EFq_2$.

Farm support price programs in the United States reveal an active role on the part of government in income redistribution, but the programs also have economic effects. As the government accumulates surpluses of the product (say wheat), pressure builds for the establishment of special surplus disposal programs. These take several forms.

232

Surpluses may be sold abroad, either directly or indirectly by the government, at less than support prices. In 1983, for example, the United States government sold a large amount of wheat flour to Egypt, receiving considerably less for the flour than it had paid the farmers for the wheat from which it was made.[64] Surpluses are also used to provide school lunches and food stamps, while some are left to deteriorate in storage, if not thrown away altogether into the ocean!

In addition to the surplus disposal problem, economists have observed that farm price supports result in much larger government payments to large, wealthy farmers than to small, poor ones; and that the smaller the output and income of the farmer, the less the amount of government payments the farmer receives. Conversely, the greater the output and income of a farmer, the greater are the payments received. It would appear that these are the direct results of supporting farm prices rather than farm incomes. Therefore, as a means of combating poverty, a price support program is an upside-down welfare program, providing more welfare for the rich than for the poor. At any rate, these support programs suggest inefficiency and waste on the part of the government, something which is rather in sharp contrast to the Japanese case.

This form of inefficiency is to be anticipated from the perspective of Lindblom's analysis. If government policy is the product of the objectives of powerful capitalist groups, instead of the "national interest," then we would expect that U.S. policies would differ systematically from those of the other countries that we have discussed.

CONCLUSION: RESEARCH IMPLICATIONS FOR SAUDI ARABIA

Western, and especially American, social theorists commonly oppose political and economic forms that feature the dominance of authority relations. There are economic theories that argue against "monopoly," and a general philosophical opposition to the dominance of political elites such as royal families and aristocracies. Authority is associated with coercion and the violation of the public interest; authority is thrown into the same pot with "authoritarianism" of the Soviet or fascist model. However, traditional forms of social authority have usually justified their policies in terms of the collective interest. For example, the Saudi Arabian policy toward the development of wheat production was not designed in response to political pressure from wheat producers; it was developed for the achievement of national goals. And in Japan the industrial and agricultural sectors of the economy are actually creations of the state, not servants of particular interest groups. The leaders of traditional societies such as Dahomey would have thought it absurd to assume that the outcome of the struggle of private interest would give rise to anything other than domination by the strongest group, creating a form of authority that may not be bound to traditional concepts of fairness.

Furthermore, the issue of "authoritarianism" within traditional systems, while potentially problematic, did not arise in the case of Dahomey because the state sphere was focused on foreign economic relations, allowing lower level village or family institutions to govern much of economic life. In fact, the role of custom (or local "traditions") in traditional systems seems to be parallel to the role of markets in capitalist systems in the sense that customs, like markets, reduce the need for central direction.

Each of the systems discussed in this paper contains something that could be called a private business sector, and in each case there are incentives of various kinds offered by the state. But the merchant classes of traditional systems are never in a position to control governmental interventions into the economy to the extent that they are in the American economy. On the contrary, merchants tend to be illegitimate and are often despised and feared by authority. Merchants are known to have had low status (in spite of considerable wealth) in feudal Europe and in imperial China. In Saudi Arabia capitalists are largely encouraged by the availability of state resources, but since their activities are likely to be consistent with the objectives of state policy the typical hostility of the traditional state toward private capitalists does not arise.

Lindblom's theory recognizes the inefficiencies in public policies associated with allowing greater dominance from the private sector, but for him the avoidance of a dominating central authority is a primary goal; he seems willing to forgo the search for the collective interest in order to avoid authority of Type One, while submitting to authority of Type Two.

The contrast between traditional and capitalist policies is clearly joined on questions of income distribution. Traditional policies address income distribution as a primary goal, because each social group is believed to deserve a certain "fair" distribution from the collective product. The management of such a system of collective production with fair distributions tends to conflict with the needs of capitalists who seek an environment in which they can define the national interest.

Bell's theory of allocations within traditional systems is one that accepts their value-perspective as a point of departure, and presumes that there is a collective interest that can be defined by authorities. His theory then defines the principles that should govern the specification of (fair) responsibilities and rewards within such systems.

Of the four societies that we have discussed, pre-colonial Dahomey was the most authority-driven. The king was able to earn the respect and fealty of the public because he, by controlling (and limiting) the export of slaves, and by regulating the activities of the private sector, was able to provide for the society as a whole. The Kingdom of Saudi Arabia is the second most centralized in structure. Here again, the wealth of the Kingdom depends largely upon the export of wealth to other countries, so that the government is in a position to control economic activities and assure that a fair allocation of consumption goods is available to each social category.Then there is the Japanese case, where traditional values of collective consumption continue to hold within a highly industrialized economy. The concept of "Japan Incorporated" is a manifestation of this traditional perspective. However, since the wealth of the economy does not flow through the hands of the government, the government must exert its direction on the economy in a more indirect fashion—by control of essential central organs of economic planning, and its influence on monopolistic structures that require coordination with government policy. And, finally, there is the United States, where there is considerable involvement by government in the private sector, but where the traditional values associated with collective production have been strongly denied. In this case, a polyarchy of powerful economic interests are able to focus public policy toward business (and agricultural businesses in particular) in terms of the objectives of special interests.

Contemporary conditions do not require that the social system be dominated either by authority relations, or by market relations. Both may be at work, as is demonstrated by the remarkably successful government-business relationship in Japan, where traditional values and modern values have been combined without sacrificing efficiency and technical skill. The case of the United States shows that government involvement in the private sector, while quite pronounced, is subject to the dominance of private interests in the determination of public policies.

To the extent that a society adopts the ideology of free enterprise we would expect that society to accept, in addition, the idea that governmental bureaucracy should follow the Weberian model, treating persons and businesses with an impersonal impartiality, focusing on the use of rules

235

and law. However, traditional forms of authority tend to require more "particularistic" concerns, and greater sensitivity of public management to the needs of specific social groups. Hence, the characteristics of governmental involvement in the private sector, and the criteria of efficacy that should be applied to that involvement, may differ along the traditional/capitalist continuum.

There is a tendency to accept unquestioningly the appropriateness of the Weberian model for a national administration that accepts the values of traditional society, but this may not be wise. Indeed, Japan seems to have resolved this question by encouraging "achievement" orientations within the context of traditional values of cooperative production.

For Saudi Arabia the central importance of family and friendships, of loyalty and generosity, and of religion and the Holy Places of Islam, should continue to be essential guides to the behavior of public institutions. Our task is to preserve these values while managing the public sector in an increasingly complex and technologically developing society.

Footnotes

1. Perhaps the best theoretical statement on this issue is found in Lindblom's widely debated book *Politics and Markets: The World's Political-Economic Systems*, 1977.
2. Although this paper will largely focus on structural issues one way of assessing the variations would be through focusing on the concept of organizational culture which has recently emerged as a "contenting concept", see *Administrative Science Quarterly*, September issue of 1983, where there is a rather thorough discussion of the concept of organizational culture.
3. Ibid., see also Johan Galtung's "Methodology and Ideology" in *International Peace Research Institute*, Volume 1, 1977, pp. 13-40.
4. See Duran Bell's Essay on *"Production ad Distribution Within Hierarchically Structured Groups,"* *Journal of the Steward anthropological Society*, Vol. 16, #1, November, 1987.
5. Ibid., p. 3.
6. Ibid., pp. 9-12.
7. Professor Bell argues that socialism and communism are forms of traditional systems, being based ideologically on the principles of co-operative production.
8. Datta-Chaudhuri, M.K., **Industrialization and Foreign Trade: The Development Experiences of South Korea and the Phillippine.** in Eddy Lee, (eds.) *Export-led Industrialization and Development*, 1981.
9. This is a view which would seem to agree with the Madisonian framework of factions or groups as being the major unit of association in a pluralist society, see the *Federalist Papers, No. 10 and 51.*

236

10. For a comprehensive study of Dahomey, see Melville J. Herskovits, *Dahomey An Ancient West African Kingdom*, 1938. Also see Kary Polanyis, *Dahomey and the Slave Trade: An Analysis of an Archaic Economy*, 1966.

11. See Herskovits, op. cit. pp. 51-136.

12. See Bell, op. cit. pp. 1-3.

13. Ibid., p. 3.

14. Karl Polanyi, *Dahomey and the Slave Trade: An analysis of an Archaic Economy*. 1966, p. 32.

15. Ibid., p. 34.

16. Ibid., PP. xxi-xxii.

17. Ibid., pp. 34.

18. ds stores in

19. See Bell, op. cit. pp. 3-9.

20. Polanyi, op. cit. p. xxii.

21. I.A. Akinjogbin, "Dahomey and Its Neighbors 1708-1818," *Cambridge University Press*, 1967, pp. 108-109.

22. J.D. Fage, *A History of Africa*. Hutchinson of London, 1978, p. 273.

23. Ibid., p. 265.

24. See Ibrahim M. Al-Awaji, *Bureaucracy and Society in saudi Arabia*, Unpublished Ph.D. Dissertation, University of Virginia, 1971, pp. 82-97; 143-146.

25. Ibid., pp. 53-74.

26. Before the 1970s, oil income increased slowly, and the government did not have revenues sufficient to finance.

27. See Darrell R. Eglin's "The Economy of Saudi Arabia" in Richard F. Nyrop (ed.) *Saudi Arabia: A Country Study*, 1984.

28. See Vahid Nowshirvani's "The Yellow Brick Road: Self-Sufficiency or Self-Enrichment in Saudi Agriculture," *Middle East Report*, March/April 1987, p. 8.

29. For a comprehensive description of Saudi agricultural projections and the general agricultural setting of the country, see Howard Bowen-Jones and Roderick Dutton, "*Agriculture in the Arabian Peninsula*," *Economist Intelligence Unit Special*, Report No. 145, 1986.

30. For a detailed description of the various land distribution policies and laws see E.G.H. Joffe "*Agricultural Development in Saudi Arabia: The Problematic Path to Self-Sufficiency*," in P. Beaumont, and K. Mclachlan (eds.), *Agricultural Development in the Middle East*, 1985.

31. See Vahid Nowshirvani, op. cit. p. 10.

32. Haitani Kanji, *The Japanese Economic System*, pp. 33-40.

33. Ibid., p. 40.

34. Ibid.

35. Ibid., pp. 47-53.

36. Ibid.

37. See Lockwood op. cit. pp. 55-93.

38. See Japan Culture Institute, *Politics and Economics in Contemporary Japan*, 1979.

39. See U.S. Department of Commerce, Bureau of International Commerce, *Japan: The Government/Business Relationship*, 1972.

40. Ibid., pp. 35-42.

237

41. Ibid. See also Japan Culture Institute op. cit. p. 23.
42. U.S. Department of Commerce, pp. 103-8.
43. Ibid., pp. 11-15.
44. Ministry of Agriculture Report, Japan 1979, p. 15.
45. Ibid.
46. See White Papers of Japan 1984-1985, "Annual Abstracts of Official Reports and Statistics of the Japanese Government," *Japan Institute of International Affairs*, 1986.
47. See "Agriculture and Food in Japan," Ministry of Agriculture Report, 1976.
48. See OECD Economic Survey of Japan, 1984.
49. Ibid.
50. See "Agriculture and Food in Japan" op. cit. p. 37.
51. See C. Wright Mills, *The Power Elite*, 1956.
52. This is one underlying argument of Lindblom's *Politics and Market*, op. cit., and one which he seeks to counter.
53. See for example, John Goodman, and Edwin Dolan in their discussion of farm policy in the United States in their book, *Economics of Public Policy*, 1985.
54. Lindblom, op. cit., pp. 38-51.
55. Ibid., p. 48.
56. Ibid., p. 194.
57. See Bale E. Hathaway's *Government and Agriculture: Public Policy in a Democratic Society*, 1983, pp. 84-85.
58. See Adam Smith (Cannon Edition) *The Wealth of Nations*, p. 164.
59. See John goodman, and Edwin Dolan, op. cit., pp. 91-104.
60. See Ansel M. Sharp, and Richard H. Leftwich, *Economics of Social Issues*, 1986, p. 39.
61. Ibid., p. 98.
62. Ibid., pp. 98-103.
63. Ibid., pp. 96-97.
64. Ibid., pp. 42-43.

A SYSTEM DYNAMICS MODEL FOR SAUDI ARABIAN INDUSTRIAL DEVELOPMENT

by Hussein Murad Reda, Ph.D.

I. Introduction

Industrial development is a complex process which involves interaction among a multitude of economic, social and physical factors. (1)(5)(9) Both its structure and its pace vary over time and from nation to nation. At the macro level, industrial development is usually the result of broad or dramatic changes in cultural, social and economic behavior. It may involve changing values, interests or demands of a given population. Great differences have been found between patterns of industrial growth in developing and developed countries.

Due to its inherent complexity, industrial growth has often proved a difficult subject for research. Key variables and their interaction have been hard to identify, specify and analyze. On the whole, however, three general approaches to research have been used: broad and descriptive, narrow or single variable, and system dynamics modeling. The descriptive approach has generally involved looking at whole sets, components or "systems" of society and their interactions over a period of development. Most often works of this type have been mainly theoretical with little emphasis on empirical hypothesis testing or experimental modeling. Furthermore, they have tended to concern themselves with a wide variety of topics in industrial development and as a result have been fragmented and unstructured. A second common approach has been to focus on a single or major aspect of development such as a particular economic or social change variable. The idea has been to identify a few crucial factors in interaction. On the whole studies of this type have yielded valuable information of a quantitative nature and proved capable of empirical testing. Where they have been weak is in their tendency to oversimplify the complex process of development. A third approach has been to quantify descriptive variables where possible from a broad range of areas, and to develop analytic models. This "system dynamics" approach has the advantages of both quantifica-

239

tion and complexity, of a broad focus, and the possibility of seeing the influence of single variables on others. It is the approach the author used to obtain the prototype model for Saudi Arabian industrial development presented in this paper below.

System Dynamics

Briefly defined, system dynamics is a structured methodology for modeling complex systems. The basic modeling structure is based on the concept of causal feedback looping. A causal feedback loop consists of two more system variables. A change in any one variable causes a series of changes whereby each variable in the loop influences the rest, thus causing the initiating variable to change again. Based on this concept, a computerized mathematical model can be developed to simulate the system behavior patterns dynamically. The model can be employed for understanding the system component interaction leading to the design of a more effective system. (2)(3)

System dynamics models are usually constructed to answer specific structural questions regarding system environment and behavior. Such models serve as analytic tools which can be used for design and testing as well as tools for policy planning and decision making. To date, system dynamics models have been used to study such a wide variety of subjects as urban systems, industrial systems, and economies of communities, regions, countries and the globe.

An Industrial Development System Model for Saudi Arabia

There are many reasons why a system dynamics model for the Saudi Arabian industrial system should be developed and would prove useful and fruitful for researchers and policy makers alike. Primarily, such a model could serve as an experimental tool to test the effect of various development strategies and policies. It could capture the essence of the dynamic structure of the economy and reflect the true behavior of the system it represents, provided it included true system components. Furthermore, if adequately designed, it could serve as an experimental decision tool. In this sense, various industrial development policies and objectives could be tested by the model.

As far as the model being a tool for development strategies, it is clear that Saudi Arabia has already embarked on ambitious development plans,

240

the wide ranging effects of which can at this point only be speculated. Development goals for Saudi Arabia include a diversified economy, an increased productivity of the workforce, and a smooth transition of the economy and society from the present to a future state which will combine the benefits of industrialization and high standards of living with traditional social and moral values.

To achieve these goals requires the application of complementary policies to various interrelated sectors of the socio-industrial system. The selection of which policies to implement requires projecting the effects of individual development policies, and especially the effects of entire policy sets on numerous components of the complex system. Therefore, in designing a system dynamics model which could serve as a tool to test alternative plans for industrialization, it is critical to identify specific variables important for achieving development goals. Among these goals are those of economic diversification, manpower development, and agricultural development:

The country's oil wealth provides the most important means for its economic growth. It provides Saudi Arabia with the potential to develop a strong industrial base that will maximize the returns from its oil, and will provide stable employment for the Saudi population in the future. Investment in industrial capital will lead to the development of the desired industrial base. However, a smooth development of industry and other sectors of the economy requires adequate infrastructure facilities and adequate supply of labor. Too rapid growth of manufacturing capacity without appropriate growth in infrastructure could result in idle capacity and bottlenecks. This rapid growth of manufacturing would also compete for a limited supply of labor.

Another important factor in the Saudi development process is the lack of a large enough and properly trained labor force to satisfy rapid industrialization demands. Excessive reliance on foreign labor to satisfy demands can have negative effects on the social and cultural climate of the country. Thus, the increase of worker productivity is an integral part of the industrial development process.

Agricultural development is another major goal which a dynamic model could address. As population and standards of living increase, the demand for food will grow. Shortages in domestic agricultural production are satisfied through food imports which may cause a drain on the country's foreign exchange capital. The development of the agricultural sector would result in creating increased competition for scarce resources of water and manpower.

241

Thus a useful system dynamic model of Saudi Arabia could be designed to include the basic sectors of the economy in its multi-feedback loop structure. Among those sectors are the agricultural sector, manufacturing and industrial sector, and population and labor sector. Within each sector a multitude of factors which affect the sector output would be represented. For example, the agricultural sector would include factors such as water availability, demand for agricultural products, agricultural output, fraction of the total labor employed in agriculture, and capital allocated for agricultural development. Similarly, the manufacturing and industrial sector would include factors such as raw material availability, demand for manufactured goods, industrial output, fraction of labor force employed in industrial production activities, and capital allocated to industrial development. The population and labor sector would include factors such as population growth rate, domestic labor force, proportion of skilled labor, share of foreign labor in the labor force, and capital allocated for man-power development.

These are but a few examples of how a dynamic model of the national economy could accommodate some of the industrial development issues. However, these examples give some indication of the extent to which specific objectives can be accommodated in system dynamics models.

As regards using the system dynamics modeling approach for an experimental decision tool, it is possible that various projected Saudi policies could be incorporated into the model and subsequently simulated. The model would indicate the system reaction to these decisions. Systems' reaction (defined as parameter value changes) could be observed either graphically as trends and fluctuation, or numerically, or both as appropriate.

As an example of such a use of the model, let us assume that during the process of development, situations arise where trade-offs have to be made between capital-intensive and labor-intensive investments. The allocation of limited resources of capital and labor is particularly critical when such investments extend far into the future and may require committing large portions of national resources. The government has two choices. It may decide on a strong commitment to capital-intensive programs and the high-level of technology that is usually associated with it. This might mean that capital will not be sufficiently available for other development sectors. It also might mean greater dependency on foreign skills, in the short and medium terms, until domestic skills are developed. To develop indigenous expertise requires investments in higher education and training capacity, which in turn involves committing further capital and prolonging the time needed for young Saudis to enter the labor force. On the other

242

hand, the government might decide on a strong commitment to labor-intensive programs in the agricultural and services sectors to increase self-sufficiency of food supplies, and to provide services that are essential to the welfare and security of the people. The draw-back here is the low return on investment usually associated with such labor-intensive development and naturally, the increased drain of scarce labor.

The model as an experimental tool would thus address the interrelated issues of population, education, training, capital, agriculture, industrial production, services, and infrastructure to name just a few of the model components. It would help policy makers to see the wide ranging effects of decisions in one or two areas on a multitude of other areas.

A Prototype Industrial Development Model

Given the validity of the numerous arguments presented for applying a system dynamics model to the Saudi Arabian situation, the author developed a prototype. (10)(11) This prototype is briefly presented in the pages that follow in terms of its structure, and through an illustrative simulation run of the model. In this model, a general development system is described by boundary, component, and activities. The system is represented by ten major activity sectors. (Figure 1) They are grouped into three classes:

1. Driving Sectors, consisting of population and capital sectors.
2. Production Sectors, consisting of software and hardware production sectors. The software sectors include services, technology, and social infrastructure, while the hardware sectors are resources, manufacturing, agriculture and physical infrastructure.
3. An Outlet Sector, consisting of import and export trade activities.

The material flow between these sectors is depicted in Figure 2. As shown, population provides the production sectors with labor, while the capital sector supplies them with funds to acquire and operate the factors of production. In this model, capital is defined as financial assets that are saved and are available for, or employed in, production activities. It is generated by population savings.

The seven production sectors serve as the core of the development process. Output from the production sectors is classified as either hardware or software production. They are explained as follows:

1. The resources sector uses labor, capital, physical infrastructure, and

243

MODEL'S MAJOR SECTORS

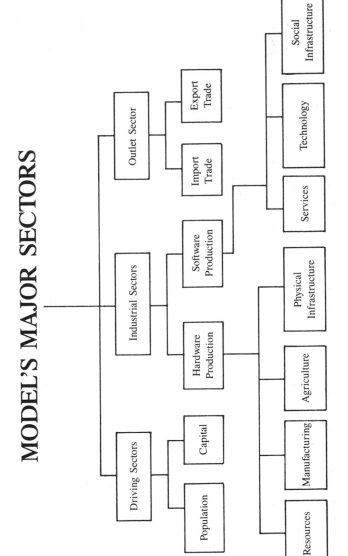

Fig. 1: Classification of Model's Sectors

244

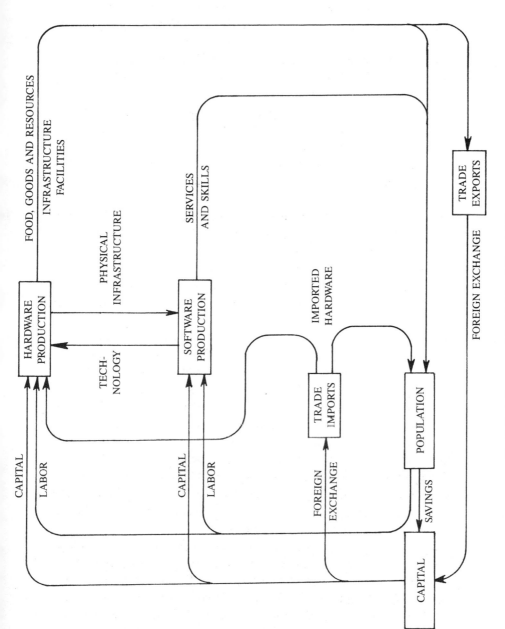

Fig. 2: Basic Structure of the Model and Material Flow

245

technology to produce extracted and processed resources. Resources are defined as exhaustible substances deposited or existing within the system boundaries. They include coal, petroleum, natural gas, and minerals. Forests and ground water are also considered as resources since there is usually a long time period before they can be renewed. Activities of the resources sector include mining, oil and gas production, forestry, and well-drilling.

2. The agriculture sector uses capital, labor, technology and manufactured goods (fertilizers, pesticides, farm equipment, etc.) and produces food. Activities of the agriculture sector include farming, fishing, food processing and agricultural services (such as animal husbandry, pest spraying, etc.)

3. The manufacturing sector uses capital, labor, resources, physical infrastructure facilities, and technology to produce consumer and capital goods. Manufacturing is defined as the mechanical or chemical transformation of substances into new products (except for food processing which is considered an agricultural activity.) Activities of the manufacturing sector include metal and non-metal industries, equipment and machinery, wood products and by-products, glass and china, etc.

4. The physical infrastructure sector uses capital, labor, technology and manufactured good to yield infrastructure facilities. Activities of the physical infrastructure sector are those related to the hard public utilities. They include transportation and communication networks, power generation and transmission, construction, storage, and rural and urban municipal functions (sewerage, water supply, etc.)

5. The services sector uses labor, capital, technology and infrastructure (physical and social) to produce services to the population. Activities of the services sector include financing, insurance, real estate, wholesale and retailing, restaurants and lodging, repairs and maintenance, and general business services (such as legal counseling, accounting, auditing and advertising.)

6. The technology sector uses labor, capital and social infrastructure to produce technological capabilities as represented by labor skills, managerial capacity, engineering and scientific knowledge and know-how; all of which lead to efficiency and competitiveness of the production sectors. Activities of the technological sector include engineering, architectural and technical functions, research and development, and the development of professional practices and institutions, standards and procedures, and ethics and codes of conduct.

246

7. The social infrastructure sector uses capital, labor, physical infrastructure and social infrastructure to provide the population with social and community services. Activities of the social infrastructure sector include education, health care, welfare, religious and cultural affairs, public information and recreation (television, radio, libraries, parks, etc.), and public administration and defense (such as judicial and legislative functions, police and national security, etc.)

The outlet sector is represented by trade activities. It serves as a gateway between the national economy and the international community. All interaction between the model's sectors and sources outside the system boundary take place through the trade sector. Thus, trade is a two-way process. It involves the sale of domestic products to foreign purchasers, or exporting; and the purchase of foreign products by domestic agents, or importing. Traded items thus include raw and processed resources, agricultural products and manufactured goods. Table I summarizes the sector's input-output relationship.

Table 1 Sectors Input-Output Relationship*

Output of Input To	Population	Resources	Agric.	Mfg.	Physical Infras.	Services	Tech.	Social Infras.	Export	Trade Import	Capital
Popu.	–	–	Food	Consumer Goods	Public Facilities	Services	–	Social & Community Services	–	–	–
Res.	Labor in Res.	–	–	–	Transport Storage	–	Extraction Techniques	–	–	Import Res.	Invest. in Res.
Agri.	Labor in Agri.	–	–	Mfg. Goods	–	–	–	–	–	Import Food	Invest. In Agri.
Mfg.	Labor in Mfg.	Stock Material	–	–	Infra. Facilities	–	Production Tech.	–	–	Import Goods	Invest. in Mfg
Phys. Infra	Labor in Phys Infra	–	–	Mfg. Goods	–	–	–	Design & Construc-techniques	–	–	Invest. in Phys. Infra.
Ser.	Labor in Service	–	–	–	Construction Transport, Communication	–	Tech. of Conduct	Public Administ.	–		Invest. in Ser.
Tech.	Labor in Tech.	–	–	–	–	–	–	Education Legislation Info.	–		Invest. in Tech.
Social Infras.	Labor in Social Infra.	–	–	–	Construction Facilities	–	–	–	–	–	Invest. in Soc. Infra.
Export Trade	–	Resource for Export	Food for Export	Goods for Export	–	Services for Export	Tech. for Export	–	–	–	–
Import Trade	–	–	–	–	–	–	–	–	–	–	Foreign Exchange
Capital	Capital Savings	Resource Sale	Agri. Prod. Sale	Goods Sale	Infras. Facilities Use	Services Sale	Tech. Use & Sale	Social Infras. Use	Foreign Exchange	–	Invest. in Capital

*Rows read sector input; columns read sector output.

247

Using these components as major variables, the author then constructed an elaborate mathematical model to simulate the general workings of an industrial dynamics system. Several prototype simulation runs were produced through the application of plausible sets of model parameters reflective of the general characteristics of a developing economy.

An Illustrative Model Run

The simulation program was executed for an 80 year period, from the year 1960 to 2040. Several model variables were plotted over the simulation time period for observation. Figure 3 is a plot of population, POP, population living standard, POLVST, and income per capita, INPC. As shown, population maintains a steady exponential growth pattern. It doubles after 23 years from the simulation starting time. By the year 2010, its growth rate declines and for the next 30 years population increases by only 75 percent of its size. The other variables, POLVST and INPC, are functions of population.

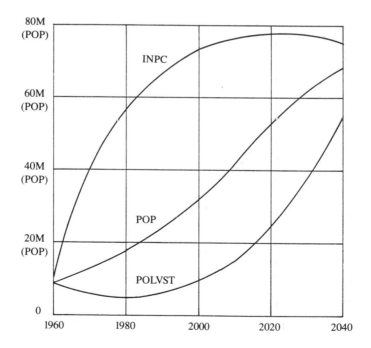

Fig. 3: Population (POP), Pop. Living Standards (POLVST), and Income Per Capita (INPC) Plots.

POLVST depends on the per capita share of several production levels. It declines slightly during the first 20 years of the simulation time, and then about 1980 it begins a steady upward trend. On the other hand, INPC rises sharply during the 1960 to 1980 period, after which its growth rate slows down. INPC remains stationary from 2000 to 2020, and then it begins a slow downward trend. The behavior of POLVST and INPC can be explained in relation to the two main driving forces: population and investment capital. As capital investment increases, the system production levels also increase. Nevertheless, POLVST does not begin to rise until 1980. This can be attributed to two factors: time lag between investment and benefits realization, and high population growth rate. After that time POLVST rises steadily in response to increased production levels and slower population growth rate.

On the other hand, INPC responds quickly to the increased capital investment. This is attributed to increased labor participation in the production activities which brings direct income benefits to the population. However, the change in the INPC curve from growth, to equilibrium, and finally to a decline, is caused by resource production rate changes.

Population Growth Rate Effects on Systems Performance

The population growth rate influence on system performance was investigated by increasing the population birth rate normal, BRN, from 0.035 to 0.040 and 0.045.

Figure 4 shows the effect of the changes in BRN. As shown, population grows in a 100 year period from an initial 10 million to 90, 180, and 440 million for a BRN of 0.035, 0.040, 0.045 respectively. The effect of these changes on system performance was mostly quantitative, while its qualitative behavior was generally the same. This behavior is attributed, in part, to the system's initial state specification which reflects plentiful supply of resources and agricultural land. This initial system state is supplemented by a relatively high capital savings rate of 10 percent which generated investment capital for various system development activities.

Savings Rate Effect on System Behavior

In the model, investment capital is generated from population savings. The fraction of population income allocated to saving, SAINM, was set to 0.10 in the first simulation run. The model was then run with the SAINM

249

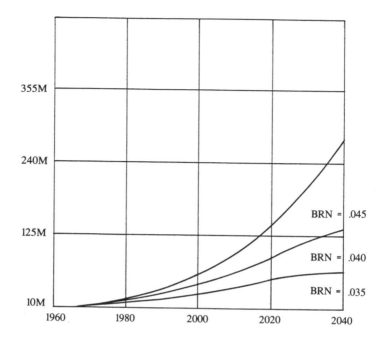

Fig. 4: Birth Rate Effect on Population Growth

set to 0.05 and 0.20. The effect of these changes on the model behavior was substantial. Figure 5 shows the performance of several system variables when SAINM was set to 0.05. As shown, population in the year 2040 is 180 million, which exceeds that of the initial run by over 100 million. Consequently, population living standards and income per capita fall below those of the initial run.

The system behavior was almost reversed when the SAINM was set to 0.20. Figure 6 shows the plots of population, living standard and income per capita. As shown, population growth rate slows as POLVST rises. During the first 30 years of the simulation, population doubles in size (from 10M in 1960 to 20M in 1990). However, for the next 50 years it grows only to 1.6 of its size (from 20M in 1990 to 32M in 2040.) POLVST rises steadily during the simulation in response to higher capital investment in the system production activities and lower population growth rate.

250

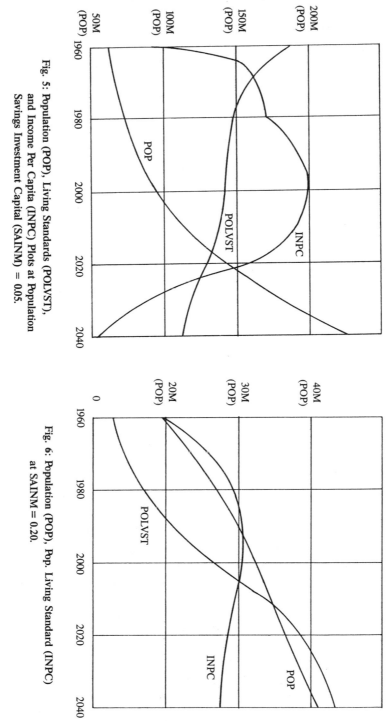

Fig. 5: Population (POP), Living Standards (POLVST), and Income Per Capita (INPC) Plots at Population Savings Investment Capital (SAINM) = 0.05.

Fig. 6: Population (POP), Pop. Living Standard (INPC) at SAINM = 0.20.

251

Policy Alternative for Capital Investment

The basic model structure assigns investment capital to the various system activities according to a uniform proportionate policy. The simulation run described earlier shows the model behavior under that policy. In addition, several capital investment policies were investigated by assigning investment priority to selected development sectors. During the early simulation run, the model's major production levels demand-to-supply ratios were observed. It was found that among the highest ratios were those of the manufacturing production capacity, technology, physical infrastructure, and social infrastructure levels.

In view of these findings, the capital investment policy was changed such that a selected sector's demand for investment capital was filled first. However, capital investment in the priority sector was not allowed to exceed 25 percent of the total available investment capital. Investment capital remaining after the priority sector's share was then distributed proportionally between the other sectors. The capital priority policy was then applied to each of the four levels identified as development bottlenecks.

Four simulation runs pertaining to capital priority investment in the technology, TECH, social infrastructure, SOIN, manufacturing, MFG, and physical infrastructure, PHIN, sectors were executed and various system parameters were observed. Subsequently, several performance variables from each of the four priority policy simulations and the initial run were plotted for comparison. Figure 7 shows population growth under the five capital investment policies. As shown, the MFG priority policy led to the highest population level, while the lowest population resulted from the SOIN priority assignment. The effects of these policies on the population living standards are shown in Figure 8. The highest POLVST is accomplished by the SOIN priority policy, while its lowest measures are from the MFG priority. Income per capita is at its highest when priority was assigned to TECH, figure 9, until the year 2023 when the MFG priority yielded the highest INPC. The lowest INPC, however was caused by the PHIN priority until 2005 when its rank was taken over by the SOIN priority.

252

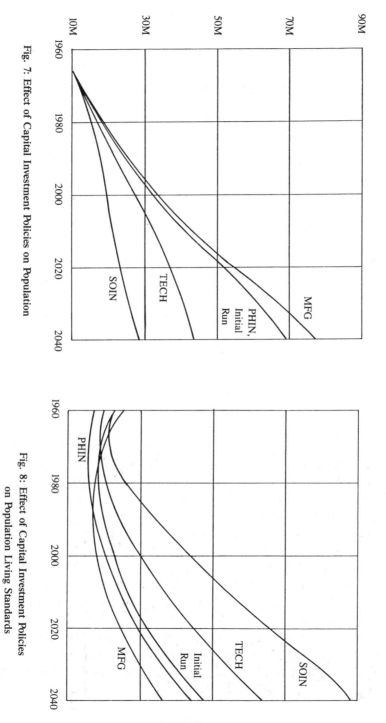

Fig. 7: Effect of Capital Investment Policies on Population

Fig. 8: Effect of Capital Investment Policies on Population Living Standards

253

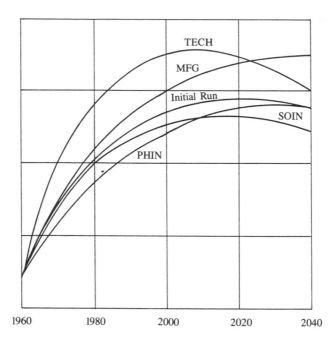

Fig. 9: Effect of Capital Investment Policies on Income Per Capita

High Income Development Example

An example of a high-income developing economy was simulated (10). A high-income developing economy is characterized by high resources and investment capital levels and relatively low population level. In this example, the development behavior trends were observed over an 80 year period (1980-2060.) Figure 10 shows the population, living standard, and income per capita plots. Population living standard remains relatively stable throughout the simulation time. However, INPC rises slightly between 1980 and 2000, then it follows a relatively smooth stable curve. INPC declines between 2020 and 2050 and then begins an upward trend. Figure 11 shows the manufacturing capacity, MFGC, agricultural production, AGP, technology, TECH, and social infrastructure SOIN, growth level trends. As shown, MFGC grows steadily due to high levels of investment in the manufacturing sector. AGP rises sharply during the first 15 years of the simulation, remains stable between 1995 and 2035, then begins an upward trend. TECH and SOIN show steady growth levels throughout the simulation time.

254

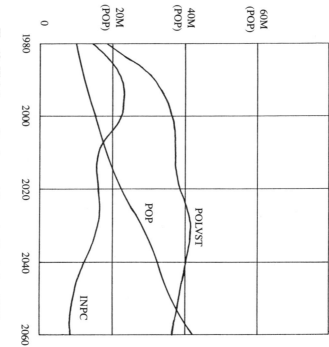

Fig. 10: High-income Development Example. Population (POP),
Living Standard (POLVST), and Income Per Capita
(INPC) Behavior Trends.

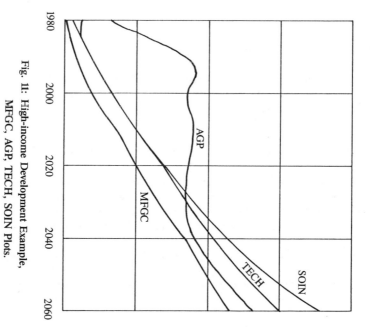

Fig. 11: High-income Development Example,
MFGC, AGP, TECH, SOIN Plots.

255

Conclusion

There are clearly strong and valid reasons for the construction of a system dynamics model for the process of industrial development in Saudi Arabia. Most importantly the model would serve the following objectives.

1. Provide an understanding of the industrial development system behavior and the interactions between its components.
2. Serve as a laboratory for examining various behavioral modes of the development process.
3. Aid in the analysis and design of general industrial development strategies and policies by providing some insight into their potential impact.
4. Identify the factors most critical to industrial developmental progress and show how they would react to different stimuli.

REFERENCES

Ansari, Jared A. and Singer, Hans W. *Rich and Poor Countries*, George Allen and Unwin, London, 1977. (3rd ed. 1982)

Forrester, Jay W. *Industrial Dynamics*, MIT Press, Cambridge, Mass., 1961.

Forrester, Jay W. *Principles of Systems*, Wright Allen Press, Cambridge, Mass., 1968.

Forrester, Jay W. *Urban Dynamics*, MIT Press, Cambridge, Mass., 1969.

Forrester, Jay W. *World Dynamics*, Wright-Allen Press Inc., Cambridge, Mass., 1971. (2nd ed., 1973)

Meadows, Dennis L., Donella H. Meadows, Jorgen Randers, and William W. Behrns III. *The Limits to Growth*, Universal Books, N.Y. 1972.

Meadows, Dennis L., William W. Behrens III, Donella H. Meadows, Roger F. Nail, Jorgen Randers and Erick K.O. Zahn, *Dynamics of Growth in a Finite World*, Wright Allen Press Inc., Cambridge, Mass., 1974.

Montjay, Alan B. *Industrialization and Underdeveloped Countries*, Willey-Interscience, N.Y., 1971.

Piccardi, Anthony C. "A Demographic and Economic Growth Model for Bolivia," Simulation, April 1973, pp. 109-118.

Reda, Hussein M. "A Theory for National Industrial Development Presented in a System Dynamics Model," Ph.D. dissertation, Virginia Tech., Blacksburg, Va., USA, 1985.

Reda, Hussein M and T.J.Green. "As Prototype Simulation Model for the Study of Socio-Economic Development Systems," Proceedings of the 1986 Summer Computer Simulation Conference, Reno, Nevada, USA.

Sharif, Nawaz and Pakron Abdulbhan, ed. *Systems Models for Decision Making*, Pergamon Press Inc., Oxford, England, 1978.

Sharp, J.A. "System Dynamics Applications in industrial and Other Systems," *Operations Research Quarterly*, Vol. 28, 3, pp. 489-504.

PART V:

MULTINATIONAL CORPORATIONS: RESPONSIBILITY & LEADERSHIP

INTRODUCTION:

Trade has been known since early history, and the Arabian Peninsula witnessed, in the third millennium B.C., a high volume of international trade by the standards of the time (as indicated in the introduction to Part I). Multinational corporations (MNCs), however, are the 20th century vehicle for such international commerce. MNCs play a significant role in the global economy, including both industrial and developing countries.

However, few countries in the world today enjoy the stability, security, progress and participation (SSPP), which Saudi Arabia does. This has provided an encouraging environment for MNCs to invest and produce in Saudi Arabia, both for the Saudis and for global welfare. In this process, MNCs assume economic activities and shoulder social burdens.

"THE SOCIAL RESPONSIBILITY OF THE MULTINATIONAL CORPORATIONS OPERATING IN SAUDI ARABIA" by Mohammed Farid Y. Kurashi, as summarized here by Constance B. Joy, is the first study of its kind to explore, in depth and from a scientific approach, the impact and influence of the many MNCs operating in Saudi Arabia in terms of social responsibility. Dr. Kurashi approaches the subject from three perspectives: (1) theoretical, (2) empirical, and (3) personal. He closes with his recommendations for the future. Contribution of MNCs to the economy of Saudi Arabia is recognized, and the author presents actual statistics on their number, their countries of origin, and the variety of ways they have contributed to the country's development.

Responses to the various questions in the study were categorized and analyzed for both Saudi and non-Saudi respondents. As might be expected, the Saudi responses were more protective in nature, with a greater tendency than non-Saudi to blame MNCs for social problems and to feel that the MNCs should do more in terms of contributing to the well-being of society. Paradoxically, one of Kurashi's findings in the study was that wholly-owned Saudi companies were no more concerned for the social responsibility of their companies than other MNCs.

Kurashi's recommendations for change and improvement in the area of corporate social contribution are both logical and responsible. Many could be implemented with little more than a greater awareness of the situation, as brought to light by this study, and very little commitment of resources.

Further, the Saudi business community should demonstrate more patriotism in their investment and contribute to the Saudization of the workforce in the private sector. The end result would certainly be one of benefit to the companies and the people of Saudi Arabia.

On the organizational level, Dr. Abdul-Rahim Al-Gattan, in his article "TEST OF THE PATH-GOAL THEORY OF LEADERSHIP IN THE MULTINATIONAL DOMAIN," examines the relationship between leadership style (directive, supportive, participative, achievement-oriented, and maintenance), and employee performance and satisfaction. This leader-subordinate relationship is tempered by numerous forces and factors including characteristics of employees and features of the work environment, both internal and external.

Employing several and different types of organizations, and subjects from various nationalities working in Saudi Arabia, Dr. Al-Gattan sits to test theories of organizational behavior, and proposes a contingency model of leadership based on the subordinate's task, growth need, and locus of control. These three factors, Dr. Al-Gattan asserts, moderate the relationship between leadership style and subordinate performance and satisfaction. In short, he emphasizes the significant correlation between leader behaviors and employee satisfaction, and hence the universal applicability of the path-goal theory.

THE SOCIAL RESPONSIBILITY OF THE MULTINATIONAL CORPORATIONS OPERATING IN SAUDI ARABIA

Dissertation by Mohammed Farid Y. Kurashi, Claremont Graduate School, 1984

Summary of the dissertation by Constance B. Joy

Since 1970 Saudi Arabia has experienced an enormous rise in wealth and a subsequent rapid expansion of its economy. This has been especially true since the increase in oil prices in the early seventies. Hundreds of government projects have been funded and innumerable new private businesses have been established. Many of these businesses, large corporations in particular, have been multinational and they have consequently had a substantial impact not only on economic growth, but also on social, educational and cultural change for the Saudi Arabian people. Mohammed Farid Kurashi focuses in his study on that impact with special attention to the social responsibilities which multinational corporations incur, or are perceived to incur, by virtue of locating in Saudi Arabia and being in a position to train, educate and aid employees and society at large. The study assesses corporate social responsibility from several perspectives: a theoretical perspective, based on literature in the field; an empirical perspective based on interviews with and questionnaire responses from both Saudis and non-Saudis connected with multinational corporations in Saudi Arabia; and a personal perspective based on the results of his empirical and theoretical work, as well as his recommendations for the future.

Kurashi's study is the first to explore multinational corporations (hereafter referred to as MNCs) in terms of social responsibility in any sort of depth from a scientific point of view. His chief concern was to obtain empirical data on four primary subjects of interest:

- the number and types of MNCs operating in Saudi Arabia;

- Saudi and non-Saudi opinions as to what the social responsibilities of these firms should be;
- actual participation of MNCs in Saudi Arabia in programs reflecting social responsibility roles;
- Saudi opinions as to the impact MNCs were having on various aspects of Saudi life.

The first information he was able to gather from government sources in Saudi Arabia, primarily the Ministry of Commerce statistics. Data for the other areas he obtained by conducting his own survey of 160 firms and managers, and from interviews with top echelon government and university officials in the Kingdom.

According to statistics gathered by the author, the number of commercial firms operating in the non-oil government and private sectors in Saudi Arabia quadrupled during the late 1970s, a staggering commentary. In 1977 there were 43,817 companies and establishments registered with the Department of Commerce, of which some 57 were joint ventures with foreign countries and seven were branches of foreign businesses.[1] By 1981 the total number of firms had reached 172,298, and by the end of 1982 MNCs accounted for 1,794 of these firms representing three basic types: 794 joint ventures, 777 firms contracting with government agencies, and 38 branches of foreign companies.[2] The total value of capital for joint venture firms in 1980 was about 5,154 million Saudi riyals and the total value of contracts with government bodies about 160,702.5 million.[3]

These companies represented a large number of foreign countries, and as a consequence brought quite a variety of foreigners into the Kingdom. In 1982 there were 56 countries which had joint ventures and 41 which had government contracts. The USA had the highest total number of each (182 joint ventures and 117 contracts with government agencies), but Korea, with 49 government contracts, ranked first in the value of its contracts (32,901 million Saudi riyals or 20.5% of the total) largely due to its predominance in the field of construction. During the years from 1975 to 1980 there was a sharp rise in the value of joint venture contracts from 252 to 5154 million Saudi Riyals. The Saudi share gradually increased to 56.29% during that time while the non-Saudi share gradually decreased.

The MNCs were involved in wide variety of activities, but by far the greatest number of contracts were in construction and infrastructure installation. Almost half the foreign branches were involved in contracting (44.7%), the rest being primarily concerned with planning (15%), maintenance, soil tests and other services. Joint ventures concentrated in four main fields: construction (46.8%), manufacturing (21.2%), maintenance and technical services (14.9%), and marine services (5.34%). Government contracts heavily emphasized basic infrastructure projects and were concentrated in housing, water and sewage, seaports, military works, telegrams, post and telephone, airports, water desalination, roads, government and administration construction.[4]

According to legal type, practically all joint venture MNCs were designated as limited liability companies. 979 companies were of this type; 47 were joint liability companies; none were joint stock companies; 33 were mixed liability partnership companies; and none were mixed liability partnership companies by shares. All MNCs are required by law to conform to one of the legal forms and, as contractors, to have a Saudi agent.

Kurashi states that the meaning and value of social responsibility as it applies to the corporation has undergone considerable evolution over the last century. Until 1930, social responsibility was not generally considered by the public or by businessmen to be a concern of business organizations. Profit maximization was their key concern and owners, not companies, might make the choice to be philanthropists, but were not obligated to do so. Then in the 1950s public responsibility and business morality became social issues, and by the 1970s (at least in the US) corporations were often called upon not only to give to charity, engage in special training programs and offer education scholarships, but to solve such social problems as racial discrimination and pollution. At present, many large corporations feel it is their duty and role to be socially responsible and to allocate resources for a variety of social purposes.

In his own research, Kurashi gave the following operational definition to the term "social responsibility" for firms operating in Saudi Arabia: It is "the obligation of these corporations [is] to pursue their defined economic activities; to serve the interests of the stockholders (i.e. make a reasonable profit), the manpower within the organization (the internal environment), and the Saudi people in the Saudi environment (the external environment); and [to be] responsible for the impact of the corporations' activities on Saudi society in all aspects that do not violate Saudi government regulations."[5]

Kurashi hypothesized that, on the whole, Saudis would be more likely than non-Saudis to believe that MNCs should hold socially responsible roles in Saudi Arabia, but that this might vary by education, age, years in the corporation and other variables. He further conjectured that very likely MNCs were doing little to initiate programs which reflected concern for social responsibility. Finally, he speculated that Saudis were likely to have mixed feelings regarding the impact of MNCs on their lives, depending on whether social effects were seen as impinging on family, education, religion, crime rate, ethics, etc.

The Empirical Study

Methodology

In order to test his hypothoses Kurashi sent questionaires to 201 Saudi corporations and 509 foreign MNCs. The Saudi corporations were selected on the basis of having a high percentage of foreign managers and therefore could be regarded as multinational. Kurashi defined an MNC to be "a firm operating through ownership or management, or both, in more than one country. In reference to Saudi Arabia, this term includes all firms working in Saudi Arabia whose homes are entirely abroad, and corporations that are partially owned by the Saudi Arabian people or government but jointly managed by foreign firms or managers, or corporations that are wholly owned by Saudis but managed by non-Saudis."[5] Kurashi had a return rate of 56.7% of the questionaires for the saudi corporations, of which 21.9% were useable. They represented 44 Saudi firms in total. 49.3% of the foreign MNCs returned questionaires and 31.4% were useable, representing 148 firms.

In addition to the questionaire, the author conducted several personal interviews with prominant university and government officials. The results of these talks were used in the study for descriptive purposes only, not for statistical analysis, but they helped to flesh out the study and to make meaning of some of the results as viewed from differing perspectives.

Sample

The sample consisted of two main groups: Saudi (110 respondents), and non-Saudi (144 respondents.[7] The Saudis composed three sub-groups of respondents: managers or owners (50.6%), government officials in ministries or agencies (13.6%) and elites working in large educational institutions with graduate degrees of MA or higher (35.5%). 75% of Saudi respondents worked in Saudi corporations and 80% had bachelor's or higher degrees. The non-Saudis composed five subgroups: Americans (17.9%), Europeans

(19%), Southeast Asians (10.5%) and Arabs (10.5%). The answers by Arab respondents were excluded from most analyses as they tended to agree with Saudi answers. Therefore non-Saudi also meant non-Arab for most answers.

Concerning corporation form, the large majority of non-Saudi firms were joint venture firms in the service area, except the southeast Asian firms which tended to be branch offices in construction and engineering. The Saudi firms spread themselves evenly over services (32.5%), trade (37.5%), and manufacturing (25%), with only 5% in construction. American, European and Asian firms were most likely to be in the service area and Southeast Asian firms overwhelmingly in construction.

As far as employees were concerned the great majority of the sample was composed of firms dominated by non-Saudi workers. 84% of the foreign MNCs had fewer than 25% Saudi employees and 56% of the Saudi firms had these few. 69.1% of foreign MNCs had fewer than 25% Saudi managers while Saudi firms tended to spread themselves out where nationality of managers was concerned: 28.9% had fewer than 25%, and 28.6% of firms had 75% or more Saudi managers.

The Hypotheses and the Results of the Study

Ten basic research hypotheses were tested, each consisting of one or more statements. Responses were rated on a 4 point scale as follows: $1 =$ strongly agree, $2 =$ agree, $3 =$ disagree, $4 =$ strongly disagree. A low mean indicated agreement while a high mean indicated disagreement with the statement. Several tests were conducted on the results, including t-tests of significance of difference, ANOVA, and correlations between variables. The group means and the results of the t-tests are presented in table one at the end of this article. Where the results of other tests are particularly interesting, they are presented within the context of the discussion below.

Hypothesis One:[8] Saudis are more in agreement than non-Saudis that MNCs are concerned with their own self-interest than the interest of Saudi society. This hypothesis was tested by responses to five statements and was generally supported. (see table one)

statement 1 (variable 19): "The corporation, acting in its own self-interest will help the public good in society." Saudis tended to agree with this statement significantly less than non-Saudi respondents, although both tended to agree. A correlational analysis showed that better educated Saudis were

265

more likely to agree than less educated Saudis. Also, for non-Saudis, those from larger corporations tended to agree while those from corporations which expected to continue operations tended to disagree.

statement 2 (variable 20): "MNCs operating in Saudi Arabia are protecting and enhancing the interests of Saudi society and the public at large." Here Saudis tended to disagree while non-Saudis tended to agree. The difference was significant. A correlational analysis showed that for Saudis, two variables correlated positively at a significant level: the percentage of Saudi employees, and the number of Saudi managers. These groups of Saudis were more likely to disagree. For non-Saudis the only group significantly different from the others and likely to disagree with the statement was from companies which had been in Saudi Arabia for a longer time.

statement 3 (variable 21): "Multinational corporations are highly concerned with profit maximization." Both Saudis and non-Saudis tended to agree with the statement, but Saudis significantly more than non-Saudis. For Saudis, the statement correlated positvely with the number of years in the corporation and for non-Saudis with higher education. In both cases they were less likely to agree. Kurashi suggests this reflects Saudi and non-Saudi managers' and owners' reluctance to see their firms accused of such a highly charged assertion.

statement 4 (variable 32): "Multinational corporations have contributed significantly to the economic development of Saudi Arabia." Both Saudis and non-Saudis agreed, but non-Saudis significantly less than Saudis. The statement correlated positively with only one variable for non-Saudis, that of number of years with the corporation. Strangely, this group tended to disagree with the statement although they had lived in Saudi Arabia longer and consequently were more likely to have seen the effects of economic development.

statement five (variable 54): "Multinational corporations should provide their stockholders with reasonable profits." Saudis and non-Saudis tended to agree with this statement, but Saudis were in significantly higher agreement. For non-Saudis, those working with a company for a longer time tended to be more likely to agree.

In conclusion, the first hypothesis was supported. Saudis differed significantly from non-Saudis on each statement. They differed most often with Europeans (4/5 comparisons) and Southeast Asians (3/5 comparisons), and least with Americans (2/5 comparisons) or Arabs (1/5 comparisons), according to Tukey B test results.

Hypothesis Two: [10] Saudis are higher in agreement than non-Saudis that MNCs have a negative impact on Saudi society. This hypothesis was tested and supported by responses to three statements.

statement six (variable 24): "The flow of foreign laborers has increased the crime rate in Saudi Arabia". All respondents tended to agree with the statement, but Saudis agreed significantly more than non-Saudis. Moreover, Saudi responses were significantly different from those of Europeans and Southeast Asians, but not from those of Americans and other Arabs. Those Saudis with higher education and employed by larger companies were less likely to agree. It seems they might consider "crime" to be a function of other variables as well, possibly increased Saudi national income. Among non-Saudis, those working longer in Saudi Arabia and those with a larger number of Saudi managers were more likely to agree with the statement.

statement seven (variable 25): "Transfer of technology benefits foreign laborers more than Saudis." Both Saudis and non-Saudis disagreed, but Saudis were significantly less likely to do so. Saudis with higher education were the most likely to agree with the statement and Kurashi speculates that this is because they observe MNCs giving technical jobs to skilled, cheaper paid expatriates, rather than giving Saudis the chance and time to be trained. Non-Saudis from companies expecting to stay longer in the Kingdom were more likely to disagree.

statement eight (variable 33): "The existence of Multinational Corporations in Saudi society has made Saudi people more materialistic and less spiritual." In responding to this statement Saudis tended to agree while non-Saudis tended to disagree. The difference is significant only between Saudis and Americans, not other nationality groups. For Saudis, the response did not correlate with any other variable studied. However, for non-Saudis, those who were older, had worked in Saudi Arabia longer, and had a higher percentage of Saudi employees tended to disagree more with the statement. Kurashi thought this might be because non-Saudis saw the practices of prayer, fasting, etc. as indicators of continued spirituality, but that Saudi respondents agreed with the statement because they felt such practices did not necessarily reflect spiritual feelings.

Hypothesis Three: [11] Saudis are in higher agreement than non-Saudis that MNCs should provide medical care and housing for their employees. This hypothesis was tested via three statements and was also supported.

statement nine (variable 43): "MNCs should provide medical care for their employees." Both Saudis and non-Saudis tended to agree with the statement, but Saudis more so, and educated Saudis the most of all. The differences were significant.

statement ten (variable 44): "Medical care for Saudi employees' families should be provided by MNCs." Both Saudis and non-Saudis agreed, but Saudis significantly more so.

statement eleven (variable 45): "MNCs have a responsibility regarding housing for Saudi employees." Saudis were in significantly higher agreement than non-Saudis in responding to this statement. The differences were significant between Saudis and each other nationality group, but the statement did not correlate with any other variable for Saudis. For non-Saudis the statement correlated negatively with percentage of Saudi employees, suggesting those with more Saudi workers are more likely to agree.

Hypothesis Four:[12] Saudis are more in agreement than non-Saudis that MNCs should contribute in the area of training, research and education. This hypothesis was tested through responses to nine statements and was also supported.

statement twelve (variable 35): "Scholarships for Saudi students should be provided by MNCs."

statement fourteen (variable 37): "Grants for Saudi researchers should be a part of MNCs social responsibility in Saudi society."

statement twenty (variable 46): "School facilities should be built by MNCs."

For all three of the above statements Saudis tended to agree while non-Saudis tended to disagree. The differences were significant. For statement twelve, Saudis with a higher level of education were more likely to agree, and non-Saudis in large companies and with more Saudi employees were also significantly more likely to agree. For statement fourteen, Saudis from large companies with a larger number of managers were less likely to agree, while non-Saudis from large companies were more likely to agree. These patterns seem to suggest that big companies abroad are more likely to have such programs as grants and scholarships, and therefore employees find it not unusual to agree. Saudis might be agreeing out of self-interest.

statement thirteen (variable 36): "Scholarships for Saudi employees should be provided by MNCs".

statement fifteen (variable 38): "MNCs should cooperate with Saudi researchers."

statement sixteen (variable 39): "MNCs should have on-site training for Saudi managers in the corporations."

statement seventeen (variable 40): "MNCs should provide training for Saudi managers in the corporation."

statement eighteen (variable 41): "MNCs should provide training for Saudi managers in foreign countries."

statement nineteen (variable 42): "Summer training for Saudi students should be provided by MNCs."

Both Saudis and non-Saudis tended to agree with all six of the above statements, but in each case Saudis were in significantly higher agreement. For statements fifteen, sixteen and seventeen, non-Saudis who had been in the country a longer time were in higher mean agreement. On the other hand, Saudis from larger companies were less likely to agree with statement fifteen, those with more managers were less likely to agree with sixteen, those who had worked for the company for a longer time were more likely to agree with seventeen, and those with more Saudi managers tended to agree with eighteen. For Saudis, some of the agreement appears to stem from self-interest and the perceived possibility that better training might mean more promotions in the Saudization process of the companies.

Hypothesis Five:[13] Saudis are in higher agreement than non-Saudis that Saudis should hold key managerial positions in MNCs. This hypothesis was tested via a single statement and was supported.

statement twenty-one (variable 53): "Key managerial positions should be held by Saudis." Saudis were in significantly higher agreement with this statement than non-Saudis. correlational analysis showed that both Saudis and non-Saudis who had worked in their corporations longer tended to be more likely to agree. Also non-Saudis who were older and had more Saudi managers were more likely to agree. It appears that non-Saudis who had more experience in the Kingdom, or with Saudis, were more likely to take the Saudi viewpoint.

Hypothesis Six:[14] Saudis are in higher agreement than non-Saudis that MNCs should provide non-profit organizations with financial support, and technical and administrative assistance. This hypothesis was tested through the use of two statements and was supported. In examining group differences through analysis of variance tests however, it was found that the significant differences existed only between Saudis and one other nationality group, the Europeans.

statement twenty-two (variable 31): "Multinational corporations should

269

financially support humanitarian, cultural and social organizations in Saudi society." Saudis tended to agree with this statement while non-Saudis tended to disagree. A correlational analysis showed that for non-Saudis those from large companies were significantly more likely to agree, probably since they know such a policy is common for large companies in their own countries.

statement twenty-three (variable 48): "Technical, administrative and consulting assistance to Saudi humanitarian, cultural and social organizations should be a part of MNCs social responsibility in Saudi society." Both groups tended to agree with this, although Saudis significantly more so. Saudis with more education and in corporations with more Saudi employees were more likely to agree. Non-Saudis who had worked in Saudi Arabia longer were also more likely to agree.

Hypothesis Seven:[15] Saudis are in higher agreement than non-Saudis that MNCs need to follow written guidelines and to have their own long-range plans concerning their role in Saudi Arabia. This hypothesis was tested via four statements and was only partially supported.

statement twenty-five (variable 26): "Multinational corporations should have long-range plans addressing their social impact on the Saudi society."

statement twenty-six (variable 27): "The Saudi government should provide multinational corporations with written guidelines on their roles in Saudi society."

statement twenty-seven (variable 28): "Multinational corporations need to prepare a formal written policy in regard to their roles in Saudi Arabia."

statement twenty-eight (variable 56): "Multinational corporations should have long-range plans on the corporations' roles in Saudi society."

Regarding statements 25, 26 and 28, both Saudis and non-Saudis tended to agree, but the difference between them was significant only regarding the first statement. For statement 27 Saudis agreed while non-Saudis tended to disagree that there should be formal written policies, and the difference was significant. Saudis from corporations with more Saudi employees were significantly more likely to agree, while non-Saudis from larger corporations were more likely to agree. As far as statement 28 was concerned, Saudis from larger corporations and with more Saudi employees thought MNCs should have long-range plans, as did non-Saudis who had worked in Saudi Arabia a longer time. However, older non-Saudis were significantly less likely to agree.

270

Hypothesis Eight:[16] Saudis have different expectations of MNCs' social responsibilities from non-Saudis. This was tested via three statements and was not supported. There were no significant differences between Saudis and non-Saudis on two out of the three statements.

statement twenty-nine (variable 29): "Multinational corporations must have the authority from the Saudi government to become involved in social, cultural and humanitarian activities if they are to perform in a socially responsible manner." Both Saudis and non-Saudis tended to disagree on average with this statement, but an ANOVA test of group differences showed that Americans and Saudis tended to disagree, while Europeans and Southeast Asians tended to agree. Saudis who were older and had worked for corporations longer also tended to agree.

statement thirty (variable 30): "Not all American MNCs operating in Saudi Arabia should be concerned with supporting humanitarian, cultural and social Saudi organizations."

statement thirty-one (variable 55): "MNCs should be involved in solving social problems."

Both Saudis and non-Saudis tended to disagree with the above two statements. There were no significant differences between them.

Hypothesis Nine:[17] Saudis are in higher agreement than non-Saudis that MNCs should cooperate with government agencies and Saudi companies in activities other than their defined ones. This hypothesis was tested by responses to two questions and was only partially supported.

statement thirty-two (variable 49): "MNCs should provide technical, administrative and consulting assistance to Saudi companies." Both Saudis and non-Saudis tended to agree with this statement, but Saudis significantly more than non-Saudis. A correlational analysis showed that Saudis working for corporations with a larger number of managers were less likely to agree, perhaps meaning that Saudi managers tend to adapt the non-Saudi majority viewpoint. However, Saudis with more work experience and higher education were more likely to agree.

statement thirty-three (variable 50): "MNCs should provide technical, administrative and consulting assistance to Saudi government agencies." Both Saudis and non-Saudis agreed with this statement and there were no signficiant differences between them. More educated Saudis and non-Saudis who had worked in the Kingdom longer had the highest average levels of agreement.

271

Hypothesis Ten:[18] Saudis are higher in agreement than non-Saudis that MNCs should contribute to introducing Saudi culture to their non-Saudi employees and workers. This hypothesis was tested via three statements and was partially supported.

statement thirty-four (variable 51): "MNCs should teach the Arabic language to their non-Arab employees." Both Saudis and non-Saudis tended to agree with this statement with no significant differences between them. Saudis who had worked longer with their present corporations were more likely to agree, perhaps reflecting the fact that English continues to be a problem for many where the majority of managers are non-Saudi.

Statement thirty-five (variable 52): "MNCs should have programs for explaining Saudi law and culture to non-Saudi employees." Both groups tended to agree, but Saudis were in significantly higher agreement than non-Saudis. Saudis from companies with more Saudi managers were less likely to agree, possibly feeling less need, while non-Saudis with more education and working where there were more Saudis also were less likely to agree, perhaps meaning they found other ways to gain such knowledge. On the other hand, those non-Saudis who had worked in the Kingdom longer were more likely to agree, suggesting they had run into, or heard about, problems because they were uninformed.

In conclusion, Kurashi found that six of his hypotheses were supported and four partially supported. Of 34 statements, 82% showed significant differences between Saudis and non-Saudis. For Saudis, years of education and percentage of Saudi employees or managers were most often found to correlate with the attitude statements. For non-Saudis, those who had worked longer in the Kingdom tended more often to hold views similar to Saudis.

In addition to hypothesis testing, Kurashi asked each respondent to list the actual programs relating to social responsibility his corporation provided. His results are reported by nationality and type of ownership form, but only the first are reported here (see Table 2 at the end of this paper). In general, he found that only a small minority provided scholarships or cooperated with Saudi researchers. More had training programs and gave donations to non-profit organizations, but still only a minority. A majority provided medical care for their employees, but a minority for Saudi employees' families. Kurashi also asked each respondent to suggest ways of funding social, educational and humanitarian programs. By far the most favored response was as a percentage of profit. 48% of Saudis, 33% of Arabs, 34% of Americans, 38% of Europeans and 60% of Asians liked

272

this approach best. Most respondents, furthermore, suggested that MNCs should spend less than 3% of profits for funding such programs (36% Arabs, 50% American, 57% European, 68% Southeast Asian). However, only 16% of Saudis favored such a low percent—the majority favored between 3% and 10%.

Since theory and observance suggested that MNCs were having an impact on a broad variety of aspects of Saudi life, Kurashi decided to ask his Saudi respondents if this was so in a questionnaire given to them only in Arabic. For 27 variables he found the following results:[19]

—The majority of Saudis felt that MNCs have no effect on the following six aspects: family ties, marriage, Saudi housewife, the application of the Islamic law, humanitarian organizations, and consumer protection.

—The majority of Saudis (50-73%) felt that MNCs have positive impacts on the following five social aspects: development of technical skills, development of managerial skills, research and development, employment in the private sector, and Saudi economic policies. Also, 37% to 47% of Saudis associate positive effects with MNCs on the following four aspects: national wealth of Saudi Arabia, preserving old architecture, Saudization of key positions, and the use of foreign languages.

—The majority of Saudis associated negative effects with MNCs in relation to the following seven aspects: ethics in Saudi society, commitment to Islamic values, materialistic luxuries, use of the Arabic language, traffic, foreign labor, and company camps.

—The opinion of the majority of Saudis was divided in regard to the effect of MNCs on the following aspects: working women, ethics in work environment, materialistic necessities, housing and environment protection. Opinion seems to be influenced by individuals' convictions on such activities. For example, some who favor Saudi women working outside the house felt that MNCs have positive effects on working women, while those who felt that women should only be housewives felt that MNCs have negative impacts on working women.

—Of all social aspects that many Saudis seem to associate with MNCs, foremost is the existence of a large number of expatriates in Saudi Arabia. The empirical study indicated that the majority of Saudis view negatively foreign labor in Saudi Arabia. Several magazines and newspapers have discussed the problems associated with foreign laborers and recommended reduction in their size. Saudi government officials as well as Saudi elites have called on various occasions for cutting the number of foreign laborers in the country. In fact, the current and the fourth development plan have called for the same thing.

—Finally, the study indicated that the majority of Saudis do not perceive the impact of American MNCs differently from MNCs in general."

Discussion of the Study

In summarizing the results of his study and the results of his interviews with Saudi government officials, businessmen, teachers, school children and citizens, Kurashi makes several additional interesting points:

1. Differences in his study between Saudis and non-Saudis were greatest where statements were made suggesting corporate social responsibility should go beyond the workplace. Saudis were more likely to think they should, whereas non-Saudi respondents thought in narrower terms.

2. Wholly-owned Saudi companies were no more concerned for the social responsibility of their companies than other MNCs and usually less so. Kurashi explains this as perhaps due to the fact that other MNCs find it necessary to promote their names and are more concerned for their continued existence in Saudi Arabia.

3. The fact that there was little concern by MNCs for training for management positions and human development and Saudization was partly due to cost and partly because foreign managers do not relish their replacement by Saudis, the eventual result of training and of course contrary to self-interest.

4. Most MNCs played little role in supporting humanitarian, social, cultural and educational organizations, but this was not due solely to their own attitudes and policy. In interviews with government officials and heads of charity organizations, Kurashi found that these people avoided asking MNCs for funds. This also was true of directors of three major research centers whom he approached at King Abd al-Aziz University. Only one director had tried asking for funds, and this in a very limited way. Furthermore, in interviews with Saudi citizens, Kurashi heard many stories concerning Saudi businessmen who were opportunists themselves and were very little concerned with issues of social responsibility, either for themselves or for MNCs. Some Saudi businessmen have been caught violating Ministry of Commerce regulations, many hire non-Saudis over Saudis, and few are concerned with charity. On the other hand, some have indeed been remarkable "model" businessmen. Kurashi cites a few businessmen who

274

have given more than 20% of their profits to humanitarian non-profit organizations and names SABIC as a model corporation in this respect.

5. In general, the media in Saudi Arabia endorses and fosters the point of view that humanitarian organizations should approach individual businessmen or banks for funding, not MNCs or businesses themselves. This may also in part explain the reluctance to ask MNCs for charity donations or funding for research projects.

6. Kurashi believes that MNCs, and especially the increase of foreign labor they have brought with them into the country, have had a much greater impact on life in the Kingdom than the results of his empirical study would indicate. Regarding the family, he feels that the common use of foreign household labor, many of whom do not even speak Arabic, has resulted in a great deal of internal change in family life, values and habits. Also, many statistics show a rise in several types of crime, such as drug and alcohol use, theft, adultery, rape, prostitution and traffic violations, as well as an increase in sexual disease. Most of these crimes are attributable to foreigners, although some are committed by Saudis. The increase may in part be due to better reporting of these crimes and better methods of recording and gathering statistics. However, many experts agree that these crimes were almost unknown in the Saudi Arabia of 50 years ago, a conservative religious society with few foreigners and mostly small towns and villages. Big anonoymous cities and enormous differences in wealth also account for some of the differences, but don't explain why foreigners commit most crimes.

7. Saudi government officials seem to agree that MNCs are doing little toward fulfilling socially responsible roles, however they disagreed on what the scope of those roles should be. For instance, the Minister of Planning thought MNCs' responsibility should be limited to economic activities whereas the Vice president of SABIC thought roles should be broader. Others interviewed were also divided on their opinions.

Recommendations

In order for MNCs to play an important role in Saudi society that is consistent with the goals of Saudi development plans and that serves the Saudi national interest, Kurashi makes several recommendations, mostly based on the results of his study and interviews.[20] A few are included below:

—Saudi board directors need to ensure setting policies and implementing them regarding MNCs social responsibilities, and not leave such activities up to largely indifferent non-Saudi managers.

—Studies on the social, economic and political impact of MNCs, and on the current laws that regulate MNCs, are a paramount need.

—Saudi businessmen need to have more confidence in hiring nationals and developing promotion programs for them. They also should become more concerned with donating to humanitarian institutions and forming businessmen's associations where they can get involved with community issues.

—Government agencies need to become more efficient in dealing with MNCs. Kurashi suggests opening up a special MNC department within the Ministry of Commerce, separate from the Department of Companies, since MNCs have special needs which most companies don't. The agencies also should establish clear government guidelines for the role of MNCs in Saudi society.

—Officials in the Ministry of Social Affairs should hold conferences for people who work for non-profit organizations and teach them how to solicit funds from business firms. Government officials should also approach businesses and encourage them to contribute. The government should publish statistics on amounts of contributions and names of contributing companies in the annual reports. The agency of Zakat should require all corporations—including MNCs—to indicate in detail their contributions and the names of their benefactors.

—The goals of Saudization of managerial positions and reduction of foreign labor in the Kingdom need to be implemented.

—Community centers to introduce foreigners to Saudi culture and society should be established in urban centers.

—MNCs should get involved in organizations which may indirectly help their workers. These might include the Saudi national organizations which help free prisoners or pay medical care for traffic victims, etc. They should also get involved with media projects that help improve the image of Saudi Arabia abroad.

—The international schools in Saudi Arabia should establish better programs to introduce Saudi Arabian language and culture to their students.

—The various Saudi chambers of Commerce should become involved in conducting research on MNCs and make the results of their studies available to the public. They should also establish "charity funds" to which businessmen can contribute, and they should do more about promoting the image of Saudis abroad.

—Foreign commercial attaches should be more concerned with motivating MNCs to be socially responsible and influencing them to promote better relationships between their home countries and Saudi Arabia.

Footnotes

All footnotes are cited from pages in the dissertation.

1. pp. 86, 116.
2. pp. 113, 116, 123.
3. The statistics in this and the following paragraph are found on pages 116 and 120.
4. pp. 124, 127.
5. p. 35.
6. p. 14.
7. See pages 172-187 for a complete sample description.
8. p. 191.
9. p. 198.
10. p. 199.
11. p. 206.
12. p. 212.
13. p. 222.
14. p. 223.
15. p. 227.
16. p. 232.
17. p. 237.
18. p. 241.
19. p. 312.
20. p. 315*ff.*

TABLE 1

Saudi and Non-Saudi Differences on Hypotheses Statements

(t-tests)

Statement		Saudi			Non-Saudi		
	n	x	SD	n	X	SD	t
Hypothesis One							
Concerns for self interest to help public good (v19)	102	2.41	.87	105	2.06	.93	2.83**
MNCs in SA protecting the public good (v20)	92	2.68	.85	95	1.93	.70	6.65***
MNCs in SA are chiefly concerned with profit (v21)	102	1.50	.64	108	1.87	.83	3.62***
MNCs contribution to econ. devel. plans (v32)	94	1.88	.51	116	1.54	.64	5.31**
Reasonable profit for owners (v54)	93	1.60	.63	105	1.78	.46	2.26*
Hypothesis Two							
The flow of foreign laborers to SA (v24)	97	1.79	.71	87	2.16	.79	3.33**
Transfer of advanced technology (v25)	100	2.42	.08	112	3.13	.07	6.66**
Saudis become more materialistic (v33)	89	2.07	.86	84	2.54	.87	3.55
Hypothesis Three							
Medical care for employees (v43)	108	1.25	.46	106	1.71	.55	6.61**
Medical care for family (v44)	107	1.42	.60	93	2.10	.78	6.79***
Housing for Saudi employees (v45)	107	1.44	.62	84	2.41	.84	8.85**
Hypothesis Four							
Scholarships for students (v35)	103	1.72	.76	94	2.37	.92	5.43**
Scholarships for employees (v36)	106	1.62	.70	96	2.15	.70	5.34
Grants for researchers (v37)	101	1.67	.76	85	2.37	.78	6.08**
Cooperation with Saudi researchers (v38)	106	1.38	.49	106	1.74	.46	5.49**
On-site training (v39)	108	1.31	.46	115	1.68	.63	5.06**
Training for managers in the corporation (v40)	107	1.36	.48	113	1.69	.58	4.66**
Training for managers in foreign countries (v41)	108	1.53	.62	107	1.89	.60	4.32**
Summer training (v42)	106	1.57	.60	93	1.95	.70	4.13**
Building school facilities for Saudis (v46)	96	2.07	1.00	93	2.66	.83	4.34**

Note. Each question was scored from 1 ("strongly agree") to 4 ("strongly disagree") with "undecided" responses excluded.

**p < .01   < *p .05

278

TABLE 1 (continued)

Saudi and Non-Saudi Differences on Hypotheses Statements

(t-tests)

Statement	Saudi				Non-Saudi			
	n	x	SD	n	X	SD	t	
Hypothesis Five								
Key managerial positions for Saudis (v53)	98	1.47	.63	78	2.17	.73	6.81**	
Hypothesis Six								
MNCs financial assist to nonprofit orgs. (v31)	103	1.89	.71	87	2.28	.77	3.55**	
Technical and financial assist. to non-profit org. (v48)	103	1.71	.74	95	1.96	.56	2.69**	
Hypothesis Seven								
MNCs should have long range plans (v26)	93	2.04	.85	98	1.99	.73	.47ns	
Government should provide written guidelines (v27)	102	1.51	.71	110	1.96	.71	4.55**	
MNCs need a written policy (v28)	97	2.08	.64	94	2.02	.69	.57ns	
Long range plans on the corporate goal (v56)	91	2.08	.64	94	2.02	.69	57ns	
Hypothesis Eight								
MNCs must have the authority from govt (v29)	89	2.63	.83	98	2.20	.80	3.57**	
Not all MNCs should be concerned with s-r (v30)	100	2.53	.92	85	2.52	.85	.09ns	
Solving social problems (v55)	89	2.73	.84	88	2.72	.90	.11ns	
Hypothesis Nine								
Tech. and admin. assist. to Saudi companies (v49)	98	1.61	.59	101	2.06	.63	5.18**	
Tech. and admin. assist. to Saudi govt. (v50)	98	1.81	.74	104	1.96	.62	1.62ns	
Hypothesis Ten								
Arabic language programs (v51)	102	1.64	.59	99	1.80	.62	1.87ns	
Programs for explaining Saudi law and culture (v52)	104	1.43	.50	107	1.66	.53	3.26**	

Note. Each question was scored from 1 ("strongly agree") to 4 ("strongly disagree") with "undecided" responses excluded.

**p < .01   < *p .05

279

TABLE 2
Actual Programs Undertaken by MNCs Operating In Saudi Arabia by Nationality

Actual Programs	American			European			Southeast Asian			Total
	Do Not Have	Have	Total	Do Not Have	Have	Total	Do Not Have	Have	Total	
Scholarships for Saudi Students	91.5% 54	8.5% 5	100% 59	90.9% 50	9.1% 5	100% 55	96.4% 27	3.6% 1	100% 28	142
Grants for Saudi Researchers	96.6% 57	3.4% 2	100% 59	96.4% 53	3.6% 2	100% 55	96.4% 27	3.6% 1	100% 28	142
Cooperation with Saudi Researchers	59.3% 35	40.7% 24	100% 59	76.4% 42	23.6% 13	100% 55	78.6% 22	21.4% 6	100% 28	142
Training Programs for Saudi Managers	61.0% 36	39.0% 23	100% 59	65.5% 36	35.5% 19	100% 55	53.6% 15	46.4% 13	100% 28	142
Summer Training Programs	62.7% 37	37.3% 22	100% 59	69.1% 38	34.7% 17	100% 55	64.3% 18	35.7% 10	100% 28	142
Medical Care for Employees	30.5% 18	69.5% 41	100% 59	47.3% 26	52.7% 29	100% 55	17.9% 5	82.1% 23	100% 28	142
Medical Care for Family	61.0% 36	39.0% 23	100% 59	65.5% 36	34.5% 19	100% 55	60.7% 17	39.3% 11	100% 28	142
Financial Donation to Humanitarian, Cultural and Social Organization	71.2% 42	28.8% 17	100% 59	80.0% 44	20.0% 11	100% 55	64.3% 18	35.7% 10	100% 78	142
Technical Administrative and Consulting Assistance to Humanitarian, Cultural and Social Organizations	71.2% 42	28.8% 17	100% 59	80.0% 44	20.0% 11	100% 55	64.3% 18	35.7% 10	100% 28	142
Introduce Saudi Law and Culture	66.1% 39	33.9% 20	100% 59	76.4% 42	23.6% 13	100% 55	71.4% 20	28.6% 8	100% 28	142
Long-Range Plans on the Corporation's Role in Saudi Society	84.7% 50	15.3% 9	100% 59	89.1% 49	10.9% 6	100% 55	67.9% 19	32.1% 9	100% 28	142
Technical Training for Saudi Employees	96.6% 57	3.4% 2	100% 59	96.4% 53	3.6% 2	100% 55	92.9% 26	7.1% 2	100% 28	142

TEST OF THE PATH-GOAL THEORY OF LEADERSHIP IN THE MULTINATIONAL DOMAIN*

by Abduhl-Rahim A. Al-Gattan

Relationships between leader behaviors and subordinate satisfaction and performance, moderated by task scope, growth need strength, and locus of control, were tested in Saudi Arabia and the United States. The results appear to support path-goal theory's hypotheses in terms of satisfaction but fail to support them in terms of performance.

Studies of the universality of management theories have provided contradictory results. Some researchers believe that management theories developed in the United States are applicable in other countries (e.g., Haire, Ghiselli, and Porter, 1966; Heller & Porter, 1966; Richman & Copen, 1972). For instance, Richman and Copen (1972) believe that much of the management practices developed and applied in United States can be effective and is needed in India and other developing countries. On the other hand, Hofstede (1980) questions the assumption that management theories are universally applicable. He collected data from 116,000 employees of subsidiaries of one large U.S.-based Multinational Corporation (MNC) in forty different countries. According to his findings, it is more practical to adapt American management theories to local cultures than vice versa. He contends that because Likert and Vroom, for example, developed their system 4 management and expectancy theories, respectively, within the U.S. cultural context, it is naive to expect to generalize those theories to significantly different cultures. The objective of this study is to test the path-goal theory of leadership through the use of subjects from different countries working in a number of organizations in Saudi Arabia. Results of this study will be compared with the results of a similar study conducted in the United States (Al-Gattan, 1983).

Recently, the path-goal theory of leadership has evolved as a basic paradigm for the study and analysis of individual behavior and attitudes in the work environment (e.g., House, 1971; House & Mitchell, 1974;

Szilagyi & Wallace, 1980). The theory asserts that the leader-subordinate relationship is moderated by characteristics of the subordinate such as locus of control, growth need strength, and ability and by the characteristics of the work environment such as the tasks and work group of the subordinate and other organizatioinal factors (e.g., rules, procedures, and policies). In its original form (House, 1971), the theory described two types of leader behavior: directive and supportive. However, in its current form (House & Mitchell, 1974), the theory describes four types of leader behavior: directive, supportive, participative, and achievement-oriented.

The path-goal theory has never been subjected to a complete test. Portions of the theory, however, have been tested. Some supportive empirical studies of the theory are evident (e.g., Al-Gattan, 1983; Greene, 1979; Griffin, 1980; House & Dessler, 1974; Johns, 1978; Szilagyi & Sims, 1974; Valenzi & Dessler, 1978). Previous research, except Al-Gattan's, used samples from one or two U.S. organizations. Hence, the external validity of the results is questionable. Results cannot be generalized to other than the host organizations. For theories of organizational behavior to be applicable in all types of organizations of different countries, they must be developed and tested in all different types of organizations, as is the case in this research. Participants were full-time workers from different countries employed by a variety of organizatioins in Saudi Arabia. Furthermore, previous studies, except Griffin's and Al-Gattan's used the Ohio State Leadership scales to measure leader behavior. Accordinig to Schriesheim and Kerr (1974), the Ohio State leadership scales have some psychometric deficiencies and measure only initiating structure and consideration. Initiating structure and consideration, according to House and Dessler (1974), differ from directive and supportive leader behaviors, respectively.

More recently, Griffin (1980) and Al-Gattan (1983) operationalized the current form of the path-goal theory through the use of a new instrument. In addition, they used a new form of leader behavior, namely, maintenance leader behavior. This new style was originated by Griffin (1978) and modified by Al-Gattan (1983). It is similar to the concept of "substitute for leadership" (Kerr & Jermier, 1978).

Based on the path-goal theory of leadership and Griffin's work, Al-Gattan (1983) proposed a conceptual model that assumes that the appropriate style of leader behavior depends on three contingency factors: the subordinate's(a) task, (b) growth need strength, and (c) locus of control. These contingency factors moderate the relationships between the leader's style (independent variables) and the subordinate satisfaction (with job and supervision)

282

and performance (dependent variables). The objective of this study is to investigate, for this sample, the relationships between leader behavior (achievement-oriented, participative, directive, supportive, and maintenance), and the subordinate's satisfaction (with job and supervision) and performance, as moderated by the subordinate's task scope, growth need strength, and locus of control.

The moderating variables are, in reality, continuous variables, but to be used as moderators they will be dichotomized. In this case, tasks will be either high (unstructured) or low (structured) in scope. Similarly, growth need strength will be described as high or low, and locus of control will be described as internal (I) or external (E). This classfication permits the description of eight possible situations (cells) and suggests a number of testable hypotheses. Based on Al-Gattan's (1983) work, Table 1 presents a description of the eight cells in terms of the moderating variables, predicted leader behaviors, and the relationships between predicted leader behaviors and satisfaction and performance. The following eight hypotheses were tested:

(H_1) In the situation where task scope is high, growth need strength is high, and locus of control is internal (Cell 1), achieivement-oriented and participative leader behaviors will be more positively related than other leader behaviors to high levels of satisfaction and performance.

(H_2 In the situation where task scope is high, growth need strength is high, and locus of control is external (Cell 2), participative and directive leader behaviors will be more positively related than other leader behaviors to high levels of satisfaction and performance.

(H_3) In the situation where task scope is high, growth need strength is low, and locus of control is internal (Cell 3), participative and directive leader behaviors will be more positively related than other leader behaviors to high levels of satisfaction and performance.

(H_4) In the situatioin where task scope is high, growth need strength is low, and locus of control is external (Cell 4), directive leader behavior will be more positively related than other leader behaviors to high levels of satisfaction and performance.

(H_5) In the situation where task scope is low, growth need strength is high, and locus of control is internal (Cell 5), participative and supportive leader behaviors will be more positively related than other leader behaviors to high levels of satisfaction and performance.

(H_6) In the situation where task scope is low, growth need strength is high, and locus of control is external (Cell 6), directive and supportive leader behaviors will be more positively related than other leader behaviors to high levels of satisfaction and performance.

(H_7) In the situation where task scope is low, growth need strength is low, and locus of control is internal (Cell 7), participative and maintenance leader behaviors will be more positively related than other leader behaviors to high levels of satisfaction and performance.

(H_8) In the situation where task scope is low, growth need strength is low, and locus of control is external (Cell 8), maintenance leader behavior will be more positively related than other leader behaviors to high levels of satisfaction and performance.

METHOD

Sample and Procedure

The 466 subjects for this study were all males engaged in a variety of jobs in many organizations (e.g., oil industry, hospitals, government agencies, construction, hotels, public utilities, travel agencies, and others) in Saudi Arabia. Participants were full-time employees from different countries (e.g., Saudi Arabia, Pakistan, India, United States, Europe, the Philippines, South Korea, and other Arab countries). Questionnaires were administered to the subjects at their work sites. They were completed by the subjects during their own free time. More than 95% of the participants had completed at least some college education. Approximately 84% of the subjects were between 21 and 39 years of age.

Measures

Leader behavior. Based on factor analysis results presented by Al-Gattan (1983), Griffin (1978), and House and Dessler (1974), five items to measure achievement-oriented behavior, four items to measure participative behavior, five items to measure supportive behavior, five items to measure directive behavior, and two items to measure maintenance behavior were included in the leader behavior questionnaire. Griffin (1980) noted that these leader

284

behavior scales demonstrate very good construct validity and higher reliability. The scale reliability (Cronbach's alpha) for the five scales were as follows: Achievement-Oriented (.70); Participative (.66); Directive (.71); Supportive (.78); and Maintenance. (.42).

Task Scope. Task variety, identity, autonomy, and feedback were measured by the Job Characteristics Inventory (JCI) developed by Sims, Szilagyi, and Keller (1976). The JCI provided indices of each of these four characteristics with five, four, six, and six items, respectively. The scale reliabilities (Cronbach's alpha) for the five scales were as follows: Autonomy (.71); Feedback (.69); Identity (.73); Variety (.73) and Task Scope (.83)

Growth Need Strength. Individual growth need strength was measured by a 12-item subscale of the Job Diagnostic Survey (JDS) developed by Hackman and Oldham (1975). Al-Gattan (1983) noted that this scale demonstrated good reliability (alpha = .70).

Locus of Control. I-E locus of control was measured by Rotter's (1966) instrument, using 20 of his original 23 items. Three of Rotter's original items (numbers 5, 10, and 23), which deal with academics, were omitted as being inappropriate for this study. Al-Gattan (1983) found that this scale demonstrates high reliability (alpha = .81).

Satisfaction. Satisfaction with job and supervisioin was measured by subscales of the Job Descriptive Index (JDI) developed by Smith et al. (1969). Psychometric properties of the JDI were evaluated by Robinson, Athanasion and Head (1969). Al-Gattan (1983) noted that satisfaction with job and supervision demonstrate reliabilities of .84 and .86, respectively.

Performance. Qualitative performance of each participant was measured by self-evaluation. Each participant was asked to self-evaluate performance on four items (see Al-Gattan, 1983). Factor analysis of the scale resulted in a 3-item single factor with coefficient alpha of .79.

Statistical Analyses

The two most popular techniques to test moderating effects are moderated regression and subgroup analysis. The former was dismissed because researchers (see Zedeck, 1971, pp. 301-302) have found that moderated regression was less effective than subgroup analysis. Subgroup analysis (Zedeck, 1971) involves dividing a heterogeneous population into homogeneous subgroups on the basis of the moderating variables scores. Hence, the predictor-criterion relatioinship for some subset of these subgroups will be significantly different from that in another subgroup.

285

The three moderating variables (task scope, growth need strength, and locus of control) were scored according to the a priori format, and the median of each moderating variable was calculated. Then the total sample was distributed into eight subgroups according to the individual's task scope, growth need strength, and external locus of control scores as they were related to the sample medians. The Pearson Product-Moment correlation was used to test the eight hypotheses.

RESULTS

Table 2 presents correlations between predicted leader behaviors and dependent variables on a cell-by-cell basis. The data appear to support the relationships between most of the predicted leader behaviors and satisfaction (with job and supervision) as moderated by task scope, growth need strength, and locus of control. For instance, results appear to fully support, in terms of satisfaction, Hypotheses 1, 2, and 5 and partially support Hypotheses 3, 6 7, and 8.

The results indicate no significant correlations between predicted leader behaviors and performance. However, it appears that directive leader behavior was negatively correlated with performance for Cell 3 ($p < .01$) and Cell 4 ($p < .05$).

DISCUSSION

The primary objective of this study was to test partially the path-goal theory of leadership in Saudi Arabia (this study) and to investigate the applicability of some U.S. management theories in some foreign countries. To achieve that objective, a conceptual model, which is based on the path-goal theory of leadership and Griffin's (1980) work, was tested in Saudi Arabia (Study 1), and compared with the results of the same conceptual model that was tested in the United States (Study 2). The model assumes that the appropriate style of leader behavior depends on three contingency factors: the subordinate's (a) task, (b) growth need strength, and (c) locus of control. These contingency factors moderate the relationships between leader behavior and subordinate satisfaction (with job and supervision) and performance.

Study 1 and 2 indicate, for the total sample, that there were significant

286

correlations between leader behaviors (i.e., Achievement-Oriented, Participative, and Supportive) and Satisfaction with Job as shown in Table 3. Furthermore, there were significant correlations between all forms of leader behavior and satisfaction with supervision for the total sample for both studies as presented in Table 3. In addition, results of Study 1 and 2, on a cell-by-cell basis, appear to provide significant correlations between leader behaviors and satisfaction as shown in Table 2. In general, data tend to support, for both studies, the relationships between leader behaviors and satisfaction.

This means that the path-goal theory is applicable, for this sample, in significantly different countries. Despite cultural differences, participants had similar attitude toward leadership styles. One explanation for this similar attitude might be that participants either studied in U.S. universities or were educated by U.S. educated instructors in their countries. Hence, they were influenced by U.S. or Western civilization. The influx of U.S. technology, managerial practices, and others to the participants' countries might be another explanation for holding similar attitude.

Previous studies (e.g., Downey, Sheridan & Slocum, 1975; Szilagyi & Sims, 1974; Griffin 1980) did not support the path-goal theory in terms of performance. In general, Study 1 and 2 are not exceptional. Only Hypothesis 2, in terms of performance, was partially supported. Study 2 revealed a positive relationship between participative leader behavior (Cell 2) and performance ($p < .1$). Further, as revealed by previous studies (e.g. Downey et al., 1975; Szilagyi & Sims, 1974), Study 1 appears to provide support for the negative relationships between directive leader behavior and performance (Cell 3, $p < .01$; Cell 4, $p < .05$) as shown in Table 2.

There could be several reasons for the lack of support for the relationships between predicted leader behaviors and performance. First, self-rated performance is not a valid measure. This explanation is rejected for the following reasons: (1) Lawler (1967, p. 371) argues that "self ratings are relevant because the individual's self-perception is an important determinant of future behavior, in addition to the fact that he probably has more information about his own behavior than anyone else." (2) Several relationships between different forms of leader behavior and performance were supported in Study 1 and 2 as shown in Tables 2 and 3.

A second explanation might be that neither leader behaviors nor the moderating variables (i.e., subordinate's task scope, growth need strength, and locus of control) relate to performance. This explanation can not be accepted because some researchers (e.g., Steers & Spencer, 1977) found

287

that performance iis an appropriate dependent variable. Further, some significant correlations were obtained for the total sample as well as for several nonhypothesized relationships as shown in Table 3 and Table 2.

The third explanation is that the predicted forms of leader behavior, on a cell-by-cell basis, may not be appropriate for the samples. The researcher based his studies' hypotheses on previous studies of the path-goal theory of leadership (e.g., Downey et al., 1975; House & Dessler, 1974, Griffin, 1980). Most of the previous studies attempted to investigate the leader-subordinate performance relationship through the use of subjects with low educational levels from one or two organizations, especially manufacturing firms (e.g., Griffin, 1980; Schuler, 1973). Further, they attempted to investigate the preceding relationships as moderated by one or at most two variables.

These studies have investigated the above-mentioned relationship as moderated by three variables through the use of subjects with high educational level. For instance, the U.S. sample had an educational level with a mean of 16.27. Further, subjects were employed by a variety of organizations. Thus, lack of support for the predicted relationship might be attributed to the unique characteristics of the studies. However, future research should consider all of the preceding explanations. Future studies that examine a more comprehensive model of the path-goal theory, use qualitative as well as quantitative measures of performance, and use subjects with different educational levels in order to discern the relationship between leader behavior and subordiinate performance, may yield the greatest insights.

TABLE 1
Prediction of Satisfaction and Performance
from Leader Behavior, Task and Individual Variables

| Cell | Moderating variables | | | Independent variables | Relationship of leader behavior & outcome variable |
	Task scope	Growth need	Locus of control	Leader behavior	
1	High	High	I	Achievement Participative	Positive Positive
2	High	High	E	Participative Directive	Positive Positive
3	High	Low	I	Participative Directive	Positive Positive
4	High	Low	E	Directive	Positive
5	Low	High	I	Participative Supportive	Positive Positive
6	Low	High	E	Directive Supportive	Positive Positive
7	Low	Low	I	Participative Maintenance	Positive Positive
8	Low	Low	E	Maintenance	Positive

289

TABLE 2
Pearson Product-Moment Correlations Between Leader Behavior and Dependent Variables for Study 1 and 2[b]

Cell and Leader Behavior[a]	Satisfaction with job	Satisfaction with super-vision	Performance
Cell 1 (n_1 = 85)			
(n_2 = 30)			
Achievement-oriented	.336^{xxx}	.437^{xxxx}	-.176
	.025	.292^x	-.083
Participative	.235^{xx}	.319^{xxx}	-.048
	.422^{xx}	.510^{xxx}	.145
Directive	.116	.197^x	.015
	.279	.386^{xx}	-.089
Supportive	.183^x	.459^{xxx}	-.158
	.348^{xx}	.512^{xxx}	.014
Maintenance	.024	.107	.039
	-0.68	.214	.506^{xxx}
Cell 2 (n_1 = 45)			
(n_2 = 29)			
Achievement-oriented	.236	.435^{xxx}	-.277^x
	.367^{xx}	.511^{xxx}	-.279^x
Participative	.396^{xxx}	.524^{xxxx}	-.042
	.522^{xxx}	.514^{xxx}	.246^x
Directive	.250^x	.407^{xxx}	-.006
	-.117	.071	.122
Supportive	.218	.627^{xxxx}	.185
	.452^{xxx}	.695^{xxx}	.377^{xx}
Maintenance	.0613	.121	-.102
	.124	.391	-.177
Cell 3 (n_1 = 62)			
(n_2 = 17)			
Achievement-oriented	.309^{xx}	.477^{xxxx}	-.165
	.124	.056	.191
Participative	.251^{xx}	.183	.081
	.292	.435^{xx}	-.044
Directive	.081	.179	-.380^{xxx}
	.310	.029	.232
Supportive	.515^{xxxx}	.191	-.090
	.389	.766^{xxxx}	.176
Maintenance	.174	.177	.320^{xx}
	-.319	-.060	-.338x

TABLE 2 (Continued)

Cell and Leader Behavior[a]	Satisfaction with job	Satisfaction with super-vision	Performance
Cell 4 ($n_1 = 41$)			
($n_2 = 21$)			
Achievement-oriented	.317^{xx}	.078	-.231
	.284	.663^{xxxx}	.310
Participative	-.180	-.096	.186
	.249	.619^{xxx}	.467^{xx}
Directive	-.015	.013	-.372^{xx}
	-.182	.309^{x}	-.067
Supportive	-.205	-.122	-.072
	.353^{x}	.888^{xxxx}	.416^{xx}
Maintenance	-.077	-.116	.461^{xxx}
	.073	-.044	.170
Cell 5 ($n_1 = 79$)			
($n_2 = 20$)			
Achievement-oriented	.331^{xxx}	.231^{xx}	-.089
	.473^{xx}	.681^{xxxx}	-.272
Participative	.317^{xxx}	.345^{xxx}	.004
	.473^{xx}	.838^{xxxx}	-.147
Directive	-.017	.280	-.143
	-.166	.028	.139
Supportive	.350^{xxx}	.550^{xxxx}	-.040
	.351^{x}	.720^{xxxx}	-.115
Maintenance	-.215^{x}	.055	.118
	.167	.439^{xx}	.067
Cell 6 ($n_1 = 40$)			
($n_2 = 16$)			
Achievement-oriented	.283^{x}	.363^{xx}	-.027
	.126	.543^{xx}	.277
Participative	.099	.375^{xx}	.111
	.081	.422^{x}	-.123
Directive	.221	.178	-.034
	-.562^{xx}	.258	.219
Supportive	.349^{xx}	.403^{xxx}	-.018
	-.058	.868^{xxx}	.001
Maintenance	.154	.361^{xx}	-.078
	.266	.680^{xxx}	.090

(continued)

291

TABLE 2 (Continued)

Cell and Leader Behavior[a]	Satisfaction with job	Satisfaction with super-vision	Performance
Cell 7 (n_1 = 46)			
(n_2 = 30)			
Achievement-oriented	.135	.450^{xxx}	-.127
	.476^{xxx}	.496^{xxx}	.178
Participative	.124	.567^{xxxx}	-.005
	.172	.353^{xx}	-.175
Directive	.107	.556^{xxx}	-.073
	.176	.157	.002
Supportive	.196	.697^{xxxx}	-.044
	.139	.664^{xxxx}	.141
Maintenance	.209	.339^{xx}	.117
	-.132	.087	.123
Cell 8 (n_1 = 68)			
(n_2 = 32)			
Achievement-oriented	.241^{xx}	.394^{xxxx}	.058
	.163	.164	-.169
Participative	.155	.391^{xxx}	.050
	.170	.619^{xxxx}	-.045
Directive	.278^{xx}	.354^{xxx}	.012
	.043	.102	.026
Supportive	.364^{xxx}	.595^{xxxx}	-.037
	.268^{x}	.671^{xxxx}	-.171
Maintenance	.171	.437^{xxxx}	-.122
	.173	.521^{xxxx}	.059

a. Predicted leader behaviors for each cell are starred.
b. Study 1 (Saudi sample) correlations are listed above Study 2 (U.S. sample) correlations.
x = p < .1; xx = p < .05; xxx = p < .01; xxxx = p < .001.

292

TABLE 3
Pearson Product-Moment Correlations Between Leader
Behavior and Development Variables for the Total Sample for Study 1 and 2

	Satisfaction with job	Satisfaction with super-vision	Performance
Achievement-oriented	$.327^{xxxx}$	$.434^{xxxx}$	.009
	$.369^{xxxx}$	$.450^{xxxx}$	.087
Participative	$.262^{xxxx}$	$.396^{xxxx}$	$.095^{xx}$
	$.404^{xxxx}$	$.573^{xxxx}$	.049
Directive	$.109^{xx}$	$.261^{xxxx}$	$-.116^{xx}$
	$-.173^{xxxx}$	$.103^{xxx}$	.056
Supportive	$.266^{xxxx}$	$.537^{xxxx}$	-.013
	$.309^{xxxx}$	$.722^{xxxx}$	.093
Maintenance	.036	$.098^{xx}$	$.173^{xxxx}$
	$.111^{x}$	$.299^{xxxx}$	.030

293

REFERENCES

Al-Gattan, A.R.A. *The path-goal theory of leadership: An empirical and longitudinal analysis.* Unpublished doctoral dissertation. Arizona State University, 1983.

Downey, H. K., Sheridan, J. E., & Slocum, J. W. Analysis of Relationships Among Leader Behavior, Subordinate Job Performance and Satisfaction: A path-goal approach. *Academy of Management Journal,* 1975, *18,* 253-262.

Greene, C.N. Questions of causation in the path-goal theory of leadership. *Academy of Management Journal,* 1979, *22,* 22-41.

Griffin, R. W. *The moderating effects of leader behavior on the relationship between individual task congruence and satisfaction and performance.* Unpublished doctoral dissertation, University of Houston, 1978.

Griffin R. W. Relationships among individual, task design, and leader behavior variables. *Academy of Management Journal,* 1980, *23,* 665-683.

Hackman, J. R., & Oldham, G. R. Development of the job diagnostic survey. *Journal of Applied Psychology,* 1975, *60,* 159-170.

Haire, M., Ghiselli, E.e., & Porter, L. W. *Managerial thinking: An international study.* New York, John Wiley, 1966.

Heller, F. A., & Porter, L. W. Perceptions of managerial needs and skills in two national samples. *Occupational Psychology,* January and April 1966, 1-13.

Hofstede, G. Motivation, leadership, and organization: Do American theories apply abroad? *Organizational Dynamics,* Summer, 1980, 42-53.

House, R. J. A path-goal theory of leader effectiveness. *Administrative Science Quarterly,* 1971, *16,* 321-338.

House, R. J., & Mitchell, T.R. Path-goal theory of leadership. *Journal of Contemporary Business,* Autumn 1974, pp. 81-97.

Johns, G. Task moderators of the relationship between leadership style and subordinate responses. *Academy of Management Journal,* 1978, 21, 319-325.

Kerr, S., & Jermier, J. M. Substitutes for leadership: Their Meaning and Measurement. *Organizational Behavior and Human Performance,* 1978, *22,* 375-403.

Lawler, E. E. The multitrait-multirater approach to measuring managerial job performance. *Journal of Applied Psychology,* 1967, *51,* 369-381.

Richman, B. M. & Copen, M. *International Management and economic development.* New York, McGraw-Hill Book Company, 1972.

Robinson, J. P., Athanasion, R., & Head, K. B. *Measures of occupational attitudes and occupational characteristics.* Ann Arbor: University of Michigan, Institute for Social Research, 1969.

Rotter, J. B. Generalized expectancies for internal versus external control of reinforcement. *Psychological Monographs,* 1966, *80*(1), 1-28.

Schriesheim, C., & Kerr, S. Psyhchological Properties of the Ohio State Leadership Scales. *Psychological Bulletin,* 1974, *81,* 756-765.

Schuler, R. S. *A path-goal theory of leadership: An empirical investigation.* Unpublished doctoral dissertation, Michigan State University, 1973.

294

Sims, H. P., Szilagyi, A. D., & Keller, R. T. The measurement of job characteristics. *Academy of Management Journal*, 1976, 19, 195-212.

Smith, P. C., Kendall, L. M., & Hulin, C. L. (1969). *Measurement of satisfaction in work and retirement*. Chicago: Rand McNally.

Steers, R. M., & Spencer, D. G. The role of achievement motivation in job design. *Journal of Applied Psychology*, 1977, *62*, 472-479.

Szilagyi A. D., & Sims, H. P., Jr. An exploration of the path-goal theory of leadership in a health care environment. *Academy of Management Journal*, 1974, *17*, 622-634.

Szilagyi, A. D. & Wallace, M. J. *Organizational behavior and performance*. Santa Monica, CA: Goodyear, 1980.

Valenzi, E., & Dessler, G. Relationships of leader behavior, subordinate role ambiguity and subordinate job satisfaction. *Academy of Management Journal*, 1978, *21*, 671-678.

Zedeck S. Problems with the use of "moderator" variables. *Psychological Bulletin*, 1971, *76*, 295-319.

* *Research for this article is partially funded by the University of Petroleum and Minerals.*

* *Reproduced from:*
Group & Organization Studies, Vol. 10 No. 4, December 1985 429-445; (1985 Sage Publication, Inc.).

ABOUT THE AUTHORS & CONTRIBUTORS

Khalid M. Al-Aiban pursued his college education and graduate work at USC where he earned his B.S. from the School of Business Administration, and M.P.A. from the School of Public Administration, in 1981 and 1983 respectively. In 1990, he obtained his Ph.D. from UCI in the field of public management. His dissertation deals with the impact of public expenditures on budgetary processes and administrative practices in Saudi Arabia. He has been with the Saudi National Guard Office in the U.S. since 1985. His areas of interest include finance, public policy and comparative management. In these fields, he has published several papers in administrative journals and presented research work at international conferences (e.g. Managing in a Global Economy; Hong Kong, June 1989). In the area of comparative management, he focuses on traditional and Western societies in terms of their values, structures and practices.

Abdulrahim Ali M. Al-Gattan is the present Chairman of the M.B.A. program at the College of Industrial Management at King Fahd University of Petroleum & Minerals in Saudi Arabia. He earned both his B.S. with Honors in Geology (1976) and his M.B.A. (1978) from that institution, and has been associated there since 1976. He earned his Ph.D. in Business Administration from Arizona State University in 1983. His research interests include leadership, job design, motivation and women in management.

Aisha A. Al-Husseini is currently Head of the Home Economics Department at KAU. She holds both a B.A. in Sociology (1972) and an M.S. in Educational Administration (1973) from the University of Southern California. She earned her Ph.D. in Educational Administration & Planning in 1985 from Al-Azhar University, Girls College, Cairo, Egypt. She is a member of the "Honorary Association for Women in Education" at the University of Southern California, and a board member of both the Al Faisaliya Women's Society and the Private Schools' Board in Jeddah, Saudi Arabia.

---

*KAU refers to King Abdulaziz University in Jeddah, Saudi Arabia.

Noura Khaled Alsaad is a well known journalist and writer in Saudi Arabia, and is currently a weekly columnist for a Riyadh newspaper. She has been a lecturer in the Sociology Department of Arts forGirls at KAU since 1983. Alsaad earned a Bachelor's Degree in Business Administration from KAU in 1972, her M.A. in Social & Philosophical Foundations of Education from the University of Minnesota in 1982, and is currently a doctoral student in Sociology of Education. She serves as board member of the Girl's College of Education in Jeddah and the Al-Faisalaya Women's Welfare Society. As the latter's Research & Studies Committee Head she has conducted various social and cultural activities which have included participation from the Saudi Minister of Petroleum, the head of the General Bureau of Civil Service, and other high level government officials.

Aidros Abdullah Al-Sabban is currently Assistant Professor of Public Administration at KAU, and serves also as Administrative Consultant for the Municipality of Makkah and Chairman of the Executive Committee of Coordination and Follow-up in Makkah. He has represented KAU and the Municipality of Makkah at the Second Saudi Municipal Mayors Converence, the Arabian Cities Organization 8th Conference, the 4th Saudi Civil Defense Conference, and the Convention on Highway Safety and other local & regional conference : Al-Sabban received his B.A. from the University of Riyadh in 1974, and went on to the Claremont Graduate School in California to earn an M.P.A. (1978) and Ph.D. (1982).

Alawi N. Abu Al-Saud is an Assistant Professor in the Department of Public Administration, College of Economics & Administration, KAU, and teaches courses in Organization Theory and Administrative Development. He has served as consultant for the Saudi Ministry of Foreign Affairs and is co-author of a book in Arabic entitled *Organization Theory.* Al-Saud received his B.A. from the American University in Beirut, Lebanon in 1970, his M.P.A. from the University of Arizona in 1974, and his Ph.D. in Public Administration from the University of Maryland in College Park.

Omar Abubakar Bakhashab currently serves as Associate Professor of Law at KAU and is a member of several committees within the Ministry of Foreign Affairs for Saudi Arabia. He served as Special Legal Advisor to the Meterological Environment Protection Administration (MEPA), as Legal Advisor to KAU, and as Legal Advisor and Member of the Saudi Delegation to several international conferences. Bakhashab earned his LL.B.

from Cairo University in 1975. He received his LL.M.—(1979) and Ph.D. in (1984) from Glasgow University, Scotland. He is a member of the International Lawyers Group of Glasgow, Scotland and the Scottish Group of International Lawyers.

Almed Hassan Dahlan is a lecturer at the Department of Public Administration, College of Economics and Administration, KAU and the author of *A Study of the Political System of the Kingdom of Saudi arabia*, a book which is now in its third edition. Dahlan earned his B.S. in Public Administration from KAU in 1977, his M.P.A. from Howard University in Washington D.C. in 1984. Toward the latter degree he received some graduate work at the American University and USC. Currently he is pursuing his doctorate in Public Administration at Temple University in Philadelphia, Pennsylvania. His interests lie in the areas of management of public corporations, employee and citizen participation, and productivity in the public sector.

Seham M. Saleh Fatani teaches English Literature at KAU and is author of a number of book reviews in the Saudi press. She has studied in Makkah, Saudi Arabia, as well as in Pakistan and the United States. She earned her Master's Degree in English Literature from the University of Illinois in Chicago in 1985.

Constance B. Joy is originally from the United States and lived in Saudi Arabia from 1980 to 1988 before moving to Germany to join her husband. She taught English in Jeddah at Dar al Fikr, and was Head of the English Program at Al Nahda Women's Society in Riyadh. Joy received her B.A. in German & European History from Oberlin College, and two M.A.s; one in Sociology from the University of Denver in Colorado and the second in English as a Second Language (ESL) from The Experiment in International Living, School of International Training in Vermont. Her current work is primarily in the areas of Sociolinguistics, ESL problems of Arab speakers, and computer uses in ESL.

Abdullah Hassan Masry is currently Assistant Deputy Minister for Antiquities & Museum Affairs in Saudi Arabia and Editor-in-Chief of "Atlal," the Journal of Saudi Arabian Archaeology. He earned a B.A. in Anthropology from California State University in Sacramento in 1969, an M.A. in Anthropology from the University of Chicago in 1971, and his Ph.D.

299

in Anthropology in 1973. He is widely published in Saudi Arabia, and is a Member and Fellow of a variety of cultural, scientific and reearch organizations—locally and globally.

Mohammed Kheder Oraif is presently Assistant Professor of Arabic Linguistics at the Department of Arabic in the Faculty of Arts & Humanities at KAU and has taught Arabic, both as a native and as a foreign language, at KAU and San Diego State University in California. He received his B.A. in Arabic Language & Literature from Umm Al Qura University in Makkah, Saudi Arabia in 1976, an M.A. in Linguistics from San Diego State University in 1982, and his Ph.D. in Second and Foreign Language Instruction from the University of Southern California in Los Angeles in 1986.

Sabah Muhammed Hamza Oun has been associated with KAU since 1982 as a Teaching Assistant, Lecturer in English Literature, and currently as Acting Head of the European Languages Department, Girls Campus. She earned both her B.A. in English Literature (1980) and M.A. in English Poetry (1985) from KAU.

Hussein Murad Ali Reda is Assistant Professor of Industrial Engineering & Operations Research in the Department of Systems Engineering at King Fahd University of Petroleum & Minerals in Dhahran, Saudi Arabia. He received a B.A. in Architectural Engineering in 1979 and M.S. in Industrial Engineering in 1981, both from Bradley University in Illinois. He earned a Ph.D. in Industrial Engineering & Operations Research in 1985 from the Virginia Polytechnic & State University. Reda is a member of an engineering honor society and many professional organizations. His research intrests include system dynamics modeing & simulation, industrial development, production and manufacturing systems engineering.

REVIEWERS*

* Carolyn Adams
Chairwoman of Urban Studies
Temple University, Philadelphia

* Lenneal Henderson
Director & Professor
Bureau of Public Administration
The University of Tennessee, Knoxville

* Hesham Milyani
Professor of Public Administration
KAU, Jeddah

* Charles Joiner
Professor of Public Admin.
Temple Univ., Philadelphia

* Conrad Weiler
Director of M.P.A.
Temple Univ., Philadelphia

* Seraj Zamzami
Asso. Professor of Political Science
College of Economics & Admin.
Jeddah, Saudi Arabia

* Abd al-Rahman Al-Dayel
Saudi Education Mission
   to the U.S.A.
Washington, D.C.

* Seham M. Fatani
Dept. of English Language
Girls Campus, KAU
Jeddah, Saudi Arabia

* Asma Al-Abdullah
English Language Dept.
Girls Campus, KAU
Jeddah, Saudi Arabia

* Kristin Guss
The American University
Washington, D.C.

* Khalid Bin Sayeed
Professor of Political Science
Queen's University, Canada

* Mohammad Badran
Public Administration Department
College of Economics & Administration
King Abd al-Aziz Univ., Jeddah

* Mohammad Had'dad
Professor of Public Administration
KAU, Saudi Arabia

* Maurice Woodard
Chairman of Public Admin.
Howard Univ., Washington, D.C.

* Walid A. Hashim
Department of Economics
KAU, Jeddah

* Wahid H. Hashim
Department of Political Science
KAU
Jeddah, Saudi Arabia

* Don Lehnhoff
Professional Writing
Minneapolis, MN

* Constance Joy
ESL, School of Int'l Training
Vermont

* Sabah M. Oun
Dept. of English Language
Girls Campus, KAU
Jeddah, Saudi Arabia

* Ahmed S. Gabbani
Public Admin.
USC

* Lesley Anne Tyson
Temple University

*The Associate Editors review papers for their sections.